GENDER AND THE PROFESSIONAL PREDICAMENT IN NURSING

GENDER AND THE PROFESSIONAL PREDICAMENT IN NURSING

Celia Davies

Open University Press
Buckingham · Philadelphia

Open University Press
Celtic Court
22 Ballmoor
Buckingham
MK18 1XW

and
1900 Frost Road, Suite 101
Bristol, PA 19007, USA

First Published 1995

A catalogue record of this book is available from the British Library

ISBN   0 335 19402 8 (pb)   0 335 19403 6 (hb)

Library of Congress Cataloging-in-Publication Data
Davies, Celia.
    Gender and the professional predicament in nursing/by Celia Davies.
        p.   cm.
    Includes bibliographical references and index.
    ISBN 0-335-19402-8 (pb.)   ISBN 0-335-19403-6 (hb.)
    1. Nursing – Social aspects.   2. Sexism in medicine.   3. Nurses – Public opinion.   4. Nurses – Job stress.   5. Nursing – Political aspects. 6. Nursing – Social aspects – Great Britain.   7. Sexism in medicine – Great Britain. 8. Nurses – Great Britain – Public opinion. 9. Nurses Job stress – Great Britain.   10. Nursing – Political aspects – Great Britain.   I. Title.
    [DNLM.   1. Nursing.   2. Gender Identity.   3. Professional Autonomy.   4. Education, Nursing – Great Britain.   5. State Medicine – Great Britain.   WY 16 D255g   1995]
    RT86.5.D38   199b
    610.73'06'99 – dc20
    DNLM/DLC
    for Library of Congress   94-40172
                                                                                                             CIP

Typeset by Type Study, Scarborough
Printed in Great Britain by Biddles Ltd, Guildford and King's Lynn

In memory of Marion Ferguson, 1924–1988, whose comments and companionship I have missed.

CONTENTS

PREFACE

'You can speak our language!' This was the surprised exclamation back in 1984, when I took up a post at the United Kingdom Central Council for Nursing, Midwifery and Health Visiting (UKCC) to work on Project 2000, the reform of basic education for the profession. I explained that nursing education had been the topic of my doctoral thesis in sociology. I had read each one of the many reports on the topic.

Over the next two and a half years, it became apparent that there was a great deal more to learn about the language of nursing. It was not only a matter of the specialist and clinical terms, but something more fundamental. When those in the nursing world spoke of how they saw the nature of nursing work, of their ideals, of what they needed in the way of educational and other resources to deliver optimal care, above all when they spoke of holistic care and of commitment, their words sounded out of place. They were accused of being 'unrealistic', 'sentimental', or 'muddleheaded'; they were said to be 'pretentious' in their borrowings from social science jargon, 'elitist' in their aspirations, and in particular, 'defensive' and 'hard to help'. Above all, it seemed, they were a frustration and a puzzle to their colleagues in the health field.

I left the UKCC with one lasting impression. Individually, and at the point at which they deliver nursing care, nurses are lauded and applauded, but collectively and in the arenas where policy is debated and decided, nurses are viewed in a much more ambivalent and negative light. Why is this? Why is it that the language that they speak seems almost to have a different root? I now believe that questions such as these can only be answered through coming to terms with nursing as 'women's work'. We need a feminist analysis which will consider what gender divisions mean and how they work out when nursing seeks to act as a profession and attempts to regulate its own practice within this frame. There are plenty of passing references to nursing as 'women's work', but there is no sustained attempt, at the level of a contemporary policy analysis in nursing, to explore what such an approach might offer.

I start from an assumption that gender divisions are fundamental to the organization of all areas of social life. There are cultural codes of masculinity and femininity to which we are all exposed. These shape but do not entirely determine identities and behaviour. These gender codes are also inscribed in organizations in a multi-layered way, such that it makes sense to claim that organizations and organizational relations are gendered. Starting from assumptions such as these, what appears initially as disconnected personal discontents of women as nurses gradually transmutes into the collective dilemmas of nurses as women – the dilemmas, in other words, of gender.

This book is intended for several audiences. First and foremost, it is for nurses. Some are already hungry for a gender perspective on their work and their profession. They are likely to have found campaigns for equal opportunity in employment frustratingly disappointing as far as nursing is concerned, to talk about a recurrent 'image problem' in nursing and to complain about not being taken seriously. Others, particularly those in the nursing policy world, will be deeply sceptical. They will find, however, that this book is neither a tirade against men nor a celebration of all that is female. If anything, it is a lament about the damage that gender-divided thinking does to us all.

Second, this is a book for policy-makers and health policy analysts outside nursing. At last, and after a long period of neglect, they are beginning to pay more attention to nursing. If it encourages a few people to abandon overly simple forms of 'gender talk' and to move in directions now being signposted by feminist scholars in social policy, then it will have served an important purpose.

Third, it is a book for students of women's studies. These, more than the others, will be aware of the volume and diversity of scholarship that has emerged over the last decade in this field, as in one discipline after another conventional thinking has been fundamentally challenged. They will also be aware of the potential that all this has to illuminate a world in which feminist excursions are still too few and too brief. Because the account of any one author is inevitably shaped by her history and by the particulars of her time and place, readers will need to know how I have come to the understanding of nursing presented here. It has emerged through a pathway in male-dominated industrial sociology and through the empirical traditions that are the result of long years of contract research. For many years, I strove to understand nursing using conventional sociological concepts of profession. But it was a long time before I came to realize, in the words of Audre Lorde's aptly titled essay, that 'the master's tools will never dismantle the master's house' (Lorde 1984).

My quest has been to tease out the masculine vision that is built in to our organizational life and to the process of policy-making and to realize more clearly the partial and inadequate nature of that vision. To do this is to be on the way, not only towards breaking down recurrent images of women as somehow deficient, but, even more importantly, towards creating more adequate institutions which express our human needs. Nowhere is this more important than in relation to health care, something that at one time or another we will all need, and in relation to nursing, an occupational choice that is central to the lives and the identities of well over half a million women in the UK. If what is happening in women's studies and what is happening in nursing come more closely together as a result of this book, if it stimulates debate, bringing comment from others with other histories, then it will have achieved its aims.

ACKNOWLEDGEMENTS

I received a considerable amount of help and encouragement from friends and colleagues during the period in which this book was in preparation. First, I would like to pay tribute to Jane Robinson and her colleagues in the Department of Nursing and Midwifery Studies at the University of Nottingham. A month in their company, experiencing their energy, commitment and intellectual curiosity, gave the book the best start it could have had. Others have helped in different ways. Some of the following colleagues and friends were invaluable for their guidance and information on the myriad of changes that have faced nursing since I moved away from it some six years ago, others commented, criticized and above all encouraged me to go on at moments when the task seemed impossible. I would like to thank June Andrews, Chris Brotherton, Jim Buchan, Ruth Elkan, Christine Hancock, Jalna Hanmer, Jane Lewis, Monica McWilliams, Amanda Parkyn, Eilish Rooney, Jean Orr, Pam Smith, and Maggie Wallace. Morag Stark provided not just secretarial support but editorial assistance of all kinds. The University of Ulster was extremely generous in granting that increasingly scarce commodity, a period of study leave. I would also like to thank colleagues at the Gender, Work and Organization Seminar at the University of Manchester Institute of Science and Technology (UMIST) for helpful comments and criticisms. Finally, I want to pay a special tribute to the many members of the nursing profession, who, over many years now, have answered my questions and encouraged and supported me in my quest better to understand their work. I am acutely aware that this latest use to which I have put their openess and trust will be a controversial one, and that by no means all will be convinced that the directions that I propose here will be the right ones in which to go. To follow the logic of my own argument, however, is to aim for a dialogue through difference rather than always seeking the comfort of a perspective more fully shared.

INTRODUCTION:
THE DISCONTENTS OF
NURSES

I've always wanted to be a nurse. I've always enjoyed it. I always will. I am one of those that do moan because we are short-staffed but I will get on with it. It is very, very stressful at the moment and you do get frustrated. But I don't know. I wouldn't do anything else. (Enrolled nurse)

It's something I have always enjoyed doing. It's the companionship, the feeling that you are doing something worthwhile. It's not just a job, it gets to be a way of life. And I think you get to be addicted to it. (Sister)

. . . it's so difficult to leave once you are into it – it sort of gets hold of you. I can't imagine leaving it. (Enrolled nurse)

(Mackay 1989: 135)

The dedication of nurses to nursing that is expressed in the above quotations is well known. No one is surprised when a young woman says that she has taken up nursing because it is a job that is 'worthwhile', because it is a way of 'helping people', or because it is something she 'always wanted to do'. Recruitment campaigns have traded on and romanticized this kind of commitment with slogans like 'people remember nurses' and 'good nurses are born not made'. Nurses tend to be in more prolonged contact with their patients and clients than other health care professionals; it is they who provide the continuity and the follow-up. Nurses, more than others in the public world of paid work, see us at our most vulnerable – when our emotions are often in turmoil and when, stripped of the protective trappings of status and position, our bodies are revealed for their faults and their fragilities. The image of the enthusiastic, youthful and dedicated carer, or perhaps of the motherly calm of the older, experienced nurse can be comforting at times of stress and in the face of fear.

Images such as these, of course, are images of women. Both the nurse and the work of nursing are firmly associated in the public mind with the female sex. Nursing, too, is among the most sharply sex-segregated of occupations. Men constitute less than 10 per cent of the qualified nursing labour force – a proportion that for many years has shown little sign of change.[1] The warmth and emotional contact expected of a nurse, the qualities of care, nurturing, comfort and concern, are often supposed to be inherent qualities in women, so much so that while a woman doing nursing is unremarkable, a man in the same job will be described not just as a 'nurse' but as a 'male nurse'.

A closer acquaintance with nursing, however, shatters any cosy image of women doing work that is somehow natural to them and hence being entirely comfortable in and satisfied with the role that they have chosen. Confusion, resentment and exhaustion frequently surround nurses' assessments of their work. Nurses will often report that they are not being allowed to get on with the job of nursing and that they are not gaining the respect that they should enjoy. And when one turns to those who work most closely with nurses – the doctors, the managers and the politicians – the positive image clouds further. They will say that nurses complain a lot, that they 'whinge'. They will observe that somehow nurses are 'hard to help', and that in general, they seem often to be 'defensive' and 'difficult'. The problem with nurses, you will hear, is that 'they do not seem to know what it is that they want'. Nurses, furthermore, will often themselves agree with these negative assessments. They will say that it is the divisions within their own ranks that are a root cause of the trouble, or that their lack of assertiveness and unwillingness to engage in action at any level that seems 'political' is at the heart of the problem. All this, it must be stressed, is not an alternative to the picture of dedication. Curiously, it seems to be part and parcel of it. And it adds up to what a past General Secretary of the Royal College of Nursing (RCN) has recently dubbed the 'silent frustration' of nurses that the world as they see it is not affirmed by others, and that changes that are suggested seem to miss the point as far as nurses are concerned (Clay 1987: 151).

This chapter will give a brief outline of some of the current sources of discontent in nursing, emphasizing their multiple and seemingly intractable character. For some readers, this ground will be all too familiar.

They will have their own views as to what the causes are, what the solutions ought to be and whether they are in train. For others, the issues are likely to be quite new, since the details of the organization of nursing work are not well understood outside nursing circles. For both groups, however, I hope that the chapter will give a sense of the range and depth of the issues at stake. As I toured the country in 1984–5, outlining to a wide variety of groups of nurses the aims of the UKCC's nurse education reform project, I was overwhelmed by the hopes that many pinned upon it. 'Nurses don't want a reform of education,' my diary of the time records, 'they want a root and branch reform of the nature and conditions of nursing itself.' This chapter provides a brief catalogue of some of the sources of the unease that nurses were then expressing, and some of the tensions that emerged between nurses and others in the health care arena. As problems seem to be heaped upon problems, I began to ask – how could it be that so much seems to be wrong? Must we accept the implication that so often seems to be offered, that nurses have only themselves to blame?

A full decade has now passed, and in that time the National Health Service (NHS), in which the vast majority of nurses work, has been the subject of unprecedented scrutiny and change. Yet, despite the arrival of managers and markets in the health service, notwithstanding the new vocabularies of performance, cost and quality control, and the disappearance of the old management hierarchies in nursing, and despite too the concern which has surfaced from time to time with questions of motivation, morale and recruitment, the fundamental discontents of nurses which are set out in this chapter have not been addressed in any direct way. The confetti of consultation documents, the White Papers on future health policy and organization, and the academic commentary regularly concern themselves with the place of the medical profession in a process of change. It is now being acknowledged rather more often, notwithstanding that nurses constitute over half the workforce and their services consume around a quarter of total NHS expenditure, that nursing has been 'marginal to the debates that have shaped health policy since 1948' (Beardshaw and Robinson 1990: 5). It is the reasons for this neglect of the nation's nurses, why it is that nursing can remain taken for granted and invisible and the ways in which this invisibility is sustained in policy arenas, that is the major subject matter for this book. First, however, we need to take a glimpse at the frustrations that nurses themselves express.

1   A second-class education?

The mid-1980s saw the nursing profession focused with an unprecedented determination on the reform of nurse education. Three phrases occurred with regularity in discussions I held with nurse learners in the initial stages of Project 2000. First, the learners would say that they felt that they were being used simply as 'pairs of hands' on the hospital wards. Second, they would complain about the 'gap between theory and practice', the difference, for example, between a procedure taught in half an hour in the school session, and carried out in 10 minutes on the ward. Third, they would report that they were 'thrown in at the deep end', that busy staff frequently had no time to teach them, and that they felt that they were a nuisance to everyone if they looked for guidance or explanation. It was widely recognized that this situation came about because students were part of the labour force in the hospital wards to which they were allocated for blocks of time during their training. Studies of students show the continual pressure on them to 'fit in', the constant adjustments they have to make to new settings, and the way that patient care takes precedence over learning needs (Melia 1987); studies of the work of hospital wards confirm that few of the interactions between qualified staff and learners can be classified as 'teaching', and show, not surprisingly, that the inexperience of students can bring an extra management headache where staffing is already tight (Reid 1985). Nor was the situation in the classroom anywhere near ideal. To facilitate a steady flow of student labour, schools must work with multiple intakes each year. In the bid for reform, the UKCC spoke of this as a 'constant grind . . . of repeated teaching with no time for research or professional development' (UKCC 1986a: para 1.14). The RCN referred more colourfully to an educational atmosphere 'reminiscent of a nineteenth century teachers' training college rather than a modern establishment of post secondary education' (RCN 1985: para 1.11).

A system such as this clearly has repercussions for the learner. It is not surprising if the student emerges with a lack of confidence, an eagerness to fit in, if she is not assertive and if her first instinct is to cope with issues rather than to confront them. Learners, Lesley Mackay argues, are introduced to a world that is 'narrow' and 'introverted'; they 'learn to take orders and to see themselves as at the bottom of the pile' (Mackay 1989: 34–5). They are likely to retain a sense that they have an inadequate basis on which to move to a position of confident practice of the skill of nursing. Nurses, in short, have a fundamental discontent with the nature of the education that they receive.

But the repercussions go much further than this. The system sets up a constant tension and conflict between those working in education and those working in service that produces a sense of inadequacy and a defensiveness not just amongst the learners but amongst those who teach them as well. Tutors regard the ward, which is principally about patient care, as a learning resource for their students, but they are, of course, constantly foiled in this by the immediate demands of service. From another direction, they receive pressures from the statutory bodies set up to maintain and improve educational standards. Measures for educational improvement, changes to the statutory syllabus, for example, and new requirements for areas of practice that must be covered can easily generate resentment or even despair on the part of education staff who must reconcile these with the needs of their more powerful service colleagues. Negative stereotypes of tutors abound – that they are clinically out of date, afraid to visit the wards or unrealistic in what they teach the students. Furthermore, new roles designed to ease the situation, such as that of clinical teacher or later the joint appointee between school and service, can come to be expressions of the tensions in the system rather than solutions to it, notwithstanding the achievements of exceptional and determined individuals.

One important development in this respect has emerged from the removal of some of the most energetic and able nurse educators from the hospital-based schools of nursing to become associated with university and college programmes. There are highly positive aspects to this, in the educational innovations, the development of nursing texts and research in nursing, the opportunities for advanced study and development into leadership positions (Chapman 1985). But there are also disadvantages, in the gulf that opens up between those in the universities and colleges and the rest, and in the resentment of an apparently 'academic' form of nursing by those who are not associated with it. The world of nurse education in these various ways thus emerges as full of discontents, divisions and insecurities. Much change is now under way, associated with the educational reforms known as Project 2000 (see Chapter 6). Whether the changes which have been secured will be enough to promote confidence and build bridges across the divisions produced by the old system remains to be seen.

2   Who does what?

Nor does one find a greater sense of satisfaction, unity and morale amongst qualified staff – at least in the hospital setting. Qualified nurses, of course, see the student labour system from another angle – one where the constantly changing cohorts of students are now a problem for the delivery of high quality care. These nurses are also part of a team containing a bewildering range of staff of different grades and experience. There are three-year trained and two-year trained nurses. There are permanent staff who are part of the establishment of the health authority and temporary nurses from an agency or nurse bank. There are unqualified staff. There are full-timers and part-timers amongst all of these groups of staff. Nursing means providing 24-hour cover with this highly variable mix, while at the same time trying to ensure that care does not become fragmented from the patients' point of view. Qualified staff will frequently find themselves supervising care by less qualified staff rather than giving it themselves, or moving from patient to patient to carry out those procedures that others are not competent to perform. Day-to-day reality can often be a long way from the textbook model or indeed the statutory definitions of the competence of a registered nurse, which emphasizes that a qualified nurse assesses the need for care for each patient, plans it, and, with the help of others executes it, monitors and adjusts. Such a gap is likely to give rise to feelings of stress, frustration and guilt. It seems that it is not just the students, but it is everyone in nursing who is a 'pair of hands'.

Deeply entangled with this pattern of staffing is the particularly divisive question of the future of the enrolled nurse. Two levels of nurse are recognized by statute, the three-year trained nurse who has a qualification as a registered general nurse (RGN) or is registered in a specialty and the two-year trained nurse whose title is enrolled nurse (EN), and whose function in principle is to assist.[2] The mix of registered and enrolled nurses, students and nursing assistants in any clinical setting is highly variable. Its rationale is frequently lost in the mists of time, yet continues to be reflected in the figures for a particular hospital or other care setting. In practice, as we have just seen, the boundaries between the two levels of nurse in terms of the work that they do have not been maintained. ENs can easily become angry and embittered by a system of education, formal regulation and labelling with titles and dress that stresses their place as subordinate to the RGN and by a daily practice which can use them as the equal of RGN on one day and as something more like an auxiliary on the next. Nursing journals in the 1980s regularly carried letters and articles discussing what was termed the 'misuse and abuse' of the EN. The UKCC had published a discussion paper in 1982, proposing to end entry to the EN parts of the Register, but had drawn back in face of the controversy it provoked. Once it was clear (late in 1984) that the Council had moved to a large-scale review of initial educational preparation, a steady stream of correspondence from ENs started to arrive in its offices. As Project Officer, I read all these letters. Emotions ran high; some nurses were angry, others clearly in despair. Their letters catalogued the injustices they felt about the way in which they were deployed and pointed out too that channels of advancement were almost completely closed to them. 'After years of service', one wrote, 'am I to be cast on the scrapheap?'

There were two opposing views at the time. The dominant one, which had been argued for some years by the major professional association, the RCN, was that nursing should be moving towards a single level of qualified practitioner and indeed, if possible, to an all-qualified staff. On this model, some ENs would convert to first-level registration status, others would need to be protected for the duration of their employment. The other view, advocated by the trade unions and the Trades Union Congress, harked back to the recommendations of the Briggs Committee (Committee on Nursing 1972). It envisaged a two-stage process where the student would gain a certificate after 18 months and could practise at this level with the option of going on to first-level training (UKCC 1986a: paras 5.6–12). Feelings ran high. The first strategy could be criticized as a form of 'elitist professionalizing' that denied access to many who would make good and capable nurses. The second appeared to open the door to a lowering of standards and the wholesale employment of 'half-trained' nurses.

In the event, the UKCC did recommend closure of the EN parts of the Register as part of its educational reform proposals. ENs were and are a significant proportion of the labour force in the health service, however,[3] and the recommendation sat for a long while on the table while the government consulted with health authorities as employers and deliberated about the practicalities of it. In the meantime, uncertainty remained. Conversion courses developed in earnest, though supply was often far below the level of demand. ENs still emerge in the most recent surveys as less satisfied than their colleagues and as the staff group most likely to be considering giving up nursing altogether (Buchan *et al.* 1989, Seccombe and Ball 1992). As we will see later in the book, nurses may have got a new form of initial preparation, but they are far from a new pattern of practice. The vision of an all-qualified workforce, as we shall also see later, was dismissed by the government as entirely impractical. The alternative, of greater access to and diversity in nursing, still jostles uneasily with this hope for an all-qualified workforce delivering care. One result is a doubt about the whole notion of whether it is right to try to 'professionalize' nursing, and questioning about just what other model there might be.

Policy arguments like this, however, have little resonance for the busy nurse. In practice, boundaries between grades in nursing, and indeed boundaries between nursing and non-nursing duties seem impossible to set and nurses do whatever is necessary to ensure patient care. In truth, whatever their grade and contract, nurses feel misused, overburdened and unable to 'do nursing' properly. The depth of their frustration, the sense of being trapped and oppressed while at the same time deeply committed to the work is evidenced by the findings of a number of 'motivation and morale' surveys in the mid-1980s. The key issue that emerged in a survey of over 7000 nurses carried out in the autumn of 1987

was the lack of resources to get on with the job. Over 70 per cent said
there were not enough people to do the work and two-thirds said that not
having enough time to do nursing was their real frustration. More than
three-quarters of them said that they were mentally exhausted after work,
over half worried about work at home and felt they were under too much
stress (Price Waterhouse 1988). It was not that nurses were disillusioned
with nursing. Far from it. Nurses were often actually working through
breaks as well as staying late or coming in early so as not to let the patients
down. But they were simply not getting a chance to give nursing care in
the way they felt they were able and their patients deserved. Dissatisfaction with pay was a serious factor, but so too was lack of counselling and
support, and despair at the level of the workload. Other studies show
much the same picture (Waite and Hutt 1987).[4]

In this context, anger is vented on those who are responsible for staff
allocation and for co-ordinating the resources for patient care. Nurse
managers frequently get a vote of no confidence from nurses in the
clinical setting. Two-thirds of nurses in the 1987 national survey, for
example, agreed with the statement that nurse management was too
inflexible, and over half of them felt that they were not consulted about
decisions affecting them or given opportunities to discuss their concerns
(Price Waterhouse 1988: 41,43). The survey came not long after a major
reorganization where general management had been introduced into the
NHS to replace the previous interprofessional consensus management
teams, and the term 'management' was used perhaps too loosely by the
researchers to cover both the general managers and the variety of nursing
management structures that had been put in place at local level. The
situation thus was an unfamiliar one, very different from the past, where
from the end of the 1960s, nurse management had been organized in a
steeply hierarchical fashion, with nursing officer grades by this means
coming to find a place at every level in the NHS itself. But it is clear that
nurses have long reserved their most withering contempt for their
colleagues who move up the managerial ladder, seemingly leaving real
nursing for pay and power, especially when their presence in these
elevated posts seems to offer little support and resourcing in the clinical
setting. It is significant in this respect that while the RCN waged a strong
campaign against replacing nurse management with a general manager
structure, the heart of the profession was not in it, and the practical effect
was minimal. There is room, some feel, in the new and varied practices
that have replaced older style nurse management, for good nursing advice
to be given at health authority level, and for positive initiatives in
managing the nursing labour force, but there is also room for an authority
to ignore nursing if, as is often the case, it has a dim view of what it is that
nurses, in any role beyond the bedside, can contribute.[5] It is not only

nurses then who can promulgate the view that nurse management has turned out to be a waste of time and money.

3   A structure of opportunities?

If nursing has offered a poor educational preparation, frustrating terms and conditions of work on the hospital wards, and a management who for whatever reason does not seem firmly to have grasped the nettle of change, does it not at least give opportunities to specialize in a wide array of areas of practice, to move on to community nursing, health visiting or midwifery, as well as to develop an educational or a management role – thence to rise to posts of high pay and power in the corporate management structure of the NHS? Nurses do not see it this way. Two out of three members of the RCN reported in a recent survey that they 'did not know where their own career was going' (Seccombe and Ball 1992); in the 1987 national survey, 60 per cent said that they were not offered the right training to further their careers and almost half said that they had not received opportunities for updating (Price Waterhouse 1988: 47). What are the discontents here?

First, promotion in nursing, after a sister/charge nurse post, has long meant a move into education or management. There are courses of different types that offer opportunities to deepen knowledge and skills in clinical practice terms, but, despite campaigns, some demonstration projects in a variety of settings and the creation of a new 'clinical grading structure' for nursing,[6] there is no clear career pathway in clinical terms for nurses. Nurses, by and large, 'do their own thing', creating a career profile for themselves by adding qualifications, and by moving between jobs. Doing this means working against the grain of the system; it can result in downgrading as the nurse who has been promoted to sister/ charge nurse grade returns to a staff post in a new area. Such a move does not reflect back to the nurse a sense of growth of professional competence and worth, on the contrary, it can look like indecisiveness and lack of commitment. Tension is evident between those who make the conventional moves up the ladder and those who follow a more varied path. Since it is often men who follow the former course, and who come to be overrepresented in top positions compared with their minority status in nursing overall, this too has become a focus for anger and discontent expressed in the case of one much cited article in a question about whether there was a 'male takeover' or 'female giveaway' (Nuttall 1983).

What of the response of nursing to the needs of its majority of women members? Many nurses are likely to change jobs at some time not only at the dictate of their own career needs but in a way that is linked to those of a spouse. The majority will probably take career breaks for childbearing and many of these will be likely to want to work on a part-time basis for at least some part of their careers. Discontent is being voiced overtly here that in a profession that is so overwhelmingly composed of women, the adjustments made are so minimal. At first sight, nursing does appear to facilitate women with domestic commitments – there are return-to-nursing courses, a variety of hours arrangements and opportunities for part-time work as part of the establishment or as bank and agency nurses. But it is the full-timers and those with continuous careers who have the fuller choices and who can much more easily advance themselves and their careers. Lesley Mackay's study of nurses in a single region in England, the study from which the quotations at the start of the chapter are drawn, brings out very vividly some of the personal dilemmas and the waste that is involved. Mackay quotes the ex-sister, working nights as a bank nurse, who says that having applied for a night sister post and having not even been shortlisted, she gets on with the job but has just 'switched off'; she quotes another ex-sister who says that having returned as a part-timer she is 'ticked off' for using initiative and brains, and she draws attention to a third who points out how hard it is, having had children, to attempt to get back to where you were, in her case to a post as theatre sister. Mackay comments that 'doing part-time work is really time spent in the wilderness because it means that a nurse's career is put into abeyance' (Mackay 1989: 85). Survey findings make much the same point, emphasizing the need for a much more positive approach to the management of women's careers (see Price Waterhouse 1988, Waite *et al.* 1990).

Nurses' questioning of the arrangements that employers and their professional regulatory and support institutions are making for them as women, appears in a decade when questions of equality of opportunity, of access, of potential discrimination on grounds not only of sex, but of other factors such as ethnicity, disability, religious and sexual orientation, are all more insistently on the public agenda. The health service, as the largest employer in the UK, has been subject to repeated scrutiny for the fairness of its employment practices, and has supported a range of initiatives in terms of research and the development of good practice.[7] In this context, a growing thread of discontent amongst black and ethnic minority nurses about the treatment they have received at the hands of their colleagues has come to the fore. Harassment and abuse on account of their skin colour, discriminatory lines of questioning at interview, blocked promotion prospects for junior staff and lack of co-operation from others with those few who do reach more senior posts are among the complaints that have been documented in research reports and tribunal enquiries and have been the subject of discussion in the nursing press. Channelling of black nurses into EN training has also been subject to particular criticism.[8] Reviewing the evidence on this theme, looking too at the lack of positive steps to facilitate women's participation, at the blocks put in the way of enrolled nurses wanting to develop in nursing and the lack of any clear route for those who start as nursing auxiliaries to progress into nurse training, one observer has seen nursing as a profession particularly deeply divided along race, class and gender lines, whose leadership seems actively to be exacerbating such divisions rather than seeking policies that will ameliorate them (K. Robinson 1992). Others too are asking just what direction nursing should take in face of its size and its diversity (for example, Salvage 1985, Melia 1987, Hugman 1991). To think of controlling and shaping an occupation of half a million and more, where entrants come from diverse social backgrounds, where their initial educational qualifications may be nil, or may be degree level, and where the range of job opportunities yield a pay range, in 1993 for example, from less than £11,000 per annum to something in excess of £50,000 is daunting indeed.[9]

4   Professional divisions?

The huge size of nursing, the diversity of people and of jobs which it encompasses, is highly relevant to a further set of discontents concerning the relations between the three specialist groups within the broad umbrella of nursing, midwifery and health visiting, and also between hospital and community nursing, between general and specialist areas (as reflected in the mental illness, mental handicap and children's nursing parts of the Register), and between these and a whole array of other specialisms with different forms of recognition. Divisions opened up very sharply over the 1979 Nurses Act, designed to bring together not only the four countries of the UK, but a total of nine different bodies that served to regulate basic and more advanced qualifications in different areas of nursing, midwifery and health visiting. Behind what the outsider might be inclined to see as a relatively straightforward matter of rationalizing and simplifying an overly complex and overlapping set of arrangements, were commitments and convictions that stemmed from different histories, different circumstances and different perceptions of the nature of the work. Midwives, alert to all the difficulties of establishing a practice role in the hospital ward, wanted to preserve the position set out in their separate rules and regulations which they felt gave them a more clearly autonomous sphere. Health visitors, along with midwives, would agree that general nurse training was so disease-oriented that their training programme had to focus on a paradigm shift to health and normality, and to working with the well for the improvement of health. The placement of their trainings in colleges in the educational sector was felt to be an important gain that could be jeopardized by bringing them together with nurses. For district nurses, as with the other groups, their orientation to the needs of care in the community needed to be protected. The consultation process that preceded the 1979 legislation was protracted for these very reasons. Many felt that the fundamental premises from which they started had been misunderstood and swept aside, and that the basis of their practice was under threat in the new unified arrangements.[10] This has continued to influence relations within the nursing profession into the 1990s.

All this finds expression in an apparently trivial concern with matters of terminology and with issues of membership and representation. The UKCC, for example, can never refer to nurses, but must always refer to nurses, midwives and health visitors. We will see later, when we come to discuss the process of educational reform, that the Council's Education Policy Advisory Committee (a total of some 20 people), for example, could not form a subgroup to formulate new educational policy, since all interests had to be represented at all times. The question of whether it is actually feasible to hold together as a unitary profession groups of the size and diversity that are at present encompassed in our understanding of nursing might well be raised. But nurses constantly admonish themselves that they handle this badly, and see others turning away from issues that nurses regard as important, pronouncing nurses as parochial and inward-looking in their concerns. Certainly, as nurses are aware, their stances have left them at times open to mockery, to labels of immaturity and an inability to deal constructively with conflict, criticisms that they have found hard to counter in an effective way.

Overview

It is clear that to ask about nursing's discontents is to open a veritable Pandora's box. We find a pattern of education and service that seems to be intertwined to the detriment of both; we find a workforce that appears to be stretched beyond the limits of what is tolerable; we find a management that apparently cannot cope and a leadership that is accused of being out of touch. All this is before we even begin to look at the questions of opportunity, access and discrimination and at the position of specialist groups within nursing, and the arguments of those in midwifery and in health visiting and district nursing who feel that it would be better if they were not associated with nursing at all. Nurses frequently display the dedication and devotion to their work that is the stuff of the public image, but they combine this with an uneasy sense of their own oppression and a seeming belief in their own inability to tackle some of the fundamentals that would enable nurses to practise as they would wish.

To what extent is it fair to lay the blame for the unresolved issues that have been described and the tensions they generate at the feet of nurses themselves? Could nursing ever have put its own house in order? Has it had the power to do so? These are important questions. Before we look at divisions, doubts and unease, before we start asking what is wrong with nurses, we must understand the nature of the ground on which struggles for understanding and efforts to develop nursing practice actually take place. This ground, it will be argued, is a gendered ground. If we can uncover rather more than other authors have done, something of the form of this gendering and the ways in which it is sustained, we will be able to see the discontents of nurses in a new light, as a reflection of a much broader societal devaluation of women and of the work that they do. The character and scope of this devaluation, not at this stage in terms of nursing directly but in terms of a broader 'gendered world', is explored in Part One. A look at the cultural codes of masculinity and femininity that are found in this gendered world and how these serve to oppress women will provide the context for a closer and very different approach to some of the discontents outlined here.

We should note at once, however, that there are several different ways in which a discussion of gendered worlds such as is set out in Part One could be presented. We could, for example, derive understanding from a discussion of literary texts, or from representations in art, and other media where feminists have identified and analysed the male gaze. We could consider the work of feminist historical scholarship that traces the separation, ideological and material, of the public and private spheres, a separation that reaches its apogee in the bourgeois ideal of leisured lady in the Victorian era. The selection of texts in the two chapters which follow is one that represents the way that my own understanding has developed and inevitably reflects my own experience and biography. It is what I shall bring to bear in my attempts in later parts of the book to understand what we might mean when we say that we need a gender analysis of policy development in nursing, and it is one way, though not the only way, that such an analysis might develop. It should be noted too, that the argument will be conducted in fairly abstract terms, treating masculinity and femininity, for the moment at any rate, as though they are both unitary and fixed. In practice, there are many cultural codes, many specific masculinities and femininities and they will vary according to historical and class factors.[11] The way that individual women and men relate to cultural codes of masculinity and femininity will likewise be affected by a host of historical and contextual factors, and these themes will be picked up again at a later stage in the book.

Notes

1 There is no single published source of statistics about the UK nursing labour force from which a satisfactory picture can be gleaned. Figures for England for 1988 show men as 9 per cent of the total number of qualified staff working in the NHS (Department of Health 1990). Figures of around 10 per cent have been reported for male nurses for some time in more localized studies of the NHS. Training statistics tell a similar story (see UKCC 1986a).

2 The position concerning two- and three-year trained nurses is complex and involves a terminology that is confusing unless one understands something of the history. The Nurses Register was set up under legislation in 1919, and provided for nurses with a recognized training to be on a list maintained by the General Nursing Council. The legislation allowed for general registration and for a number of supplementary registers to denote more specialist areas. The growing recruitment of untrained nurses and continued questions of nurse shortage resulted in the approval in the early days of the NHS of a trained assistant. Placing names on a Roll rather than the Register was an attempt to indicate a clear difference of status between the two. Under the 1979 Nurses, Midwives and Health Visitors Act, however, a single Register was created. This included parts for general nurses, children's nurses, mental nurses and mental handicap nurses (all three-year trained 'first level' nurses), together with parts for enrolled nurses in the general field, in mental illness and in mental handicap (two-year trained 'second level' nurses). Enrolled nurses are thus today on the Register. The further complexities of the Register, to cover dual qualifications and differences in Scotland, Wales and Northern Ireland, and the registration of health visitors and midwives, are explained in UKCC (1986a).

3 ENs as a proportion of the total qualified nursing labour force in Britain had been shown to have risen considerably from the mid-1960s to the mid-1980s (see UKCC 1986b: annex 2, figure II:iv). Figures for the NHS in England for 1988 show them as 30 per cent of the qualified workforce and 18 per cent of the nursing workforce as a whole (Department of Health 1990).

4 A substantial volume of survey data concerning the motivation and morale of nurses became available in the late 1980s, prompted by fears about likely shortages due to wastage and turnover in the context of a declining recruitment due to the demographic dip in the population of 18-year-olds. This material offers a wealth of information on the ways nurses view their work. Management consultants Price Waterhouse, commissioned by the Regional Health Authority Chairmen, carried out a survey exercise on a massive scale, covering 7600 nurses, midwives and health visitors working in the NHS, leaving the NHS and in the private sector (Price Waterhouse 1988). The independent research body, the Institute of Manpower Studies (IMS) was

commissioned by the RCN to survey College members; this it did on six occasions between 1986 and 1991, producing a number of detailed reports. These surveys, alongside other research findings, particularly those of researchers associated with the Health Research Centre at the University of Lancaster (Mackay 1989; see also Francis *et al.* 1992, Williams *et al.* 1992) confirm that there is indeed a wide-ranging problem of 'motivation and morale' that needs to be explored.

5 For a good account of the range of views, largely negative, which abounded in a number of settings as general management was being put into place in the late 1980s, see Strong and Robinson (1990: ch. 3, and esp. ch. 4).

6 A new grading structure was negotiated for nursing in 1988. A furore erupted over the regradings, with employers being overwhelmed by the large numbers of appeals from individuals who felt that their gradings did not reflect the level of responsibility that they exercised in their work. Debate over this rather than any real discussion over the opportunities for new roles dominated the period at least until 1990. It is clear that local experimentation with a clinical nurse specialist role predated the grading review by a decade and more and that concepts of clinical specialist, advanced practitioner and nurse practitioner have all been advanced at different times, with no overall consensus or route forward being clear (Castledine 1986; Markham 1988). There is scope in the grading structure, and particularly with the freedoms of the new NHS Trusts as employers, for new departures here.

7 In September 1991 the Department of Health became the first government department to join the 'Opportunity 2000' campaign to increase the quantity and quality of women's participation in the workforce. It set up a Women's Unit within the NHS Management Executive and set eight initial goals to be achieved by the end of 1994 (see NHSME 1992). For recent discussions of NHS employment policies and women see Equal Opportunities Commission (EOC 1991), and Goss and Brown (1991); practical suggestions about policy development in this area are available in a number of manuals and guides, for example, National Steering Group (1987–9), Nursing and Midwifery Staffs Negotiating Council (no date).

8 Examples have been collected together in a vivid way in Baxter (1988). A good overall account can be found in King Edward's Hospital Fund for London (1990), and further relevant material has been collected together in Davies and Conn (1994).

9 Salaries for some executive nurses in post in NHS Trusts were rumoured to exceed those of senior officers at Health Department level.

10 No extensive review of the circumstances leading to the 1979 Act has yet been published, though a brief account including comments on failure to impose a common culture can be found in Dingwall *et al.* (1988).

11 Hearn (1992) argues for use of the plural – masculinities, public domains, patriarchies – in order to underline that there are different and overlapping social constructions here, involving class, ethnicity, age and other factors, and offers an analysis of the different spheres and contexts in which the theme of 'public men' can be deconstructed.

part
one

GENDERED WORLDS

two

ON GENDER, IDENTITY AND ACTION

The assumption that all social relations are gendered . . . changes the nature of the debate from an exclusive focus on women to a focus on how gender shapes and is implicated in all kinds of social phenomena. . . . I think we are only at the beginning of working out what we mean, in concrete terms, when we say social relations and processes are gendered.

(Acker 1989: 77)

Any group of students, set the task of producing a list of adjectives under the headings of women and men will have little trouble in quickly filling a page with common sex stereotypes. Men are strong and women are weak; men are rational, women are emotional; men are active, women passive; the list goes on. A little more discussion is likely to produce the observation that these qualities are not simply complementary, but in most cases are imbued with positive value on the side of men and negative value on the side of women. Somewhere along the line, someone will propose that all these so-called sex differences are the result of outmoded and prejudiced views, that they are disappearing in the worlds of work, education and politics where today, after all, merit is the key to individual achievement, and sex discrimination, should it occur, can be met with legal remedies. True, it might be conceded, there are obstacles to equal opportunity for women; but more flexible hours, jobsharing, state supported childcare, the chance of return to equal seniority after a career break, all these are being introduced and serve to facilitate women's greater access and participation. Some members of the student group would probably endorse the idea of providing a course in confidence-building and assertiveness for the more reticent of women – others would object either on the grounds that this would give women an unfair advantage, or on the grounds that there were unassertive and reticent men too. At this point the class is likely to be thoroughly confused; action of some sort would seem to be indicated, especially if they have to hand any of the multitude of statistics that could be produced to show the tiny proportions of women in senior positions in just about every sector of public life (see for example, Hansard Society 1990). But, someone would surely say, no one was seriously going to argue, were they, that all men possessed the one set of attributes and all women the other?

A discussion such as this brings us straight to the heart of the 'difference debate' which continues to plague feminists both at the level of theory and practice.[1] Conceding any ground to a position that accepts that there is sexual difference risks the charge of 'biologism' or 'essentialism'; and if there are indeed qualities that the two sexes have, 'by nature', are women then to be seen as naturally inferior? Suppose that we retreat a little, and regard these qualities as emerging from socialization into sex roles, are women then to be seen as major agents and willing victims of a process resulting in their own oppression? Starting from a position of no difference, resolutely arguing that men and women are the same, exposing sexual difference as a set of out-of-date and prejudiced attitudes, at first sight is much more defensible. Historically, such a position has provided a basis for women's successful political claims to hold property in their own names and to suffrage, and more recently has underpinned the outlawing of sex discrimination. And an assumption of 'the same until proved different' has also underpinned a myriad of challenges to bias in scientific thought and practice. On reflection, however, things are not so easy. Women do have a range of interests and claims arising from their roles, biological and social, in reproduction, and the ready catalogue that can be provided of a clear sexual division of labour in the home as well as in many other areas of social life, lends some credence to the suggestion that at present at any rate, women and men do seem to inhabit rather different worlds, and will be likely to bring different perspectives to bear. Then there is the matter of those lists of qualities; why is it that they continue to have so familiar a ring?

The approach outlined in this chapter will suggest that there is an escape from this dilemma, provided that we turn the spotlight (as Acker suggests in the opening quotation) from women to gender, and provided too that we make a clear distinction between real women and men on the one hand, and masculinity and femininity on the other. In this other way of thinking, masculinity and femininity are not 'attributes' that all men and all women in some simple way possess, nor are they in any straightforward sense 'scripts' that we have learned. Recent work, as we shall see, has suggested that masculinity and femininity are better understood as cultural codes or representations of gender and that gender, in this cultural sense, pervades our earliest experiences and shapes our sense of identity. Gender also, as later sections make clear, shapes the way in which we relate to each other and structures social institutions – not only those relating to the family, sexuality and reproduction, but also those which are apparently gender-free and which operate in the public domain of work and politics. Indeed the public/private split is itself a fundamental part of this cultural gendering. Furthermore, masculinity and femininity, the chapter will show, must be understood in constant reference to each other; they are not separate and complementary; rather they wrench apart the diversity and richness of our human qualities, assigning the masculine set a privileged status and containing, denying and repressing the feminine.

This argument will be pursued by reference to three particular authors. Nancy Chodorow, unusually for a sociologist, is steeped in an understanding of psychoanalytic feminism. A brief examination of some of her key themes provides an important starting point, emphasizing as it does the way in which gendering, though a cultural artefact, is also locked into some of our earliest experiences and deepest senses of identity. Carole Gilligan, a psychologist, relying to an important extent on Chodorow, has produced a highly accessible study of so-called sexual differences. It is important for giving more content to the notion of an alternative and feminine way of thinking and for the storm of controversy that continues to surround it. Roslyn Bologh at first sight will be the oddest choice of the three. A political scientist writing a scholarly treatise on a nineteenth-century theorist is certainly not the most obvious person to consider in such detail. Yet, she is the most important of the three. She provides an understanding of how masculinity and femininity relate to each other and of how this relation denies and denigrates the feminine. She also makes a crucial link between the masculine vision of organizing and the problems we still face today in designing organizations in which the totality of human needs and potentialities can be expressed. It is Bologh's work that I will build upon towards the end of the next chapter, to develop an understanding of the gendered vision at the heart of our current thinking about bureaucracy and professions. It is this that can help us to see that when nurses complain that no one speaks their language, that is because public language and the vision of proper public conduct that it expresses is saturated with gender. This chapter takes the first steps in explaining what this means. By the time we come to Part Two, we will be ready to deal with some of the immediate policy debates in which nursing comes, uncomfortably and uneasily, face-to-face with the gendering of social identities and institutions.

1   Two developmental pathways

The work of Nancy Chodorow (1978, 1989) provides an account of the development of gendered personalities. By drawing as it does on the object relations school of psychoanalysis and by being informed as it is by the ongoing critique of Freud provided by feminists,[2] it has proved to be particularly attractive to those looking for a theoretical stance that not only dismisses any notion of fixed biological attributes of the sexes but also goes beyond a simplistic social psychology that states that we are merely socialized into sex roles. Masculinity and femininity, she argues, are reproduced in complex ways both at the level of social organization and at the level of individual development. At this latter level, the level of acquisition of gender identity, or of 'a cognitive sense of the gendered self', attention needs to be focused on the family, and more specifically on the mothering that women do.

Object relations theory in psychoanalysis posits that all children begin life by experiencing a unity with a parent, only gradually relinquishing undifferentiated infantile attachment and acquiring a self as apart from the parent. The process of separation involves stages in which the initial sense of oneness with the mother gives way to separation and to the integrity of the individual self. This psychosexual process is seen as complex, by no means automatic, and as dependent both on physiological developments and on the capacity of the parent to make and elicit an appropriate response at each stage. Pinpointing inadequacies in this process for specific individual people, bringing them to conscious awareness in adulthood and tracing them through to the adult mode of response, is, of course, the stuff of much psychoanalytic therapeutic practice. A key part of Chodorow's contribution is to insist, in the context of a division of labour that allocates the parenting process overwhelmingly to the woman, on different developmental pathways for the two sexes as a consequence of this. The different pathways that she proposes accept and address directly the observation, common across different traditions of psychoanalytic thought, that the period of attachment to the mother lasts longer in girls than in boys.

Now, if we proceed, as many do at this point, to take the male as the norm, we will quickly start to conclude that girls have a slower or less complete developmental process than do boys. Chodorow does not do this. She argues instead that the fact that both boys and girls are raised by mothers places them in a different position in relation to the mother and gives each a distinctive developmental task.[3]

What does this entail? Chodorow explains:

> Mothers tend to experience their daughters as more like, and continuous with, themselves. Correspondingly, girls tend to remain part of the dyadic primary mother–child relationship itself. This means that a girl continues to experience herself as involved in issues of merging and separation, and in an attachment characterized by primary identification and object choice. By contrast, mothers experience their sons as a male opposite. Boys are more likely to have been pushed out of the preoedipal relationship, and to have had to curtail their primary love and sense of empathic tie with their mother. A boy has engaged, and been required to engage, in a more emphatic individuation and a more defensive firming of experienced ego boundaries . . .
>
> (Chodorow 1978: 166–7)

Chodorow stresses the different inner worlds and the different 'relational capacities' that this involves. Elaborating in particular on the position of the woman, she notes:

> Girls emerge with a stronger basis for experiencing another's needs or feelings as one's own (or of thinking that one is so experiencing another's needs and feelings). . . . From very early then, because they are parented by a person of the same gender (a person who has already internalized a set of unconscious meanings, fantasies and selfimages about this gender and brings to her experience her own internalized early relationship to her own other), girls come to experience themselves as less differentiated than boys, as more continuous with and related to the external object-world and as differently oriented to their inner object-world as well.
>
> (ibid.: 167)

When a girl does 'turn to the father', Chodorow argues, she does so 'every step of the way . . . while looking back at her mother – to see if her mother is envious, to make sure that she is in fact separate, to see if she can in this way win her mother, to see if she is really independent' (ibid.: 126). Girls, in other words, do not make so clean a break with the original object of their attachment, they retain a strong sense of connection to others, and display the empathy that goes with it. A girl's psychic structure, involving the full triad of mother, father and child, is more complex than a boy's, since the latter, experiencing the earlier and more complete 'pushing away' by the mother, attends to issues of separation and autonomy. Men for this reason are likely to find the expression of connection with another more threatening.

Chodorow's achievement here is two-fold. First, she takes us away from any idea that women have particular characteristics by nature. Her account encompasses much that appears in traditional psychoanalytical approaches to women's psychology without assuming that there is something anatomical or constitutional about this (ibid.: 168). Social arrangements, the sexual division of labour in the family and the process of mothering are what start this process in train. These are in principle alterable, and indeed Chodorow ultimately argues for a shift towards more shared parenting. Second, she shifts from gender as role to gender as identity. She is talking about personality or character formation; about the way in which a deep psychic structure is put into place. Her work demonstrated, in the words of Hester Eisenstein, who has provided a useful brief account of her overall argument, that the 'very process . . . by which infants acquired the most fundamental sense of self, was in fact a process that differentiated girls from boys' (Eisenstein 1984: 90). To change social relations that depend on gender will not be a simple matter of slipping into or even consciously learning a new role, it will involve aspects of personal identity that have been laid down in the unconscious in the earliest of childhood experiences.[4]

There is, of course, much more to Chodorow's overall contribution than this; her work, in any case, is concerned more to answer the question of why it is that women continue to engage in mothering than to elaborate on the gendered nature of personality structures as such. Not surprisingly, she has her critics, both of the mothering thesis as a whole and of this concept of gendered personality.[5] What is important here is not to pursue these as such, but to pay attention to the leave that the work of Chodorow has given for others to begin to elaborate a difference theory, to explore the theme of separation versus connection and to use it to break away from a constant comparison which renders the male normative and the female inferior, to develop instead a view of a distinctive 'women's worldview', internally coherent in its difference. (More strictly, however, we should speak of a worldview of femininity, or a cultural code of femininity, rather than imply that this worldview in any simple way equates with that of women.)

Carol Gilligan (1982) provides what is probably the most prominent, influential and controversial example of such thinking in her study of ethics and moral reasoning among women and men.[6] Her reliance on Chodorow is made very plain at the outset; it gave an important stimulus not only to see the negative and dismissive account of female psychology that was contained in much conventional theorizing, but also to start to replace it with something more positive and direct – something, furthermore, that could give new insights into the development of male and female children and adult women and men. The goal of her study she explains is to use the group that has been left out to expand understanding and to call attention to what is missing. The book is intended to encourage psychologists to go in a different direction but it is also written for a more general readership among women.

Gilligan describes how, about half-way through a period of 10 years of research listening to how children talk about moral issues and using a framework stressing distinct developmental stages through which the child passes,[7] she became increasingly uneasy. Girls and women were being depicted as remaining at what was deemed to be a 'lower' stage of contextual reasoning and as not moving to the 'higher' stage of the logical application of abstract rules. Thus, describing the experiments that had been designed, she notes how, given an ethical dilemma to resolve, the boy at age 11 would treat it almost as a mathematical problem, deducing a solution from general principles, and firmly and articulately arriving at his decision. The girl at the same age seemed altogether less confident, and would often conclude that 'it all depends'.

Some excerpts will give the flavour of this. They concern part of the responses of two children, Jake and Amy, to 'Heinz's dilemma' – whether to steal a drug he cannot afford to buy in order to save the life of his wife. Gilligan describes Jake, at 11, as clear from the outset that Heinz should steal the drug:

> For one thing, a human life is worth more than money, and if the druggist makes only $1,000, he is still going to live, but if Heinz doesn't steal the drug, his wife is going to die. (Why is life worth more than money?) Because the druggist can get a thousand dollars later from rich people with cancer, but Heinz can't get his wife again. (Why not?) Because people are all different and so you couldn't get Heinz's wife again.

Gilligan then comments that Amy replies in a way that seems evasive and unsure. Asked whether Heinz should steal the drug, she replies:

> Well, I don't think so. I think there might be other ways besides stealing it, like if he could borrow the money, or make a loan or something, but he really shouldn't steal the drug – but his wife shouldn't die either.

Amy pursues the question further:

> If he stole the drug, he might save his wife then, but if he did, he might go to jail, and then his wife might get sicker again, and he couldn't get more of the drug, and it might not be good. So they

should really just talk it out and find some other way to make the money.

(Gilligan 1982: 26–8)

Gilligan proposed that, far from Amy being unsure, or less developed in her thinking, there were two quite different logics at work here. The one stemmed from the perspective of maturation as a process of developing the integrity of the autonomous self, the other from a different worldview based on connectedness and intersubjectivity. Jake constructed the dilemma (as the theory has assumed that one did if one had reached a higher stage of reasoning) as a conflict between the two abstract values of property and life. He sees a consensus around a hierarchy of societal values that places life before property; he recognizes and respects that Heinz would be breaking the law, and suggests that if Heinz is caught, the judge should give him the lightest possible sentence. Gilligan comments on how Jake enjoys the encounter, sets the problem up as an equation in logic and derives a solution. 'Since his solution is rationally derived, he assumes that anyone following reason would arrive at the same conclusion' (ibid.: 28).

Amy operated differently. She was seeking a solution that did not sever the relationship between the parties and thus wanted to explore whether there could not be a win/win solution, rather than a win/lose one, and started from a belief in communication as a mode of conflict resolution. Amy obviously was not enjoying herself as Jake was, and remained unconfident. Yet her response was not more indecisive and uncertain, instead it was 'another voice', stemming from a different developmental direction, with a logic of its own. The stages of development theory, expressing the 'masculine voice', and supposing it to be universal, suppressed the feminine. Gilligan was able to uncover and valorize what seemed to be a more woman-centred and woman-friendly way of reasoning.

Later in the book Gilligan describes the extension of her studies[8] to adults' senses of self and to women's judgements in situations concerning abortion for example. Here she explores what we might see as a struggle with issues of altruism versus apparent 'selfishness' in women's accounts. The developmental process, which used to be thought of as more or less complete at adulthood begins to be seen in a different light. The data suggest that rather than linear development, it may be more appropriate to see women as engaged in a cyclical confrontation: moral values stressing altruism and connection on the one hand and on the other a recognition that these values alone threaten to erase the self, and that it is not always 'selfish' to challenge them. For men, having established the bounded sense of self early on, the issue is almost a reverse one – of making connections, of coming to terms with needs for intimacy that have been repressed. On the one hand, there is an 'ethics of justice'; this involves a clear sense that a person is autonomous, has rights and must act responsibly, that is by following a set of formal rules of behaviour, but in essence pursues self-development. On the other hand, there is an 'ethics of care', where concern for others overrides personal autonomy, responsibilities are more important than rights and altruism and self-sacrifice are important. The first can appear from the vantage point of the second as pure selfishness; the second can appear from the vantage point of the first as dependency and indecisiveness.[9]

It is possible to take this kind of reasoning some considerable distance further, and to see the view from connection and the view from autonomy as differing not just on moral reasoning but on a range of other dimensions also. Table 2.1, drawing from a number of what we might call the difference school writers,[10] sets out a number of features that might characterize the 'masculine' and 'feminine' voice (but what I will later explain I prefer to call the cultural codes of gender), showing how, prompted by these kinds of approaches it is now possible to propose characteristics for the 'feminine' that are neither negatives nor in any sense inferior.

The first heading, 'development of self', summarizes key features in

Table 2.1 Cultural codes of gender

	Masculine	*Feminine*
Development of self	Separation Boundedness Responsibility to self Self-esteem Self-love	Relation Connectedness Responsibility to others Selflessness Self-sacrifice
Cognitive orientation	Abstract, rule-governed thinking Mastery/control Emphasis on expertise Skills/knowledge as portable acquisitions	Concrete, contextual thinking Understanding/use Emphasis on experience Skills/knowledge as confirmed in use
Relational style	Decisive Interrogative Hierarchy-orientated Loyal to superordinates Agentic/instrumental	Reflective Accommodative Group-orientated Loyal to principles Facilitative/expressive

Chodorow's gendered image of child development. In the masculine cultural code, the project is separation, establishment of firm ego boundaries and the development of a sense of self and of responsibility for one's self; in the feminine, the project is relation, a situation where the girl remains connected to the mother, developing a sense through this of responsibility to the other. And where learning masculinity means striving for autonomous action, a growing confidence as an agent in the world and an accompanying growth of self-esteem and perhaps we can say self-love, learning femininity means selflessness and even self-sacrifice in orientating to the needs of others.

The second heading, 'cognitive orientation', links back to Gilligan's Jake and Amy example, showing that the two perspectives can also be seen as orientated differently in relation to a world of knowledge. On the one hand, there is a view of knowledge as abstract and rule-governed. It is thus something to be taken hold of, 'mastered' and possessed. The concept of self as expert, of skills and knowledge as acquisitions, things that are displayed and can be put to use at will, flows from this. On the other hand, we can begin to discern another view, one which derives from a concrete and contextual cognitive orientation. Here, knowledge takes on a much more provisional character. Knowledge is an under-standing that needs to be confirmed in context and in use; experience may need to accompany formal expertise, and instead of a confident feeling of possession and mastery by the self, there is a need to have knowledge confirmed and validated by others.

Some of the items under the third heading, 'relational style', make intuitive sense in terms of the lists of adjectives that opened the chapter. But here, instead of the feminine list being negative, a deliberate effort has been made to find terms that express difference in a positive way; not indecisive, for example, but reflective. The contrasts that relate to hierarchy and loyalty will not be immediately graspable at this stage. They will be developed further, however, later in this chapter, at the end of Chapter 3 and again later in the book.

It is as well at this point, however, to attend to the critics.[11] In a commentary on Gilligan, Lynne Segal (1987) puts a number of important objections. First, what does an argument of this sort achieve? Does it not in the end come full circle and reinstate the very stereotypes of sexual difference that women have tried to challenge? It is true, of course, that it presents difference positively rather than denigrating it. But politically, the only place it seems to take women is into separatism, into creating their own spaces to nurture and celebrate the 'other voice'. In the day-to-day world, arguing for difference in the public arena can also have a boomerang effect – whenever women propose that they are different, that difference is used by men to work to women's containment and disadvantage. Gilligan, Segal objects, does not indicate how the stress on difference serves to perpetuate male dominance and disqualifies women from areas where rewards are high. Next, what precisely is the status of the proposed difference? Difference arises in a social context of unequal power between the sexes. Segal would clearly prefer to see Gilligan understand difference as dynamic and changing and relating to social practices rather than producing an argument where, as she rather disparagingly puts it, difference 'reduces to some sort of basic internal personality trait'. On a related point, Segal questions whether all women and all men really behave in this way. Here she objects to a research design which, while making male and female comparisons, remains silent on class and ethnic differences that may lead to variation within the sexes. Is a study that attacks false universalizing of theory actually falling into the same trap, and falsely universalizing gender difference?

These criticisms must be taken seriously. The dangers of a difference argument, the purposes for which it will be used and the ways in which it is likely to be misunderstood, are real. But I am on the side of those who say that there is no point in denying difference; we must 'risk difference'[12] if we are to develop understanding. The point about presenting the other voice in a positive light needs more acknowledgement than Segal is prepared to give. It is a step away from the crude stereotypes that abound and are harmful to women and must be acknowledged as such. It does not take one set of attributes as normative and construct the other in a negative way as inferior to the first. It brings into focus that which has been suppressed, it suggests that there is a way of acting that 'listens to a different drummer'. This brings us to the celebration point. Gilligan does not celebrate the other voice in any straightforward sense; to the contrary, she sees implications positive and negative in both of the voices she describes, and talks, towards the end, of a balanced human development that involves a rapprochement between the two.

What then of the charges that women and men do not 'always' behave like this and that their behaviour may be more a function of power difference than of difference of gender identity? Gilligan presents an eloquent statement of an alternative way of viewing ethics and moral reasoning. She does it in a way that makes it widely accessible, that captures the imagination, draws from literature, myth, film, and cuts across the conventions of presenting an argument in the social sciences. Perhaps that was the only way, but it does leave unanswered questions and it does mean she seems to say different things at different points and that the crucial issue of the status of the 'different voices' of the ethics of justice and care and the relation of these to real women and men remains ultimately unclear.[13] My remarks at the very outset of the chapter put my position on this – that we need to engage with difference in the shape of cultural codes of masculinity and femininity, that they will map, but not neatly, on to real people. As for the question of power, it may well be that it is not a question of either/or, but that gender has to be understood as a process that operates at many levels, one of which is likely to be the gendering of identity, and that if we fail to recognize this we will fail to understand the full difficulty of accomplishing any change. The idea of gender as operating at different levels, at the level of identity, at the level of representation and at the level particularly of organizational practice, is taken up in the next chapter.

To sum up: first, the difference theorists have performed an important and probably still unfinished task of naming that which has been suppressed. That does not mean that we must accept uncritically that which they have named. The very difficulty and novelty of naming the feminine attests to the power of the masculine cultural code. It is vital that more work is done on clarifying the status of that naming as part of a set of cultural understandings of masculinity and femininity, rather than as attributes that describe women and men. One important implication of this is to recognize that women are exposed to the culture of masculinity, that women, in many instances, are likely to have a double or 'bifurcated consciousness'[14] with all the attendant advantages and disadvantages that this might bring. Second, it is important to acknowledge that celebration of difference *per se* can be important (indeed often gives the kind of safe space which is vital to elaborate the naming of difference), but that this is not the only use of difference thinking. Naming of difference, as we have noted, can also be seen as part of a project, not just of reversal but of transcendence. Sandra Harding puts this point well when she says that we may have to countenance a woman–centred hypothesis before we can imagine a gender-free one (Harding 1986: 138). Third, there is the matter of difference appearing as a pair of alternative and equally coherent worldviews; unless we quickly move to acknowledge that masculinity is hegemonic, that femininity is suppressed, we arrive at the dilemmas Segal has outlined. The key weakness of the accounts presented so far is that they do not attend to this question of the power relation between the two; they do not give attention to the way in which cultural representations of gender privilege versions of masculinity. The section which follows, shifting attention from gender as identity to gender more as vision and metaphor for action, shows how important it is to do just this.

2   The representation of gender

Men, when schooled in masculinity, will reproduce their world in ways that are gendered masculine. This is true at a practical level of the institutions and organizations they found and populate, and at the level of the theories they offer to represent, explain and justify the public worlds they inhabit of work and politics. This means that the theories of social scientists and others cannot necessarily be accepted as detached from cultural representations of gender – they may, if unwittingly, offer good insights into the content of these representations. We have already seen this in the critique that Carol Gilligan offers of certain theorizing in psychology. We now turn to another writer whose work in the traditions of political science and sociology will enable us to explore masculinity and femininity from a somewhat different vantage point and supplement and further develop the account that has already been presented.

Roslyn Bologh came, as a feminist and as a sociologist, rather late in her own life to read the classical and still highly influential corpus of work written by German sociologist Max Weber. She describes at the outset of her study the profound debt that she feels she owes to Weber. He opened up to her a world beyond her own experience, a way of looking at power and politics and at the enduring themes of historical development. Her profound admiration, however, jostled with serious alienation from Weber's worldview. Her account of Weber's thought became a struggle to clarify the masculinity in his thinking and to try to frame an alternative to it. She exclaims emphatically at the outset of her book:

> Max Weber, your vision is limited; we live in different bodies, in different times, and we come from different places. Your vision, extensive and expansive as it is, is the vision from your body, inscribed with your gender, your place, your time. It may be the vision that enables you to make your way in and through the world; but it also restricts what you can see, what you can experience and what you can know. It also restricts what you can do. It is the kind of action to which your vision leads that I find most painful. I feel too keenly the restrictiveness of your vision and its consequences. And so I struggle against it; I reread your writings and scrutinise your way, in order to carve out a way for myself.
>
> (Bologh 1990: xv)

Her project, of detaching herself from, resisting and opposing Weber, involves acknowledging his vision of the public world as a masculine one, and deepening her understanding of what this entails and what it means for women. She starts with a reading of feminist revisionary work on Freud, using accounts which largely postdate the work of Chodorow, but which offer a perspective which, while not at odds with Chodorow's, brings masculinity to the foreground and problematizes it much more, particularly by emphasizing its denial of and in some instances contempt for qualities that are culturally represented as feminine.[15] It is the denial of that which is deemed feminine which Bologh finds so clearly in Weber and that she sees as so important to uncover and resist. An account of some of the key facets of her argument, therefore, will deepen our understanding, moving us more decisively away from the sense of positive complementarity that one gets from some of the difference writing in psychology, towards a greater acknowledgement of power.

Looking not to the mother but to the father, Bologh emphasizes that children have two initial desires; a desire for love, protection and consolation on the one hand, and a desire for power, action and 'making a difference in the world' on the other. The desire for love and protection is the 'feminine' desire, a desire to surrender the self, to become an object. The desire for action is the 'masculine' desire, a desire to control one's life, to become an autonomous agent, a subject in the world. We have to choose; we cannot have both. The choice of masculinity involves and produces a public world of agency, of action and greatness, but a world devoid of any expectation of nurturance and care. This public world comprises persons (mostly men) with a strongly bounded sense of self. Each acts independently, each strives to achieve his own interest. Each is rational, that is, he thinks instrumentally in terms of means and ends. Thus far we are on still familiar ground. But Bologh goes on to tease out the assumptions about the nature of social and collective action which flow from these strongly bounded creatures.

The public world, for Weber, is a world comprised of 'hostile strangers'. It must be so. Men's impulses, he feels, are to engage in autonomous action in pursuit of their interests; towards each other they must exercise power and domination, their impulses in other words are at base violent, coercive and cruel. Could things be otherwise? Weber does consider a vision of social life that is based on brotherly love, that is, one that is based on a shared commitment to values that would command support so that men could act out of their shared interest rather than their self-interest. He rejects it. Interests, he argues, are never shared; power is zero sum, A can only have it at the expense of B, and power is never willingly foregone. This is the position as he sees it of a political realist; it expresses disenchantment with the modern world. Social life is thus 'tainted with ethical guilt'. To think otherwise, he argues, is to engage in wishful thinking and illusion.

And yet, within this world of hostile strangers, it is possible, indeed it is very important, for men to set aside their violent impulses and behave in a restrained way. This may occur in the face of fear, but it may also occur when a man espouses a cause. In pursuit of a cause, the struggle for power is ennobled and becomes worthy. The man with the cause is the hero, the leader, the one who can achieve true greatness. Here Weber sees not ordinary masculinity, but true manliness. The bleakness of the political realist position to which his own masculinist worldview has led him can by this means be overcome.

Weber is known to many people today through his comments on bureaucracy. The bureaucratic organization, with its hierarchically organized offices and its rules, is technically the most efficient of institutional structures for realizing an end. It embodies instrumental rationality and reliability of judgement. But it must also be seen in this wider picture. The bureaucracy requires the command of a leader who will direct it in pursuit of a cause. The individual bureaucrat is part of a structure of command; a cog in the machine, whose main desire is only to become a bigger cog. Bureaucracy is the organizational means, we might say, by which manliness conquers masculinity; bureaucracy imposes the hierarchical relations that masculinity accepts. That makes it reliable – but it is only a machine, and without leadership it will drift.[16]

The concept of bureaucracy will be explained further in Chapter 3, but it is important to dwell for a moment on the notion of the heroic leader, the manly man, who is so crucial to Weber's thought about the organization of the public world. He is, we have already seen, re-strained. His belief in a cause disciplines him to self-control, and to a careful weighing of courses of action in pursuit of the cause. He must use his intellect and arrive at an independent judgement (remember that the world is full of hostile strangers); he must apply rational criteria to his decision-making. He must not allow his vision to be clouded by sentiment, and in this regard must welcome and foster the distance from others that this entails. This is not naked power. Manly behaviour can involve a chivalrous attitude to protection of the weak, and it always involves a careful consideration of the consequences of action in terms of achievement of the chosen end.

In imposing his will and taking personal responsibility, the manly man must endure the distrust of others. Given the importance of the cause, he will sometimes have to sacrifice ethics, ignore the welfare of others and perhaps use violence. He must examine his conscience, maintain his dignity and his distance, sometimes keeping silent, always keeping his own counsel. He is, if you like, cold, calculating and ruthless in his relentless rationality. Yet he is more than this. He is not simply exercising his strength and power. This is mediated and re-deemed by commitment to an end, which requires him to relinquish the sympathy of others. Weber sees here a constant struggle for true heroic greatness, its tragedy being that it can only ever be achieved at the high points of life. The manly ideal, then, is not only a tough job specifi-cation, it is a set of principles of personal conduct where a man can take pride in his achievements but must live constantly with the secret of his own frequent failure. Winning friends and influencing people, strictly, does not come into it. There is no point!

What of the rest of us – the men who do not reach or aspire to the manly ideal, and the women – how are these to be seen within this masculine vision of the world? As far as men are concerned, we have already seen that Weber distinguishes between ordinary masculinity and ideal manliness. Pride in the exercise of restrained, independent judgement is accompanied by disdain for other men. They are to be controlled through loyalty and fear, they are cogs in the bureaucratic machine. The gulf between a leader and his followers is profound. Relations between men are distant, hierarchical and based on fear; the potential violence of the relations of hostile strangers is nowhere far below the surface. The position of women in this construction of masculinity is very different.

Let us return to the choices of the child as set out at the beginning of this section. The masculine desire is for action in the world, the feminine desire for love and protection. But Weber, in his masculinist worldview, has concluded that love and protection are an illusion. They require trust in others, a belief that they will be sympathetic, will orientate themselves to you, and will be concerned with your well-being. In a world of hostile strangers, femininity can only be achieved if the woman withdraws, becomes not a subject but an object in the world, remains in the private sphere dependent on the protection of a man. While masculinity requires strict self-control, femininity does not, and, safely away from the public world, can be acknowledged. 'Women,' Bologh explains, 'like unrepressed children, are expected to express enthusiasm, liveliness, sympathy, delight' (Bologh 1990: 259). These are ways of being that from the standpoint of masculinity are hopelessly undisciplined and emotional. Femininity, however, is inferior, it is not part of the 'civilizing process', it lacks that discipline and constant struggle that allows the development of the intellect. It is concerned with the day-to-day, the practical and the pleasurable. It is 'being' not 'doing'. Bologh explains:

> Because women's feelings for others obstruct 'rational' action, they are too 'soft'. They are unwilling or unable to make the hard decisions that are necessary for achieving the goal. They fall into the 'compassion trap'; they rely on intuitive judgement; they are concerned with 'the relationship' or others' feelings. Women, who *by definition* orient to the maintenance of relationships and the sustenance of human life 'do not know what the real world is like'; that hard decisions have to be made, that people have to get hurt, that if one is unwilling to hurt others, then others will take advantage.
>
> (ibid.: 257, emphasis added)

She also insists that we understand the relation of the public and the private world as a relation of repression. Masculinity's version of rational action conceives itself as autonomous and independent of the other. In practice, as is already clear, while denying the other it also needs and assumes it. In a highly insightful and crucially important passage, she observes:

> Our very concept of what it is to be a man ... presupposes repression: a certain conception of and relation to women, a relation in which women are expected to fulfil men's personal and domestic needs, needs which are then not recognised as essential to being a man. If anything, they are viewed as weaknesses, needs that actors in the public world, men, ought not to take seriously. *The very existence of the public world as we know it, presupposes, yet denies that it presupposes, the private world, and the kind of person, woman, who is defined in terms of that world.* This is not the same as saying the two are separate and complementary. Rather they are forcibly divided and the division is maintained by repression.
>
> (ibid.: 242, emphasis added)

Femininity, repressed in this way, now appears not so much as something benign and childlike, but something that is to be feared as a temptation, something that in other words is seductive but contemptible.

A brief diversion from our main interest in the construction of masculinity and its relation to the public sphere, to consider what happens in the private sphere is of interest. What then of erotic love between the sexes? Bologh points out that Weber, briefly, and in passages that others rarely acknowledge, does follow his own logic through, arguing that here too is a relation of male dominance and that there is a 'veiled and sublimated brutality that accompanies sexual love', that can 'coerce the soul' of a woman. [17] But once again there is a difference between ordinary masculinity and true manliness. If she in her womanliness strives to please him, he in manliness must strive to be worthy of this devotion. This he can do by his ever more restrained and rational action in the public sphere. In other words, she is devoted to him, and he is devoted to the cause. Does it sound familiar?

This section has considered concepts of masculinity and femininity as they emerge from Roslyn Bologh's commentary on Max Weber. At first sight, a detailed theoretical exposition such as hers of a single and no longer contemporary author may seem a strange text to include. In practice, however, it has allowed us to take the understanding of masculinity and femininity one stage further. We have seen that the masculine project of separation and firming of ego boundaries discussed in the last section means not only the creation of a series of rational and autonomous subjects, but also *the creation of a public world built on the principle of hostile strangers and of a culture of competitive, distant and hierarchical relations.* We have seen how Weber's vision of masculinity involves isolation, and a lonely struggle that sets standards that cannot often be met. We have also seen that masculinity and femininity are cultural ideas that are locked together and that masculinity is given meaning via the repression of femininity. And we have gained a glimpse of the fear of and contempt for women that is part of our cultural heritage.

Concluding remarks

I have now dwelt at some length on concepts of masculinity and femininity as they emerge in a number of different texts. Authors such as Chodorow, Gilligan, Bologh and others have different reasons for trying to probe these concepts and pursue their analyses in different ways. Nevertheless important commonalities emerge, and the net result moves us some considerable distance from the everyday stereotypes about women and men with which the chapter opened. Those stereotypes are still recognizable in the writings of these authors, but the analysis is a much deeper one. At least three elements can be singled out at this stage. First, there is the notion that masculinity and femininity can be expressed as differential developmental trajectories – the one towards separation and autonomy, the other towards connection and attachment. Second, there is the suggestion that the route to masculinity gains its coherence in important measure by denial or repression of the qualities expressed as femininity. Bringing 'feminine qualities' into focus as having a logic and a coherence requires an act of effort, of consciously working against the grain. Third, there is the proposition that masculinity is hegemonic, not just in the sense of silencing ways of thinking and ways of acting by regarding them as feminine, but also in the sense of informing action in the public sphere, that is by actively shaping institutions – the policies, practices and procedures which govern the worlds of work and politics – according to a masculine vision.

An important thread running through this account concerns the personal costs to us all of a culture gendered in the way described here. Masculinity defined in the way it has been in this chapter is not only problematic for women but also for men. The model of the distant, controlled autonomous individual, whose decisions emerge from processes of unemotional, abstract reasoning, who relies always on his own counsel, is a model few can live up to for long, and one which consigns the majority of flesh and blood men to a position of inferiority and fearfulness. It renders hierarchies and elites as the normal form of relations among men. But if few men can comfortably succeed in the profoundly hierarchical order that stems from this cultural representation of masculinity, it is at least culturally appropriate that they try. No woman, however, can succeed in the public world without in some way compromising her identity as feminine.[18]

It is the pervasiveness and the power of the vision of masculinity which has been outlined in this chapter that needs to be underlined. As was clear at the outset of the chapter, there is a level at which we understand this already. But we trivialize it and fail to understand the full implications of gender. When, for example, the grammatical and linguistic conventions that prioritize the male, that speak of man the human, that employ the male pronoun are used, when the metaphors of control that present machinery, tools, nature itself as the 'she' that is to be dominated and 'mastered' are evoked, some will see this as mere ephemeral figures of speech. Others, however, will admit that such conventions serve in a way to make women invisible and for this reason should have attention. They will acknowledge that features such as this represent a culture gendered in such a way as to neglect and disregard the feminine. French feminist theorist Luce Irigaray discusses this in a very thoughtful and accessible way in her essay 'The neglect of female genealogies'. A culture that erases the feminine to this degree must be called patriarchal. And patriarchal cultures, she explains:

> have reduced the feminine to such a degree that their reality and their description of the world are incorrect. Thus, instead of remaining a different gender, the feminine has become, in our languages, the non-masculine, that is to say an abstract, non-existent reality. Just as an actual woman is often confined to the sexual domain in the strict sense of the term, so the feminine grammatical gender itself is made to disappear as subjective expression, and vocabulary associated with women often consists of slightly denigrating, if not insulting, terms which define her as an object in relation to the male subject. This accounts for the fact that *women find it so difficult to speak and to be heard as women. They are excluded and denied by the patriarchal linguistic order. They cannot be women and speak in a sensible and coherent manner.*
>
> (Irigaray 1993: 20, emphasis added)

Ignoring difference, acting as equal is often an important strategy for women and at an individual level is sometimes a spectacularly successful one. But it leaves patriarchal cultures intact. The public world that women enter when they take advantage of their civil rights is still what Irigaray calls a 'between-men-cultural-world' and is still defined according to visions of masculinity. Women are then called on either to renounce a female cultural identity or, as we shall see in Part Two of this book, find themselves defined as female and silenced, neglected and misunderstood when they try to articulate and uphold values that do not fit with the masculine world of rational, instrumental action.

This is the dilemma that is captured by Susan Reverby (1987) in her account of the history of American nursing as being ordered to care in a society that does not value caring. Nurses are expected to uphold the values of a female identity in face of a masculinity that is profoundly ambivalent about it, and in face of institutions imbued with that same masculinity. In the next chapter we explore the overall theme further in a consideration of the gendering of work organizations and of the twin notions so relevant to the organization of nursing work, of bureaucracy on the one hand and profession on the other.

Notes

1 The debate about whether improvement in the position of women is to be secured by an insistence on equal, i.e. identical, treatment, or by a call for the recognition of difference lies at the heart of contemporary feminism. It has been tackled across a wide diversity of disciplinary areas, including history, philosophy, sociology, psychology and politics for example, and has been treated as both a practical issue of strategy and tactics and as a theoretical issue. For some insights into how working women have campaigned at different times on an equality platform and a difference one, and have met with difficulties in both, see Lewis and Davies (1992); for material on current dilemmas in terms of equal opportunity legislation in a European context see Meehan and Sevenhuijsen (1991). An important article discussing the issues at both a practical and a theoretical level is that of Scott (1988); a clear introduction to many dimensions of the debate is contained in Bacchi (1990).

2 Chodorow has been described as someone who 'helped convince American sociologists and (non–psychoanalytic) feminists that psychoanalysis was not analogous to the plague' and who has contributed to a rapprochement between sociology and psychoanalysis that has been inspired by feminists (Kurzweil 1989: 94–5). In practice, psychoanalytic writing has proved more accessible to those coming from literary and cultural analysis tradition than to those like myself with a background in sociology, and sociologists' use of it, including the use made here, is likely to be regarded as a fairly watered-down affair. Kurzweil's article makes clear the long traditions in France, Germany and Britain through which the critique and reconstruction of Freudian thought has been reformulated, a tradition that is likely to be known to British feminists in the main through the classic and influential work of Juliet Mitchell (1975). I am making no claim here to have engaged with it in a systematic way. My aim in this chapter, as already noted, is to show that masculine and feminine can be given a fairly clear content as cultural codes,

that this content has a psychic dimension which aids our understanding of some specific forms of oppression of women. Whether I have succeeded in this needs to be judged on a reading of the book as a whole.

3 Chodorow makes clear her departure from Freud in the following words: 'Freud is concerned that it takes the girl so long to develop an oedipal attachment to her father and the "feminine" sexual modes that go with this attachment. The stress is on the girl's attachment as *preoedipal* rather than on the attachment itself. It is important to stress the other side of the process' (Chodorow 1978: 66). This seems to suggest not only that there is a neglected 'other side' but that Freud's line of thought has been governed by a male interest, a concern with the development of heterosexuality in women, a point that she does not take up here (although earlier, Freud's 'blindness, contempt of women and misogyny', p.142, is addressed). The challenge to a universal stages theory, however, the insistence that we see women as different not lesser or behind, is articulated very clearly in the work of Gilligan, discussed below.

4 Eichenbaum and Orbach (1985: 192) state that the kind of 'structural psychological shift' that they favour cannot be implemented in one generation: 'Women and men currently carry with them deep feelings of misogyny and unconscious sexism. Even with changes in childrearing arrangements, these influences will have their impact on at least the first generation raised by two parents . . .' To speak of a 'deep misogyny' on the part of women and men may seem a strong claim at this point in the chapter. The argument, however, will provide progressive support for such a position.

5 There is the question, for example, taken up later in this chapter of the rage and resentment that underlies the pushing away by the mother of the boy and whether the oppression of women by men cannot usefully be traced to this. Eisenstein's juxtaposition of the work of Dorothy Dinnerstein with that of Chodorow allows her to raise this alongside other questions concerning for example the reasons why the mother/daughter dynamic should conduce to heterosexuality rather than lesbianism, and the dynamics of the triad when a son is involved (see Eisenstein 1984: 93ff, cf. Tong 1989: 153ff). Those who work in a therapy context with women both acknowledge a debt and raise criticisms. In a particularly accessible description of the way the Women's Therapy Centre evolved in Britain, written for a general audience, the authors make a brief but explicit reference to a disagreement with Chodorow concerning the ease of the separation process and also perhaps offer a differing view of the significance of the father (see Eichenbaum and Orbach 1985: 22 and fn21). For further discussion of Chodorow see also Lorber *et al.*(1981).

6 The debate prompted by Gilligan's work is voluminous. Her arguments have been taken up in psychology (her own discipline of origin) and in philosophy as well as in a wide range of feminist publications. For a few examples, see Ferguson (1984), Benhabib (1987), Segal (1987), Tong (1989: 189ff), and especially Kerber *et al.* (1986).

7 Gilligan worked first as a student and later as a colleague with Lawrence Kohlberg. The following summary indicates the thinking involved in his framework of stages of moral thinking (see Kohlberg 1969, 1973).

Stage one	*Punishment and Obedience Orientation* the child does as s/he is told	} individual
Stage two	*Instrumentalist/Relativist Orientation* the child shows limited reciprocity, satisfying own needs and sometimes those of others	need

Stage three	*Interpersonal Concordance* the child conforms to gain approval	}
Stage four	*Law and Order Orientation* the child develops a sense of duty and respect for authority	shared social conventions

Stage five	*Social Control/Legalistic Orientation* the child displays a utilitarian approach valuing individual freedom provided others are not harmed	} principled notion of
Stage six	*Universal Ethical Principle Orientation* the child uses self-imposed universal principles, e.g. justice, reciprocity, respect for the dignity of individuals	fairness

8 Gilligan's own data derive from three sources: (1) a study of 25 college students taking a course in moral political choice, interviewed twice; (2) a study of 29 women interviewed at the point of taking a decision on an abortion and again one year later; and (3) a matched sample of 144 persons of both sexes at nine points in the lifecycle, plus further interviews with a subsample of 36. The studies are not presented in the form of a conventional scientific report, instead the book 'presents excerpts' in order to develop and explore the argument. Nurses, however, might be particularly interested in an empirical application of Gilligan's thinking, concerning contrasts in ethical reasoning among doctors and nurses (Uden *et al.* 1992).

9 One writer who has expressed very clearly some of the dilemmas of a 'feminine voice' is Kathy Ferguson. The values structured into women's experience, which she lists as caretaking, nurturance, empathy and connectedness have both strengths and weaknesses. On the latter, she explains that woman's experience of herself as continuous with others results in a great need of those others and a dependency that often goes unfulfilled. She sees this as 'more honest than men's repressed affiliation' but as resulting in a vulnerability that is sometimes too great: 'It leads women to be preoccupied with the threat of loss, a fear that in its most extreme forms accounts for most of the clinical depression seen in women. It also leads women to seek to avoid risk and conflict, to be threatened by the open clashing of wills . . .' Tellingly, she goes on: 'The dialectic between connectedness and vulnerability is an essential part of what it means to be a human being. To uncover it is to uncover a tragic dimension of our existence, to see ourselves as constantly seeking a completion that constantly eludes us' (Ferguson 1984: 25).

10 Undoubtedly Gilligan's is one of the first names that come to mind in thinking of writers who explore the difference theme. Arguments are often

presented in a popular and rather loose way that attracts considerable criticism. See, for example, Tannen's (1991) lively and amusing account of lack of communication between men and women and Rosener's (1990) provocatively titled article for a management audience, 'Ways women lead'. Marshall (1984) also writing on women managers derives inspiration from an early difference publication (Bakan 1966). Gallos (1989), in an excellent review article, is unapologetic in her enthusiasm for what she sees as virtually a new psychology of woman, citing authors such as Bardwick (1980), Rossi (1980), Baruch *et al.* (1983), Belenky *et al.* (1984). Hare-Mustin and Marecek (1990) offer a collection of essays on the meaning of difference in the discipline of psychology. Table 2.1 is an attempt to draw together some of the key themes proposed by these writers and is further discussed in a paper (Davies, forthcoming).

11 See note 6. The need for a corrective to Gilligan on power is developed in particular by Ferguson (1984: 158ff).

12 Debating this very point in an exploration of the masculinity of authority, Kathleen Jones is instructive. She points to the risk of 'reinforcing the very stereotypes about representations of "woman" that feminists have intended to subvert'. She goes on to suggest that the representations must be invoked if they are to be challenged. Those acquainted with the post-modernist debates in this area will appreciate her citation of Diana Fuss to the effect that risking essentialism is a deconstructive strategy. 'What is risky is giving up the security – and the fantasy – of occupying a single subject-position and instead occupying two (or more!) subject positions at once' (Fuss 1989, quoted in Jones 1993: 106). Elsewhere she puts the project attempted in this chapter very clearly when she says: 'bringing gender into focus is not the same thing as studying the actual behaviour of women and men. . . . Noting gender and the difference it makes to the construction of knowledge should mean noting the ways that cultural codes of sexual difference structure social relations of human identity and signify relationships of power and status' (Jones 1993: 176).

13 Gilligan states at the outset that the 'different voice': 'is characterised not by gender but theme. Its association with women is an empirical observation . . . this association is not absolute . . . the contrasts between masculine and feminine voices are presented here to highlight a distinction between two modes of thought and to focus a problem of interpretation rather than to represent a generalisation about either sex' (Gilligan 1982: 2). Yet only a little further on she claims that the book aims to provide a 'clearer representation of women's development' (p. 3) and to deal with 'the group left out' (p. 4). It seems fair to suggest that she recognizes the problem of interpretation but instead of focusing it as she claims, her form of presentation serves to blur it.

14 The term is that of Dorothy Smith. See especially her suggestive use of the Hegelian analysis of the master/servant relationship and of the additional knowledge that is necessitated by the position of the servant (Smith 1987: 78ff).

15 Bologh's main sources are Van Herik (1982), Miller (1984) and Benjamin (1988); see especially Bologh (1990: 2–12).

16 The relation of bureaucracy to the process of rationalization in the modern world is an important theme in Weber's work as a whole. His ambivalence towards rationalization, the importance of formal and substantial rationality and the interplay between his sociological and moral outlooks are themes lucidly discussed in Brubaker (1984).

17 It may reasonably be objected that the account produced in this chapter underplays the sexual, the violent and the relation between these in the cultural construction of masculinity and femininity. An author who develops these themes, using Chodorow and also the work of Robert Stoller, is Nancy Hartsock (1985: esp. ch. 7 and p. 236ff).

18 The reader is referred in particular to Hartsock, for her comment that masculinity (she uses the term 'abstract masculinity') is 'both partial and fundamentally perverse' (p. 243), and her observation that it is concerned not with life but with death.

three

THE MASCULINITY OF
ORGANIZATIONAL LIFE

images of expertise . . . contain dilemmas of gender. They not only
have masculine features but help to keep in place or bestow political
and economic privilege on the bearers of culturally masculine
qualities at the expense of those who display culturally feminine
ones.

(Stivers 1993: 4)

How does gender – in the sense of the intertwined cultural codes of
masculinity and femininity discussed in the last chapter – actually enter
into work organizations? And what does this entry of gender mean for the
day-to-day conduct of organizations such as the NHS and their impact on
us both as people who work within them and who spend significant parts
of our lives in contact with them?

For around two decades now, and in most of the countries of the
West the issue of gender and organization has been seen in terms of a
problem of combating discrimination and providing more equal opportunities for women's advancement at work. Sex discrimination
legislation, giving legal remedies to the individual complainant, has
been widely implemented, and campaigns around activities to publicize
and policies to promote the cause of women's fuller and more equal
participation in work organizations have been undertaken. At the same
time, however, the limitations of this kind of approach have begun to
become apparent.

The equal opportunities formula asks for equal access but leaves the structure of the organization unexamined and intact; it does not seem to offer anything to the many women in lowly positions for whom movement up the existing hierarchy is not a realistic aspiration; and success for some is often gained at the cost of a constant juggling between demands of home and family and job position in ways that are not experienced by men. Fundamental questions about the widespread segregation of men's and women's work in organizations, about styles and ways of behaving or about the product of the organization and the process by which it is produced seem to be left in the air. Equal opportunity campaigning continues, and continues to be necessary, but there is a thread of unease.[1]

Equal opportunity thinking, furthermore, has not helped nurses in any straightforward way. Actions to get a specific percentage of women into the occupation within a set period, for example, hardly seem to make sense in an area where women occupy some 90 per cent of the posts already. In such a context, not everyone can agree with a goal of getting more women into senior positions in nursing, even though men have a share of such posts which is disproportionately large in relation to their numbers in nursing.[2] Nor is it easy to pinpoint direct benefits to women as nurses from the Sex Discrimination Act – opening midwifery to men in the strict sense made opportunities more equal, but could hardly be seen as a measure for women.[3] Using an equal opportunity framework, the problem of gender and nursing seems to slip through our fingers.

Gender and organization is now, however, beginning to be seen in a different and more challenging way, a way that calls on the understanding of masculinity and femininity as cultural codes to argue that gender is deeply embedded in the design and the functioning of organizations. This approach insists that organizations are not to be seen as sets of pre-given, gender-neutral spaces, which are only subsequently occupied by people with gendered identities; instead, they must be seen as social constructions that arise from a masculine vision of the world and that call on masculinity for their legitimation and affirmation. The aim of the analysis is thus to put gender at the very heart of understanding how organizations function, not to look for isolated acts of discrimination, or to make a special effort to encourage individual women to participate.[4]

Regarding gender as an active and continuing process in organizations in this way is often signalled by a shift from using gender as a noun to using gender as a verb. Thus it becomes possible to speak of the 'gendering' of organizations and the 'gendered' character of policies and organizational activities, and to mean by this that culturally constructed gender relations are called forth, overtly or otherwise, to enable the daily business of the organization to take place. Where does a gender analysis of this sort start, and what do its components need to be? Authors have made varying suggestions about the different levels at which such an analysis needs to work but as yet there is no firm agreement on this.[5] I will start in section 1 with some of the most visible aspects of gender in organizations and the ways in which gender is often used as a daily resource. Section 2 will deepen the analysis and begin to make a more direct link with the material in Chapter 2. This will enable us to turn in sections 3 and 4 to bureaucracy and profession, casting some new light on the way in which these, both highly relevant to the organization of nursing work, are gendered.

1 Gender on the surface

Gender in one sense is a very visible resource which structures daily life. Speech, modes of dress, and presentation of physical appearance mean that we can differentiate almost instantaneously between the two sexes. This differentiation is aided by a normal expectation that there are places, job positions and roles where we will find one sex rather than the other, and where the unexpected can produce not a little confusion. Gender in this sense is so familiar that it seems natural and is often quite taken for granted; and the fact that it is a resource for shaping roles and relationships goes unnoticed and unremarked. Here we will discuss ways in which gender is overt, visible and close to the surface, in terms of organizational structures, interactions and cultures.

Whatever the organization or sector of activity under consideration, it is more than likely that positions in the highest echelons will be almost exclusively occupied by men and that 'support' functions will be the preserve of women. It will be men who carry out the work labelled 'managerial', and women who do the work labelled 'clerical'. It will be men whose 'learned skill' enables them to set machines and repair them, and women whose 'natural dexterity' fits them for the intricate work of assembly.[6] No matter what the sector, the higher you go, the fewer the women, so that the hierarchy of pay, status and reward matches the hierarchy between the sexes. As in the organization structure, so too in the structure of occupations; a five-year-old can with confidence and ease reel off lists of women's jobs and men's jobs. It will not be a perfect representation of what the latest census figures will reveal, but it is likely to be a strikingly close approximation.

All this is readily apparent in the NHS. The spotlight which has been cast on the NHS as an equal opportunities employer means that a number of statistics are now to hand, demonstrating marked divisions in the work and responsibilities of the two sexes.[7] Women, although over three-quarters of the NHS labour force as a whole, are highly underrepresented in those occupations, particularly in management and in medicine, that carry the highest levels of status and reward, and are concentrated in clerical posts, in nursing, paramedical occupations and in many areas of ancillary work. In 1989, women accounted for just 4 per cent of district and regional general managers and only 17 per cent of unit general managers. Women held only a quarter of the jobs in medicine and constituted just 1 per cent of consultants in general surgery (EOC 1991). In nursing, with its overwhelmingly high proportion of women, the 10 per cent of men held a quite disproportionate share of the senior posts, something that has been the subject of a growing amount of commentary and concern.[8] In general, however, in the NHS as elsewhere, the more senior the post, the less the likelihood of finding a woman in it.

Undoubtedly, it can be a very helpful step, when the goal is to devise a practical change programme, to construct a detailed profile of where the men and the women are in an organization, to explore the structure of opportunities, to locate where the blockages are to women's advancement and to recommend policies to alter some of these patterns. But gender operates at levels other than this, levels that can effectively interact with and reinforce the unevenness of the statistical profile.

Our common expectation that men will be in senior positions and that women will provide 'support' has a clear bearing on the business of day-to-day interaction. Telephone callers to organizations, for example, work with a presumption that the woman answering the phone of a senior manager will be not that manager but a secretary, and the caller will act accordingly. Confusion will ensue, for example, when it is found that the man in the white coat is not a doctor but a nurse. Those who are 'out of the ordinary' in terms of the expected sexual division of labour, report how they need to develop ways of managing this, how they need to offer deliberate cues to their status and position in order to make interaction possible, and how too they make compromises when rules of gender conflict with the prescription for an opposite gender in their work roles. Women in positions of authority repeatedly report their male co-workers' unease and treatment of them as women rather than as colleagues. The interpretations that they give of this and the strategies that they use to cope are varied, but the incidents they recount run the gamut from an exaggerated courtesy and respect, through compliments and mild flirtation and teasing, all the way to unwanted sexual advances and physical and emotional threats and harassment.

The way in which gender is a resource for day-to-day interaction, is something that is actively reproduced in interaction with others, has been stressed recently by West and Zimmerman (1991). Every day, and in a myriad of settings, we 'do gender' as they put it; and this process of doing gender both creates and normalizes differences between men and women.

They challenge the view that gender is something we display alongside or in addition to the activities in which we engage; whether it is the sexual division of labour in the home or in the workplace, we constantly manage situations in gender-appropriate ways. What we do, they argue, is always accountable in terms of gender – even when we are purposely acting in gender-inappropriate ways! Nurses are familiar with this business of doing gender/doing work. The 'doctor–nurse game' has long been recognized as a ritual played out where the experienced nurse makes a show of passivity and deference to her male medical colleague; she offers oblique suggestions, hinting to the doctor what it is that needs to be done, guiding him towards appropriate action without appearing to do so (Stein 1967). Stein's article, originating in the USA, has become something of a classic, being repeatedly cited and reprinted. Gender has also, however, been studied as a resource in the handling of patients by nurses; Helen Evers (1981), for example, has provided an important and insightful discussion of the ways in which elderly women patients are treated very differently from their male counterparts. Change in some of these gender interactions has come onto the agenda; Porter (1992), in an observation study of gendered interaction between doctors and nurses on intensive care and other hospital wards, discusses the significance of the growing proportions of women in medicine and the rise of men to leadership in nursing, and the differences this makes to the dynamics of gender and interaction on hospital wards, and Stein himself has updated his discussion of the doctor–nurse game (Stein *et al*. 1990).

The close observation of gender as interaction, the meanings that people assign the ways in which this legitimates and normalizes the idea of gender difference are important contributions of these writers to our understanding of gender. There is no doubt, too, that the day-to-day acknowledgement of gender in interaction, the displays, the rituals, the courtesies that are involved, can be pleasurable for all involved. Such writing, however, tends to gloss over the cultural content of masculinity and femininity which we uncovered in the previous chapter. The 'light' and the 'dark' of these approaches remain in need of blending (Pringle 1989, Gherardi 1994).

Some of the cultural content, not so much of femininity but of masculinity, has been brought out, however, by those in the cultural school of thought in organizational analysis. They stress the part played by business leaders in creating and sustaining a shared set of understandings of 'who we are' and 'what we stand for' and 'how we go about things'. This 'corporate culture' will generate a sense of cohesion and a striving to belong and to achieve in ways that are in line with the overall mission of the organization. Subgroups and departments also have their distinctive cultures; there might, for example, be occupational group cultures or a shopfloor culture. Albert Mills proposes that organizational cultures can be teased out in the form of underlying 'rules', including 'gender rules'. He asks: 'given that powerful organizational actors are overwhelmingly males, to what extent do values of masculinity permeate understandings of organizational reality?' (Mills 1992: 99).

In answer, Mills emphasizes that different aspects of masculinity seem to be stressed in different work settings and cultures. At one end of the social scale, studies of manual labourers and of craftsmen (*sic*) demonstrate how unpleasant physical conditions, dirt, danger, and hard labour instead of being challenged as demeaning, can be celebrated as demonstrating the toughness, the physical strength and prowess of 'real men' in 'men's work'. A competitive culture, centring around physical domination is often sustained by jokes, metaphors and images that call on a particularly crude and violent portrayal of sexuality. The work is 'a bitch', the machine must be 'tamed' or 'conquered', the bosses are wimps and so on. This is further reinforced in that the images used to sell machinery and tools call up degrading portrayals of women, trade calendars serve as pinups for the workspace, and much of the talk is of sexual exploits.[9] At the other end of the social scale, accounts of the success of business leaders are couched in a language of military exploits. There are victories to be had in price wars, campaigns to be waged and competitors to be defeated; targets are set, and battles won. Tales are written in the genre of the 'epic fable' where corporate leaders become 'generalizable cultural heroes' Ramsay and Parker 1992 in charge of their own destiny, with a vision of a particular market, company or product to inspire others – 'John Wayne in pinstripes' (Ramsay and Parker 1992, citing Thompson and McHugh 1990). There are other links to be made between traits of masculinity and the form and organization of work – male protectiveness and police work, aggressiveness and military service, strength and steelmaking, and so on (Mills and Murgatroyd 1991: 77).

Organization cultures do not serve only to exclude women. Arlie Hochschild (1983: 165) has pointed out that flight attendants do emotional work that 'affirms, enhances and celebrates the wellbeing of others'. She shows how this work is developed, managed and commercialized by airline companies yet does not count as labour and is not straightforwardly recognized or rewarded. And she examines too the costs to the women who work in this way. More recently, Adkins (1992) has examined the culture and practices that surround women's work in a hotel and in a leisure park. She itemizes the differential treatment of men's and women's work, including the dress and appearance requirements that require women to be 'attractive', 'smart' and 'not tired'. She links themes of the sexualization of women and the devaluation of their work.[10] Nursing, of course, is not exempt from this with its images of nurses as 'angels, battleaxes and sex symbols'.[11]

   The question of gender and organization, as this section of the chapter has shown, is not only a matter of describing the patterns of sex segregation in the workplace, it is also a matter of seeing how people infuse them with meaning, interact in ways that call on gender codes and confirm gendered identities through their lives in the workplace. Both the cultural and the interaction approaches draw attention to this and to the ways in which it enacts power relations that secure the superiority of men. It is now clear that gender is a key part of the 'interactional scaffolding' that holds organizations together, it is not something that happens in 'the nooks and crannies of interaction'; we 'do gender' daily and it is this daily activity that helps to render gender divisions apparently so natural, normal and unremarkable (West and Zimmerman 1991). Gender, in short, is a resource that we call upon that gives meaning to and makes sense of organizational arrangements, reproducing both the people and the organizations in gender terms. There is, however, yet another and deeper level where we can find the gendering of organizations, one that draws attention not so much to the daily process of re-creating organizations as gendered, but to gender as embedded in the design of organizations and the logic of their functioning. Gender in this sense is no longer on or near the surface of our understanding, it is something that needs a process of excavation so that it might be uncovered, retrieved and subject to scrutiny.

2   Gender and the logic of organization

Joan Acker (1989, 1990, 1992a, 1992b) has been particularly important in pioneering thinking on this topic. Gender, in her words, is 'a constitutive element in organisational logic, or the underlying assumptions and practices that construct most contemporary work organisations' (Acker 1990: 168). But gender is not called upon in any overt way at all; organizational logic gives the appearance of being abstract and entirely gender-neutral. What does this mean?

   Acker starts by questioning what is meant by the notion of a job. The organization appears to us first and foremost as a set of jobs. The content of these jobs can be described in terms of the tasks to be carried out in them and of the skills and responsibilities that are attached. We also think of jobs as arranged in a hierarchy. The jobs in higher positions are those with greater complexity and greater responsibility. The exact form of the hierarchy will differ, it may have subdivisions and complexities, be flatter or steeper, but it is almost impossible to conceive of an organization without some form of hierarchy. While it seems 'obvious' to think of organizations in this way, the act of conceptualizing renders them devoid of real people. The jobs and hierarchies come first; the jobs are empty spaces, that are then filled by people who must be assessed for their competence to fill the pregiven space, motivated and supervised so that they will perform the tasks, and rewarded appropriately. The sub-divisions of tasks are treated as firmly fixed. We focus energies on improving recruitment, training and promotion processes; we do not, by and large, each time redesign the organization around the specific mix of skills the individual brings. The job, in this sense, is an abstraction.

Yet it is precisely this abstract, what Acker calls 'disembodied', way of thinking that genders jobs and hierarchies. Acker explains that we need a real worker to fill this abstract job, and such a worker cannot display other imperatives of existence that impinge on the job:

> The closest the disembodied worker doing the abstract job comes to the real worker is the male worker whose life centres on his full-time, lifelong job, while his wife, or another woman takes care of his personal needs and his children. . . . The concept 'a job' is thus implicitly a gendered concept, even though organisational logic presents it as gender neutral. A job already contains the gender-based division of labour and the separation between the public and the private sphere. *The concept of a job assumes a particular gendered organisation of domestic life and social production.*
> (Acker 1990: 179, emphasis added)

The notion of a 'job', then, is modelled on a man; a woman cannot fit the basic specification of what a job is in the way that a man can. She may already be part of the social arrangements that service men and ensure that in general it is men who can present themselves for jobs. If she is not 'encumbered' in this way, she is likely to be viewed as having the potential to be so. And where this is not the case, where she is older and single, or perhaps divorced, she still lacks the positive social support that the normal social arrangements give to men. To give herself to the job, in other words, she needs a wife!

The notion of the hierarchy turns out to be gendered in a similar way. Acker points out that those who are fully committed to paid employment appear as 'naturally' more suited to responsibility and authority, whereas 'those who must divide their commitments are in the lower ranks' (ibid. p. 171). But she also draws attention to what we mean by the greater complexity and responsibility that we so easily assign to higher rank. These, she points out are defined in terms of managerial and professional tasks, and not in terms of other activities that might, on the face of it, seem equally responsible, complex and demanding:

> The childcare worker's responsibility for other human beings or the complexity facing a secretary who serves six different, temperamental

bosses can be only minimally counted if congruence between position level, responsibility, is to be preserved. In addition, the logic holds that two jobs at different organisational levels cannot be responsible for the same outcome; as a consequence, for example, tasks delegated to a secretary by a manager will not raise her hierarchical level because such tasks are still his responsibility, even though she has the practical responsibility to see that they are done.

(ibid: 170)

This links directly to the themes of Chapter 2. Organizational logic is a masculine logic that fears, denies and contains the world of bodily needs and emotions and interdependencies and seeks to contain it in a private sphere. It is also a logic that subdivides and ranks tasks, ignoring those activities that do not lend themselves to partitioning in this way. The public world can thus appear as rational, orderly and controlled. Jobs and hierarchies are a very clear expression of the masculine vision of organizational life, one that insists that unless we relate to each other within organizations in the distant and disciplined and abstract manner of jobs and hierarchies, chaos must ensue. Acker draws particular attention to work which has suggested that 'the suppression of sexuality is one of the first tasks that bureaucracy sets itself' (Burrell 1984: 98); and she regards strict organizational logic as similarly having no place for what she calls other bodily processes, of procreation and of the expression of emotion. Not only sexuality and emotion, but pregnancy, breastfeeding, menstruation and childcare are 'suspect, stigmatised and used as grounds for control and exclusion' (Acker 1990: 173).[12]

We can take this a stage further to consider the concept of career as part of the gendered logic of organizations. Success in a career means a great deal of time outside working hours in one's early adult years spent in study. Ideally, it means a set of domestic arrangements that can accommodate and prioritize this. It can mean extra hours and weekend working to demonstrate commitment and to get the kind of results that will foster recognition and reward. It is also often likely to mean frequent geographical moves to gain the right kinds and quantities of experience. Careers are also often evaluated according to a fairly strict chronological timetable, so that there are norms in different sectors of work as to what should be achieved by particular ages and so on.

The 'golden pathway' to management success in the NHS is a good case in point. Success in professional examinations before age 30, moves between posts every 18 months or two years for around a decade – these are requirements that can be sustained by a single person, but can be helped considerably by someone with a partner who is not pursuing a career in the same sense and who is prepared to attend to day-to-day needs and remove them from the mind of the careerist.[13] The structure of career, assumes, in other words, 'that individuals can sustain a mode of consciousness in which interest in the routine aspects of bodily maintenance is never focal and can in general be suppressed' (Smith 1987: 81). In this sense, career too is gendered and gendered male.

Organizations now begin to emerge not only as arenas to which we bring and act out our gendered identities, but ones whose prior logic is a masculine one. Jobs, hierarchies and associated careers are generic features of organizations that are built on a masculine vision of how work is to be structured. In the next two sections of the chapter we will explore how bureaucracy and profession build upon and deepen masculinist visions of work organization. We will also see that their success in doing so is predicated on the presence of women in ill-defined support roles. Bureaucracy and profession are of particular relevance for nursing, and it is usual for nurses to decry the one and celebrate the other. But if both derive from a masculinist vision, this may need to be rethought.

3   The gendering of bureaucracy

As lay people, we know that the bureaucracies we encounter are imperfect. We speak of impossible delays, absurd decisions, non-communication between departments, rules that appear to defeat the very purposes that they ostensibly serve. Students of management and organization theory, however, are steeped in a legacy where bureaucracy is regarded as the most efficient form of administration. How can this be? The framework that is used relates back to Max Weber and his comparison with the past, where the traditional authority of the patriarch in the family, or the patrimonial authority which operated on a larger scale, was in essence a form of personal allegiance to a master who could give and withdraw favour at his whim. Such domination was arbitrary; it could be despotic and tyrannical in its exercise. Set against this, the rational–legal order of authority in the bureaucracy appears as an advance both in consistency and efficiency.[14]

Offices in a bureaucracy are not bestowed as a privilege, nor are they bought and sold. Specific criteria are laid down for entry to an office, and loyalty to it and a separation between official and private concerns is maintained. Offices are hierarchically arranged and co-ordinated and are specialized. Rules are the key feature of bureaucracies. Bureaucratic decisions depend not on any personal judgement concerning the details of the case, but on knowledge of and application of the rules. Where the application of the rules is in doubt, the case is passed further up the hierarchy. The primacy of the rules renders the process orderly and predictable. Ideally, all officials will act in the same way, they will not be swayed by personal mood or by anger, ridicule or other emotional display on the part of others. These are the criteria of Weber's early account and they still form the starting point for much organizational analysis and management thinking today.[15]

Let us take a closer look at this. There are three features that can be singled out: the impartiality of the decision, the impersonality of the bureaucrat and the unequivocally authoritative character of the hierarchy. First, impartial decisions: these are decisions based on universal and delimited criteria; particulars of the context or the case that are not covered by the criteria are ignored. There is no room, therefore, for the passionate personal plea or the elaboration of circumstances that would particularize.[16] Decisions that are abstract and a-contextual in this way become the 'mathematics problem' that we discussed in the previous chapter as the way the boy Jake resolved a moral dilemma. The decision process assumes a framework of broadly consensual societal values, it involves predictable steps, and conduces to clarity, orderliness and confidence on the part of the bureaucrat. Second, there is impersonality – the facelessness of the bureaucrat. The official is detached from/alienated from the decision, remaining 'outside of' or 'above' it. His is a routine decision process and he can expect it to be reviewed by his superiors in a routine way. His private thoughts and judgements, if he has them, remain private; he himself is replaceable, and indeed the physical moves of location are often part of the normal expectation of a bureaucratic career and conduce to impersonality by militating against attachment and localism. Third, the hierarchy is a means of resolving any uncertainty or dispute. Since it expresses relations of command, the bureaucracy speaks with one voice. It expects loyalty and deference not to individuals but to the offices that they occupy.

This is a resolution of the problem of organizing that attends to the cultural issues of masculinity as we discussed them in the previous chapter in at least two senses. On the one hand, it creates a stable and predictable order in which the interests of men as hostile strangers are tightly controlled. A stable and known power replaces an arbitrary and unknown one. On the other hand, it also preserves the relations of strangers. Intimacy and the exercise of emotion are no part of the vision that is bureaucratic organization. The longed-for but dangerously all-powerful mother, together with the overwhelming, engulfing, threatening character of a climate of nurturance and care, these are both set aside. Formality and distance are not only valued, but are seen as the only route to a rational decision.

There are organizational costs, however, in what is suppressed. Stability comes at the price of losing both creativity and flexibility. The innovative solutions that might emerge from a decision process that mediated and negotiated between a diverse group are foregone. Indeed, any input that might come from valuing the diversity of personal experience of the office-holders is denied. The process is necessarily inflexible; adaptability and change are a problem since the bureaucracy puts a premium on routine. Loyalty is to be had, but the kind of energy that comes from a passionate commitment to the goals and the potential for questioning and renegotiating the mission in new contexts that this commitment often produces, is missing. No contributions are forthcoming save those that are planned. The distinctions that were suggested in the diagram in Chapter 2 between organizational loyalty and principled commitment are now a little clearer.

Kathleen Jones (1993) has embarked on a project of teasing out an alternative concept of authority to that which involves bureaucratic command. She calls it 'compassionate authority', and she cites Richard Sennett's position that the modern forms of authority are destructive because they lack the capacity for nurturance and compassion. These, in his view, are the emotions that enable us to be fully aware of one another and hence to 'express the moral and human meaning of the institutions in which we live' (cited in Jones 1993: 161). Using a reading of the works of Hannah Arendt, which returns to the Greek root of the term, Jones proposes that authority could be better seen as linking to the notion of augmenting, of beginning something over which one does not have complete mastery, something that needs the help of others to complete (ibid.: 167–8).

The confirmation of male identities that is consolidated via bureaucratic action is one factor that renders it difficult to articulate alternative possibilities such as these. Mills and Murgatroyd (1991: 79) emphasize that conformity to the rules of bureaucratic behaviour has a double function, giving the male bureaucrat a sense of superiority both in relation to 'supposedly less rational blue collar counterparts' and in relation to 'supposedly irrational females'. The woman bureaucrat is not necessarily a source of challenge and can be in a dilemma. There is much material to suggest that women find it 'effortful' and difficult to know how to 'be' in bureaucratic roles that are gendered masculine.[17] Bureaucratic action, with the limits just discussed, is also perpetuated however, through the unacknowledged work of women. A pioneering study by Rosemary Pringle of the work of secretaries, has brought out the point, echoing the theme of the last chapter, that the detached decision ideal cannot actually be sustained without the contribution of women. This needs further consideration.

The observation that secretaries are 'office wives' is a familiar one. The job that they do in servicing and supporting a (usually male) boss, the wide range of often ill-defined duties certainly has some fairly clear parallels with the work of a wife. The boss/secretary relationship, as Pringle points out, directly contravenes the Weberian model:

> By having direct access to the powerful, secretaries are outside the hierarchy of authority. Far from being specialised, they can be called upon to do just about anything, and their work may overlap with that of their bosses. The relationship is based on personal rapport, involves a degree of intimacy, day-to-day familiarity and shared secrets unusual for any but lovers or close friends, and is capable of generating intense feelings of loyalty, dependency and personal commitment.
>
> (Pringle 1989: 87)

Pringle insists that this needs to be seen, not as some 'pre-bureaucratic relic' but as integral to the overall functioning. We must understand 'ordered rationality' as an illusion; we must see that 'masculine rationality attempts to drive out the feminine but does not exist without it' (ibid.: 89). It is because secretaries do attend to needs that are personal, sexual and emotional, and because they carry out work that is underconceptualized, devalued and ignored, that their bosses can continue to act in a disembodied way and can continue to present their decision processes in terms of the abstract ideal that has been described.[18]

Nor is it only work that is strictly labelled secretarial that occupies this place in organizations. In a study of administrative and clerical hierarchies in the NHS it became apparent that there was a whole array of posts held by women, with titles ranging from secretary to clerical officer and administrative assistant, that functioned as support in a similar way. The senior clerk in a small hospital, for example, had all the local knowledge at her fingertips that enabled the trainee managers to pass through without concerning themselves with 'detail'; the secretary in a clinic or in the pharmacy did a job that was in effect that of office manager, the postgraduate medical centre was staffed by a long-serving part-timer whose job had grown out of all proportion. The bosses would be full of personal praise for these women, but the work itself was never considered, being regarded as low level clerical 'support' (Davies and Rosser 1986, Rosser and Davies 1987). Decisions got made in what everyone agreed was a rational manner. Impartial, impersonal, and largely male superiority was thus sustained.

In a study in the USA, bringing together the work of clerical staff and of nurses in the hospital, Karen Saks has argued that a great deal of health care 'has always depended on the unremunerated and unacknowledged co-ordinating, administering, screening, and nurturing work of women clerical, technical, nursing and service workers' (Saks 1990: 188). Nurses and clericals are the key people who 'direct traffic', moving consumers through the system. Their jobs require a wide range of co-ordinating skills since they are on the front line of a 'bureaucratic void', working in a system which is 'made up of specialists, each of whom is responsible only for a specific task at a specific station on the health care assembly line' (ibid.: 190). Her accounts of the knowledge, for example, that a medical secretary actually deploys, or of the follow-through work done by a reception clerk, are vivid ones, made the more so by her insistence that co-ordinating the work of those higher up – without authority or status – is a recipe for conflict and stress. More of her observations, about the way unions have not taken on the question of valuing work, and about the impact of the economic crisis on this work, will be taken up again in Part Three.

This section has tried to show that some of the familiar criticisms of bureaucracy can be seen in a new way through the lens of gender. Bureaucracy's inflexibility, its tendency seemingly to forget its own mission, its lack of regard for persons, can all be understood in terms of the partial project of masculinity with which it is associated. The analysis has hinted that there might be quite other styles of decision-making, modes of rationality that will be difficult to articulate as alternatives because they draw on qualities assigned culturally to the feminine. The section has also drawn attention to work that suggests that the bureaucratic ideal is a myth in that it relies upon and yet denies the work of women. We are now in a position to turn to the concept of profession, where we will find that much the same strategy of analysis can be brought to bear.

4   The gendering of profession

At first sight, bureaucracy and profession seem diametrically opposed. The professional has a commitment to the substance of professional practice, to the exercise of expertise and skill; professional practice seems to involve a disdain for the organization and its rules, rather than a loyalty and commitment to it. The decision process of the professional, far from being the application of a rule, is presented as a more complex affair requiring a judgement that cannot be captured by any simple algorithm. Profession appears to attend to all the specifics of the individual case in hand, and to have the flexibility that the bureaucracy lacks. Above all, the true professional acts autonomously, referring a difficult case perhaps to a more experienced colleague, but emphatically not bowing to a hierarchy of offices in the way the bureaucratic model envisages. There is a longstanding literature on professional/bureaucratic conflict which serves to affirm and elaborate this framework of opposition.[19]

Yet it would be strange if there were no affinities between the two. The professional ideal, like the bureaucratic has been forged in historical processes where the key actors were men and where we might expect that cultural notions of masculinity, with the sexual division of labour that they call forth and reproduce, would again have a bearing. Its historical trajectory is different from that of bureaucracy, and recent work has begun to explore this in new ways,[20] but there are a number of indications, particularly in that work that traces women's struggles to enter the professions in the late nineteenth and early twentieth centuries, that the hurdles that entry to the professions represented was not just a matter of doors and minds being closed to women, but of the values that were embedded in the notion of the practice of a profession reflecting a masculine project and repressing or denying those qualities culturally assigned to femininity. A study of some of the pioneering women in the fields of medicine, college teaching, scientific research and psychiatric social work in the USA at the turn of the century, for example, describes successful professionals of the time not only as being 'objective, competitive, individualistic and predictable' but also as being 'scornful of nurturant, expressive and familial styles of personal interaction' (Glazer and Slater 1987: 14). The professional profile, the authors explain, was an implicitly male one, which involved being 'the model of a gentleman', as well as the possessor of an abstract knowledge and expertise. The authors bring forward a variety of material to link the forging of a concept of profession with the quest for order in a period of rapid social change and with middle-class male anxiety about proving one's self, in ways that are highly reminiscent of the themes of the masculine cultural project as outlined in broad terms in the previous chapter.[21]

There is broad agreement that it is medicine in this period and since that has been the paradigm case for our contemporary understanding of the concept of a profession. Abraham Flexner, whose report on the restructuring of medicine in 1910 was so influential in laying an institutional basis for the development of the profession,[22] offers a vivid insight into the way that the gendered organizational logic – discussed earlier in the chapter in relation to jobs and hierarchies in a bureaucratized setting can work just as powerfully, if rather differently, in a profession. He explains that:

> Professional activities are so definite, so absorbing an interest, so rich in duties and responsibilities, that they completely engage their votaries. The social and personal lives of professional men and their families thus tend to organise around a professional nucleus.
>
> (Flexner 1915, quoted in Glazer and Slater 1987: 175)

Occupational cultures of this period are notable also, however, for drawing very directly upon ideologies of gender and gender imagery to explain and encapsulate the relations between the 'professional' work of men and the 'supportive' activities of women. Eva Gamarnikow's pioneering study of turn of the century relations between doctors and nurses demonstrates that an equation between doctor/nurse/patient and father/mother/child appeared repeatedly in discussions of the time and became if anything a leitmotif of the nursing literature (Gamarnikow 1978: 110).[23] I myself have examined the distancing of health visiting work from sanitary inspection work by reference to the activity of the health visitor not as an official from the public world but as an advisor to the family, with the specific use of the term 'mother's friend' denoting a call on the world of the private and the domestic to conceptualize the work that women do and a consequent delimiting of the powers and the knowledge that the work entailed (Davies 1988). More recently, Ann Witz (1992) has provided an extensive discussion of the historical shaping of the division of labour in health care, focusing on medicine, nursing, midwifery and radiography. She shows how the very specific forms of nineteenth-century patriarchal culture influenced the professionalizing projects of these occupations, and affected the forms of closure which they could achieve. She makes clear that the struggles that took place concerned much more than the exclusion of women, and indeed involved an active search on the part of women themselves to professionalize occupations. Such professionalizing projects, however, took place on a terrain already gendered and had to relate to that gendering.

The contemporary sociology of professions displays rather less of an interest in the question of professions and gender. It is puzzling to observe that despite the considerable emphasis that has emerged shifting towards questioning the power of professions, their monopolistic position and the relevance to clients of the services they offer, few of those sociologists who have advanced a more sceptical and critical approach to professions[24] have developed a systematic gender perspective in their work. Class divisions rather than gender divisions have been the focus of recent work. Hugman (1991), however, does provide an extended recent discussion. Relying heavily on the pioneering work of Hearn (1982), he emphasizes that the spaces women could claim were those they could secure by virtue of being women and explores the current dilemmas this entails. He notes how historical legacies interact with other gendered structures, in the family for example and in the shape of welfare and social security policies and serve to reproduce patriarchal relations. His discussion, a wide-ranging one, encompasses the many levels discussed in this chapter under the rubric of the gendering of profession. What I will do here however, is to explore profession in much the same way as we have explored bureaucracy. This generates a commentary that intersects at points with the more familiar critique of the professions but does so while heading in a different direction. Below, I shall examine briefly the concept of expertise, return to the discussion of impartiality and impersonality and give attention to the theme of autonomy. It emerges that profession, at least as much as bureaucracy, celebrates and sustains the masculine vision outlined in the previous chapter.

Expertise deriving from a formalized training based on science lies at the heart of the claim to professionalism. Whereas earlier commentators stress the essential benevolence of knowledge and skill in the service of societal progress and improvement, more critical scholarship has stressed the monopolistic character of professional knowledge, the creation of a mystique amongst an elite and the dependence and disabling of those who come to the professional in the capacity as client. Through the lens of masculinity we can expand further on this. Professional knowledge is gained by dint of a lengthy and heroic individual effort. This effort is a project involving mastery, resulting in knowledge as a 'possession' of the autonomous individual. Knowledge and associated skills and techniques are exercised in a visible, tangible and agentic way to 'make a difference in the world'; knowledge thus possessed is affirmed in use and can be neither depleted nor easily shared. The project of the bounded individual in controlling others is reflected in the way that the knowledge base of expertise is developed. The profession shapes and controls knowledge, so that it is clearly bounded and its compartments respond to a logic which may not be the same as, and may indeed be at odds with that of those who are the focus of its efforts. It creates specializations, celebrating depth rather than breadth. Specialists, with their command and again mastery of an area, are more highly regarded than generalists. Taking 'first bite at the cherry' in this way, locating the problem and the solution in terms of knowledge already mastered, affirms a sense of competence and order in both knowledge and practice; the work too bounded and easy to define.

The professional encounter, at first sight so particular and contextualized, also turns out to encompass, though not in identical form, the features of impartiality and impersonality previously discussed in relation to bureaucracy. What is apparently attention to the fullest circumstances of the client/case, is in practice a sifting of information in terms of a diagnostic model and a translation into categories of action that fit the competencies of the professional. Universal values are assumed. In terms of impersonality, there are often rules of eligibility to receive service that operate at a distance from the professional encounter itself and ensure that skills can be employed in an impersonal way. The portrayal of a professional concern, the proper 'bedside manner' of the doctor, for example, keeps emotion at a distance – the lack of emotional display in the delivery of skill is a valued aspect of professionalism. Professionals offer a detached 'understanding' when clients, in what can be a highly charged context, frequently apologize for their fears and their tears.

Autonomy stands at the very heart both of cultural concepts of masculinity and of professions. The image of the exercise of professional judgement and action is of the one-to-one encounter with the client, in which knowledge and technique can be applied with a direct and visible result untrammelled by the constraints of bureaucratic rule. In practice, things are very different. It is not just a matter of a growing challenge to professions on both costs and efficacy grounds. This is something that is certainly taking place and will be taken up in Part Three under the heading of the 'new managerialism'. It is also important to recognize that professions represent themselves as autonomous only by ignoring or misrepresenting the work of others.

Take, for example, the appearance of the hospital consultant in the outpatient department or on the ward round. This involves a direct encounter with the patient, but it is a fleeting encounter. It is sustained through bureaucratic recording systems that are the work of others, through much preparatory and often considerable follow-up work with patients by others. It is only through this work that the work of the medical profession can take on its active, agentic and distant and controlling character. Autonomy, therefore, turns out to require considerable work by others and without this work it cannot be sustained. We saw this in the previous section with regard to support work of clerical and secretarial work, and noted how in the studies of Karen Saks, clerical work and nursing were seen to have similarly unacknowledged characteristics in this regard. Some of this adjunct work[25] is defined as technical, specialized and detailed; some of it concerns coping with emotions and the embodied and particular character of patients. Almost all of it is done by women. The parallel with the argument about secretaries is a strong one. Once again, the calm detachedness of the style, the very notion of what it is to act and to be competent, derives from the masculinist vision that fails to recognize its partial and dependent character. The ideal typical professional encounter, in other words, is one that 'privileges male characteristics while denigrating and/or suppressing female ones and depends for its coherence on maintaining women in a position of inequality with regard to life chances and resources' (Stivers 1993: 52).

The opportunity costs of this approach are very similar to those described in relation to bureaucracy. Particularity and diversity among clients are discounted. Dialogue with and participation of the client is blocked. The commitment and contribution from those outside the profession can only be harnessed within a narrow groove. The onus is on the professional to name solutions, and innovative and creative action stemming from elsewhere is unwelcome. The self-referring professional in some ways is the epitome of Weber's distant 'manly' man in his decision process and in his contempt for others (see pages 32–4).

We have now seen that the ways of organizing involved in bureaucracy and profession have strong parallels. Both are orientated to control and mastery, to creating order through the implementation of an abstract decision process. Both create hierarchical relations to achieve this and promote distance from and even disdain for their clientele. The application of expert knowledge, be it associated with office or the person, retains a mysterious character and calls forth deference on the part of the recipient. It has been particularly important to note that in practice, the work process can often only be accomplished in the requisite detached and impersonal manner by dint of a great deal of preparatory and servicing work which is carried out by women. Women are the first point of contact with the client. Often it is women who are there, both before and after, attending to the 'detail' which processes and shapes the client so that the professional interaction can take place. Women also attend not only to the informational, but the physical and emotional needs of the bureaucrat, the professional and the client, sustaining the sense of order, and handling tension. This work is rarely acknowledged or well conceptualized; from the point of view of the gendered professional ideal it is regarded as trivial or as 'support'.

What, finally, does all this say about nursing? It suggests that there is a sense in which nursing is not a profession but an adjunct to a gendered concept of profession. Nursing is the activity, in other words, that enables medicine to present itself as masculine/rational and to gain the power and the privilege of so doing. It has clearly not had first bite at the cherry in defining its work, and indeed perhaps we get closer to the heart of the matter in recognizing that it is trying to put a conceptual frame around just those aspects of the work of health and healing that are 'left over' after medicine has imposed an essentially masculinist vision. Nursing's long-term project may therefore be not to become a profession in the present sense of this term, but to challenge the gendered basis of the concept. This may not be as heretical as it sounds. In some ways nursing is already doing this; specialization, mastery and impersonality sit uneasily with nursing's emphasis on holistic care and there may well be seeds of an alternative vision in current writing on nursing ethics, on patient advocacy and on caring.[26] We will examine this further in Part Three. Meanwhile, it is important to turn to some of the key policy issues that nursing faces, and to show that in a world gendered in the ways suggested here, a world that has expressed that gendering through bureaucracy and profession, the dilemmas of nursing are particularly acute.

The material produced in Part One has demonstrated that gendering is at the heart of the thinking that we all share, and that it offers us a world already deeply saturated with binary gendered thought. This gendering calls on a notion of natural sexual difference yet it is replete with images of control and domination. The masculine is hegemonic; the feminine is masked, suppressed and repressed. Gender also operates at different levels, near the surface as a resource for interaction and organizational culture and buried beneath it in the logic of organizations and in the specific forms we know as bureaucracy and profession. Far from bureaucracies and professions being somehow gender-free, we have seen how a partial and masculine vision underpins them, a vision whose limitations are obscured by the work that women do in accommodating and partially ameliorating some of its weaknesses.

These are not the familiar issues of the exclusion of women from areas of work and reward that men have kept for themselves. They are less understood and more complicated issues of inclusion – inclusion of women as 'other' – as carriers of qualities that are both feared and denied. We can be sure that whenever women have been able to construct for themselves a place in the public world that is predicated on this denial, that place will be a contradictory and uneasy one. Women, in a very important sense, cannot be 'at home' in the public world – it is constructed in such a way that assumes home is somewhere else, somewhere far away and different.[27] The final twist to the argument, as we have seen, is that a masculinist vision is a fiction, it cannot be sustained without the work that women do. Because of the nature of the masculinist vision and of masculinity itself, women's work in organizations – some of it called nursing – has to be ignored, or trivialized and devalued. Patriarchal culture and the gendered institutions that we create put us in this dilemma.

This leaves nurses and nursing in a triple bind. First, nursing aspires to be a profession when the concept expresses a gendered vision that is a denial of the feminine values of nurturing that nursing seeks to espouse. Second, nursing aspires to be a profession when its own work is part of a gendered division of labour that helps to sustain 'profession' for medicine. Third, nursing has seemed, almost despite itself, to be deeply engaged with bureaucratic forms of organizing, which are also flawed by the gender division.

The message of this part of the book can now be summed up very briefly: it is that we live in a gendered world, that gender is masculine, and is importantly also misogynist. The multiple and complex ways in which gender operates to constrain us – men and women alike – are difficult to pin down. Gender is both called forth and masked; at the level of organizational logic, it is particularly deeply covered; our institutional arrangements are presented as the only rational and efficient way to proceed.

Their vocabulary has to be our vocabulary, and in trying to talk about all of this from within an area that is gendered female, we are wrongfooted, stymied by the very terms we employ to discuss the issue. Part Two will show this in action, when nurses, operating in a national arena, try to shape the overall policy framework of their work. The analysis will enable us to explore what is often seen as irresolution on the part of nurses with more critical eyes, viewing issues instead as irresolvable in terms of the contradictions of patriarchal culture that nursing expresses. The hints that have been dropped in this chapter of an alternative, a vision of ways of working that mend the gender division expressed in cultural codes of masculinity and femininity, will be picked up again in Part Three.

Notes

1 For consideration of the British legislation and workplace action programmes, see, for example, Meehan (1985), Jewson and Mason (1986),
   Gregory (1988), Webb and Liff (1988), Davies (1989), Lovenduski (1989),
   Cockburn (1991).
2 For an account of how research and action plans on equal opportunity can
   cause puzzlement and disagreement in a nursing context and yet work well
   elsewhere in the NHS, see Davies and Rosser (1986).
3 A brief account of the lifting of restrictions on men practising as midwives
   and of the subsequent entry of men to the profession is contained in Lewis
   (1989).
4 One article advocating this kind of approach explains it in terms of a vivid,
   male metaphor of the game: 'The real problem is that it is male players that
   make the game, the rules, and manufacture the arena, in accordance with their
   specialities, skills and interests. Instead of studying foul play, the effects of
   some players having a longer training and more helpful coaches, that [sic]
   referees are un- or consciously in favour of certain players and so on, the
   interesting question is to look at the game itself, and whose interests and
   preoccupations it expresses and preserves' (Alvesson and Billig 1992: 79).
5 Compare, for example, the work of Acker (1989, 1990, 1992a, 1992b),
   Alvesson and Billig (1992), the various contributors in Mills and Tancred
   (1992), Savage and Witz (1992), and for a more specific focus on the 'sexuality
   of organization ', Hearn et al. (1989).
6 A classic consideration of the social construction of skill and the devaluation
   of women's work is that of Phillips and Taylor (1980). For a brief review of
   recent work on gendered skill, see Rees (1992: 16–18).
7 See, for example, Homans (1989), EOC (1991), Goss and Brown (1991).
8 For some recent figures and a brief discussion, see Gaze (1987), and for two
   rather different studies of male career paths see Hardy (1986) and Hutt (1985).
   For a full bibliography focusing on career paths of women and men in
   nursing, see Davies and Conn (1994).

9 The classic studies linking manual labour, masculinity and skill are Cockburn (1983, 1985). Succinct reference to much available material can be found in Mills and Murgatroyd (1991).

10 There is a new debate beginning to emerge around how a gender analysis and an analysis of sexuality relate to one another. Adkins (1992) distances herself from the writings of others on this (Hearn 1987, Hearn *et al.* 1989). There is a related issue concerning the pain and the pleasure of cultural representations and organizational experiences of sexuality for women (see Rothschild and Davies 1994).

11 For a pioneering discussion see Salvage (1985). See also a more recent revisiting of these themes by Holloway (1992).

12 The distaste about what women represent in the ordered public world of men is captured very vividly in an observation by Cynthia Cockburn concerning a male physicist and his attitude to married women with children working in the laboratory. It was, she said, 'as though they would contaminate it with odours of the kitchen and the nursery' (Cockburn 1985: 256).

13 The 'golden pathway' to success in the managerial ranks of the NHS, involving just these kinds of rapid moves, together with pressure of work and intensive study, was described in Davies and Rosser (1986). The new NHS training schemes in general management for the 1990s, however, represent a step away from this by encouraging greater diversity of entrants and including routes to management from the clinical professions as well as from business. Equal opportunity themes are present in management development materials (see, for example, Davies and Parkyn 1992) as well as being promoted through the Women's Unit attached to the NHS Management Executive (see, for example, NHSME 1992).

14 This point has been emphasized recently by Pringle (1989: ch.4) whose account is discussed further below.

15 I am aware, of course, that bureaucracies in practice do not live up to this bureaucratic ideal, and that individual bureaucrats supplement and subvert them in ways that have long been the subject of sociological study. The point here, however, is first to underline the link between the bureaucratic ideal and masculinity and a little later to show that the relevance of women's contributions in gendered roles has only recently begun to emerge.

16 For an excellent and accessible critique of the concept of impartiality by a feminist political philosopher, who is able to link it to the public/private dichotomy, to describe and question the implied notion of reason that 'stands apart from any interests and desires', and to argue for a new ideal in which diversity, difference and emotion are recognized, see Young (1987).

17 The term 'effortful' comes from a study of women teaching in higher education (McAuley 1987). The literature on women in management is replete with examples of women's unease, and with responses that range from questioning to determined conformity (see, for example, Marshall 1984).

18 For a vivid example from the academic world, as related by a lecturer deputizing for her head of department, and being amazed at the protection of her time and the detailed attention to her needs for information and for coffee, see Davies (1993).

19 It is a way of thinking that served as my own introduction to the study of professions, remained with me for many years and as I now see, hindered an understanding of the dilemmas of nursing (see, for example, Davies 1983).

20 Kimball (1992) has suggested six identifiable stages whereby use of the term profession shifts in meaning from an initial use as a term for a religious vow to more modern meaning. He is highly critical of twentieth-century scholarship in this area as remaining 'in a groove that does not understand its history' (p. 17).

21 See writings on the progressive era in the USA, especially Wiebe (1968), Bledstein (1976) and the discussion of these texts in Kimball (1992), in Glazer and Slater (1987), and especially in Stivers (1993).

22 See Berliner (1975), Brown (1979).

23 Anticipating some of the more recent work described in this chapter, Gamarnikow argues that an appeal to science was not enough to secure the subordination of the nurse, and that 'genderization' in the form described was also established (Gamarnikow 1978: 109).

24 Amongst the celebrators of the professions in the British context the classic text is Carr-Saunders and Wilson (1933). The more radical literature on professions is now voluminous. For examples and critiques of the earlier era which developed into the 1970s, see for example Jackson (1970), Johnson (1972), Roth (1974), Saks (1983) and most notably in the field of health professions Freidson (1970a, 1970b).

25 The concept of 'adjunct work' has been developed by Peta Tancred-Sheriff and colleagues and is used in a rather different and wider theoretical context than is attempted here; see Tancred-Sheriff (1989) and Grant and Tancred (1992). Tancred-Sheriff does, however, note specifically that nursing, teaching and social work contain strong components of adjunct control work (1989: 55, n2).

26 At least one study (based on the work of Gilligan, see Chapter 2) has found cultural codes of gender reflected in differences of orientation among doctors and nurses. Doctors were found to talk of care dilemmas in terms of distance, isolation, paternalism and tend to be optimistic in their assessments of change; nurses stressed closeness to the patient, quality of life and patient autonomy issues and tended to be more pessimistic about change (Uden et al. 1992). While I would be wary of attempting to map cultural codes directly on to individuals in this way, the directions of the findings are interesting and lend support to the arguments being developed here and to the extensions to them contained in Chapter 7.

27 For a parallel discussion of a 'truncated theory' with a blind spot about its own gendered base, see the work of Carole Pateman (1988) on the social and the sexual contract in political theory and the consequent exclusion of women from civil life and from the very conceptualization of citizenship. There and here the implication is that women need not to argue for inclusion but for transformation.

part
two

THE DISORDERS
OF NURSING

four

NURSING MANPOWER: WHAT'S IN A NAME?

This [nursing] service is 99 per cent women, and in all truth, if we could get more men in we would have far less manpower problems and wouldn't be in such a mess.

> (Regional officer, cited in Long and Mercer 1987: 144)

The NHS was under an intense public spotlight throughout the 1980s. An economy in recession, rising public expenditure and growing doubts about the power that the public sector professions had enjoyed in the post-war era, were some of the factors that put it there. Was the NHS accountable enough? Could it be that it was overstaffed and under-managed? The questioning culminated in an invitation to Sir Roy Griffiths to bring a business mind to the problem, and led, inevitably, in so labour-intensive an activity, to an unprecedented public debate about levels of staffing. In the parliamentary session of 1980–1, the Committee on Public Accounts (PAC) noted that NHS manpower had doubled since the start of the NHS and had grown overall by more than 20 per cent in the 1970s; it declared itself concerned that the then Department of Health and Social Security (DHSS) could produce no statistics of numbers of staff in various groups, other than doctors and dentists, beyond 1979, and that the growth in staff numbers had only partly been planned at national level (House of Commons 1981: para. 6). Three years later, specific targets for reductions in staff had been set, yet the Committee felt that progress was still quite inadequate (House of Commons 1984: para. 11). At first, the issues were about resources devoted to the management of the service. This quickly changed. The direct care staff came under scrutiny and enquiries were set in train first on the question of medical manpower, then on nursing.

How was nursing seen in this most public of arenas? What was visible and what was invisible about the nature of the nursing labour force? This chapter will begin by examining the startling differences in the way that medicine and nursing were treated, and considering some of the consequences of this. It will then turn to the concepts of manpower planning and a manpower system, arguing that these are notions devised with reference to the organizational logic of jobs, hierarchies and careers that has been described in Chapter 3. As such, they effectively mask the characteristics of women's working lives and put women on the defensive. The conventional approach, as we will see, also leaves important aspects of the nature of nursing work unanalysed, thus broadening the gap between how nurses experience their work, and how policy debates are framed and conducted. An examination through the lens of gender, on the other hand, can start to bring the reality of nursing discontent into sharper focus.

1   Medicine and nursing under scrutiny

From the time of the incoming Conservative government in 1979 onwards, detailed Parliamentary attention focused on rising health expenditure. This took place through the work of the newly revised Social Services Select Committee, and through the work of the PAC. It was this latter committee, armed with reports from the Comptroller and Auditor General, that investigated what was happening both to the medical and the nursing labour force.[1] Detailed reports from the National Audit Office (NAO) whose staff had held extensive discussions with DHSS officials, had paid visits to regions and districts, and had conducted some investigations of their own, were available (NAO 1985a, 1985b). So, too, were memoranda from the relevant professional associations which the PAC in each case appended to its own report (House of Commons 1985, 1986). On the surface, the approach taken with doctors and with nurses was very similar. MPs wanted an up-to-date national picture of overall numbers, they wanted to understand the techniques that were used to estimate supply and demand and they were concerned to establish whether local variations in numbers were justifiable. In the end, they were satisfied neither with the doctors nor with the nurses and beneath the measured tones of the two reports was a strong challenge to much current professional practice. But, as we shall see below, the nature of the challenges and the lines of questioning were very different in the two cases.[2]

In looking at the doctors, the starting point was the long established central machinery at health department level for setting student intake targets (House of Commons 1985).[3] Was the DHSS confident about the current figures, running at just under 4000 per annum? The strict answer was no, but the DHSS was able to point both to the longstanding advisory machinery and to the research with its different bases for deriving the estimates. At a cost of around £100,000 for the training of a doctor, it seemed obvious that it was urgent to avoid producing a surplus and to retain an interest at Departmental level in this area. Regional variations in doctor:population ratios and difficulties in recruitment to unpopular specialties were aired. The message from the DHSS was that the issues were complex, intervention was tricky, but slow progress, for example on performance indicators, was being made. Attention then turned to the career structure in medicine and the pay of junior doctors.

There were too many in junior doctor grades and too few consultants. On average, it was taking 12 years instead of the expected 7–10 years to achieve consultant status and it was agreed that this was too long. A policy of increasing the ratio of consultants to juniors had been adopted a decade previously and had been seen to be preferable on the grounds of career opportunities and of quality of care. It had also been tentatively suggested that cost saving might ensue, since consultants were likely to call for fewer diagnostic tests and to discharge patients earlier. So, where was the study evaluating this? Officials, under questioning, emphasized technical problems. But it also emerged that a group of consultants was opposed. With fewer juniors, there would be more sessions, more emergency work and the possibility of having to stay overnight in the hospital, a position that some felt would turn them into shiftworkers and be demeaning to their status.[4] The Committee made no direct comment, but it strongly recommended that the study should go ahead, that an interest in performance indicators should be fostered and that approaches to planning should be more systematic. Looking in detail at the payment system for juniors, it concluded that this, too, was out of control and needed review.

The writing was on the wall for the medical profession. Undoubtedly, doctors were still seen as offering a highly skilled and valued resource. Clinical autonomy was not mentioned in any direct way, but the constant reference to the complexity of the issues and to technical problems with measurement were a nod in this direction. But the irritation of the PAC with the cautious approach of the DHSS was equally clear; the doctors were not called arrogant and obstructive and self-interested, but the implication was there. Ultimately, Parliament and the DHSS were going to have to take them on.[5] In the case of nursing, no such bowing to professional status occurred. The titles of the reports betrayed it; whereas that on doctors was blandly called 'NHS: Hospital-based Medical Manpower', that on nursing appeared as 'NHS: Control of Nursing Manpower'.

The question of the numbers in training, the worry over wasting valuable resources and creating unemployment for highly trained specialists that had been the starting point for medicine, did not figure at all in the Audit Office's report on nursing (NAO 1985a) nor ultimately in that of the PAC (House of Commons 1986).[6] Instead, the starting point was a 16 per cent rise in the total numbers in post over the period 1976–83. Could this be justified? The answer in large part seemed to be yes, given a reduction in contractual hours and other factors. The Committee was mollified, but not altogether convinced. Members then discovered that the DHSS did not consider it feasible or practicable to hold centrally the kind of information about nurses that they had about doctors. While the Committee evidently looked on this as reluctance to admit to any responsibility and stated with some hostility its concern that the DHSS 'do not have the information to enable them to say whether there are too many or too few nurses' (House of Commons 1986: para. 18), it did not pursue the matter further.

Questions about specialty and geographic variation in numbers available elicited much technical discussion about different techniques of calculating an optimal nursing establishment. 'Top-down' formulae, based on patient dependency, tasks, ward workload or whatever, together with 'bottom-up' methods based on the collation of professional judgements, were explained to MPs. The argument that all techniques had weaknesses and that it was impossible to recommend one was somewhat weakened by the fact that the Health Departments in Wales and Scotland had found it possible to be rather more prescriptive. Again the PAC was disparaging of the DHSS; they remarked that surely it could support a narrow range of techniques and update some very outdated guidance still in circulation.

Significantly at this point, instead of examining the career structure in nursing or an aspect of pay, which had been the key issues for doctors, the Committee concerned itself with detailed examples of staff utilization and working practices. The Audit Office had devoted considerable research resources to this and had reviewed four areas: staff rostering, the matching of staff to changing levels of demand, the use of five-day wards and the use of support staff. Their report was able to describe practices with precision and to quantify potential savings. A number of practices appeared indefensible, most notably, shift overlaps that ranged from two to over six hours. This was an issue that was to impact adversely on nursing through the summer of 1985 as the press and Ministers took up the story. Cost savings in a sample of 30 wards were worked out at £250,000 in a year. As the then General Secretary of the RCN pointed out, this did nothing for the argument of many individual nurses that they were overloaded, and it represented a major setback, in the midst of the implementation of general management in the NHS, to the nurses' campaign to retain nurses to manage nursing (Clay 1987: 99ff).

The Audit report had concluded in rather measured tones that there was 'considerable potential for the more efficient use of nurses by the periodic review of nurse manning levels and activities and by the use of comparative data' (NAO 1985a: para. 5.12). Worse than this, some of the techniques themselves were called into question, since it seemed that:

> under pressure of resource constraints, authorities managed with a little less than what the various methodologies would suggest, in general without serious adverse effects on patient care
>
> (ibid: para. 3.15)

Could this be the case? One MP began to suggest a different picture – that nurse workloads were actually increasing, that privatization had had an adverse effect and that it was difficult for nurses to engage in whistleblowing. This was not taken up.[7] The picture of the organization of nursing work that emerged, therefore, was both bleak and damning. True, the DHSS seemed to pay much less attention to issues in nursing than issues in medicine, but what had nurse managers been doing all these years that they had allowed the situation to drift in this way? Thus, alongside an apparently *arrogant* profession of medicine, using its muscle to obstruct changes in staff utilization, was a seemingly *incompetent* profession of nursing that was attempting to manage its own labour force, but doing so with highly questionable results.

The RCN attempted to shift the line of vision of the Committee. Its memorandum suggested that there was a pressing problem of recruitment and of wastage; there was the continuing reliance on a student and an untrained labour force, and there was the question of securing a return on a female labour force by, for example, maximizing the participation of women with young children and ensuring that those outside the labour force were enabled to keep their skills up to date. The PAC latched on to just one part of this, the element concerning recruitment, wastage and a looming crisis in nursing numbers, and included a section on it in its report.

The discussion of recruitment and wastage was the closest the Committee came to acknowledging that there might be a different set of issues when it came to planning and managing a predominantly female labour force. A close reading of the exchanges between the MPs and the officials on this point, however, reveals that neither group was ready for a fundamental change of thinking. On the side of the officials, there was a note of resignation, irritation even, witnessed most clearly in the observation that high turnover was, after all, inevitable amongst women. On the side of the MPs, the urgings for more 'back to nursing' campaigns, changes in the pattern of hours, flexible use of part-timers and the point that these should be the responsibility of those at the centre as well as those in the localities, were laudable enough – but they had the air of the quick fix to meet an immediate crisis. There was nothing to suggest that managing a female labour force might require a different approach or that ways of thinking about manpower might need not just adjustment but transformation when the issue in reality was womanpower. No one thought, for example, to ask what it cost to train a nurse, or followed up the question of how to maximize her lifetime participation in nursing.[8]

How are we to summarize and evaluate these events? First, there is no doubt that the doctors and the nurses had been and were being treated very differently. It emerged, for example, that the NHS knew a great deal more about its doctors than about its nurses. As far as doctors were concerned, it knew about numbers, grades and deployment; it was concerned about career opportunities and rewards; it knew about the costs of training and had put resources into attempts at planning to use a costly and valued resource optimally. In comparison, nurses had been neglected. Nursing was something seen to be handled more appropriately at local level, so that there was less statistical information and a less differentiated picture available for national-level policy construction.[9]

The PAC noted this difference, but did not dwell on its significance. Others, however, have increasingly begun to draw attention to this. Ann Marie Rafferty (1992) has recently uncovered the way in which the NHS effectively ignored nursing in a number of its early policy debates, assuming that nursing care would somehow adapt to change without the need for explicit consideration. White (1985) has argued that nurses have never had the political power that so numerically large a group might be expected to enjoy; she has noted that the RCN for example has had to fight to get media recognition, and traced, from a reading of the relevant files, what she refers to as 'obvious contempt' for nurses by the Ministry of Health in the early years of the NHS.[10] Strong and Robinson (1990) have commented on the realization that finally came to them in their contemporary review of management restructuring in the NHS of the profound unimportance of nursing in the culture of the NHS.[11] The events described here underline this; medicine is seen as a valuable profession; doctors' grades, their career opportunities and rewards are taken seriously as aspects of this. Nursing is seen as a much less important and less differentiated resource. While the PAC, at one level, was uneasy with the apparent neglect of nursing in the NHS, the structure of the reports, the selection and presentation of themes testifies to their acceptance of medicine as highly valued and as a career to be respected (but increasingly also to be managed), and to their dismissal of nursing as less valued work that needs to be clearly controlled lest total numbers get out of hand.

This explains why the Audit Office saw it as entirely right and proper that they should carry out a detailed examination of the work practices of nursing. Medicine received no such scrutiny. And it was this, as we have seen, that resulted in the damaging criticisms that presented nurse management in the end, not as power-hungry or arrogant as one might begin to infer that the doctors were, but as inept, passive and incompetent – as not really able to manage. The damage that this did to the confidence and reputation of nursing has already been noted. It must be said that none of the three protagonists, the doctors, the nurses or the Department officials, came out well from the this set of investigations. But the others were not undermined in the way that the nurses were.

Could there have been a different view? We have seen that the memorandum prepared by the RCN tried to supply one, indicating that the Committee should pay attention to recruitment, wastage, student labour and use of untrained staff as components of the 'manpower' problem in nursing. Some might be inclined to see this as a standard case of an occupation trying to gain greater control over its own work by seeking to exclude those with little or no training. Undoubtedly there is something in this. The following sections will argue, however, that conventional 'manpower' thinking draws attention away from the linkages between the different elements highlighted by the RCN. A change of this thinking, and perhaps too a change of terms,[12] is needed if we are to gain a better appreciation of the ways in which nursing work is never fully on the agenda or discussed and comes to occupy that ambiguous and unbounded space described in the last chapter as a gendered adjunct to medicine. Section 2 examines why it is that nursing sits so uneasily with 'manpower' thinking; section 3 begins to explore what might emerge when these conceptual blinkers are set aside.

2   Cherchez l'homme...

What is it that manpower planning seeks to achieve? Introducing its report on medicine, the PAC explained that the purpose in that instance was 'to ensure that the right number and kind of doctors with their various special skills are available in the right places at the right time' (House of Commons 1985: para. 13). On the one hand, there is the matter of formulating demand, determining, that is, the number of staff and the mix of skills and experience that is required in view of the catchment population and of an estimated number of cases. On the other hand, there is the matter of understanding and controlling the likely supply of skilled staff to meet this demand. This means predicting the flows into and out of the system, including inward movements from initial training, outward movements due to retirement and the net effect of job moves. Ideally, and in abstract terms, the idea is very simple. A box and arrow diagram can represent the total picture, quantifying all the elements of stock and flow.[13] This abstract quantifying overview takes place at one remove from the day-to-day management of manpower where actual recruitment, promotion and deployment of people takes place. The terminology here, of 'human resource management' is apparently more gender neutral.[14]

The appealing simplicity and rationality of manpower planning quickly become blurred. There is a complexity in the hierarchies that represents the internal flows between job positions; there is the nested character of levels, so that what are losses at a lower level are gains at a higher one. Also, and since the ideas of strategic planning, including manpower planning, have come late to the NHS,[15] routine information systems rarely do the job that is needed. Much as we might admire or be mystified by the technical complexities that are used to produce the forecast, that forecast can only be as good as its basic data and its assumptions, and these often leave much to be desired. The specialists regularly warn for these reasons that theirs is an inexact science. The PAC and the Audit Office more than once made a similar point.

What happens on the ground, therefore, can be a very different matter from the basic model. There has been, as Long and Mercer (1987) have shown, some movement towards more objective and systematic approaches to estimating staff requirements and managing the size and shape of the NHS labour force. To a large extent, however, decisions on planning and managing the labour force are a political process, where the interests of professional groups in securing new staff and their relative power positions shape events. The government's imposition of overall manpower targets in some cases has also overridden local work towards more systematic forecasting of supply and demand. In the main, as their survey showed, it was a matter of day-to-day decisions about staffing, of responding to immediate pressures, rather than of adhering to an overall plan. Turnover and retention issues only came on to the agenda at crisis points. Ironically, given the criticisms of nurses that we have catalogued earlier in this chapter, it was the nurses more than other groups who were found to be more likely to appeal to a method of workload measurement to calculate demand. They did this not necessarily, however, because they had faith in the methods as such, but so that 'a veneer of scientific objectivity is imposed on a subjective process' (Long and Mercer 1987: 131). Thus, had those involved in the policy debate at national level looked a little more closely, they might not have had cause to single nurses out as in need of special criticism – the whole concept of manpower planning begins to take on an air of unreality in the context of the real world mechanisms of staffing the NHS.

But there is more to it than this. Managing a female labour force is undoubtedly more difficult than managing a male one. You cannot assume that women will have a continuous attachment to work throughout a lifetime, that they will wish in all cases to work full-time and that they will be able to predict at all times the priority of paid work in their lives. Some of the respondents in the Long and Mercer's survey were downright hostile to women workers. The quotation at the head of this chapter, referring to 'less mess' with men, is one example of this sentiment relating directly to nurses. In such a context, managerial adjustments to a female labour force were seen, not as part and parcel of the business of managing a labour force that is three-quarters female, but as second-best. Long and Mercer's empirical data demonstrate thinking that sees, for example, flexible hours as an inadequate overall solution and part-time work as a necessary evil when committed full-timers would be ideal.[16] It is as though, if women do not fit the model, we would rather modify (or maybe eliminate) the women, than modify the model! Why should this be? To answer this we need to look more closely at what lies behind the kind of thinking that brings manpower modelling to the fore.

Figure 4.1 suggests that there are at least six assumptions built into the process of manpower planning that will give rise to difficulty when we start to consider nursing (or indeed a number of other kinds of 'women's work'). Take the assumption, on the supply side, that entry will follow training. At first sight this gives no problem, since nurses, like doctors, undergo an initial training. But nurses have also traditionally been an important part of the labour force while in their initial training. The PAC's question about doctors, 'Are we recruiting the numbers into training that the service in future will need?' cannot be asked in the same way. There is a different question, 'Are we recruiting the number of students that the service currently needs to deliver care?' The system is driven by present need for labour, not by any strong notion that that labour, once trained, is a valuable resource. Planning transmutes into recruitment. We will take this point further in the next section to describe a constant recruitment, high intake/high waste model of womanpower, in contrast to the low intake/low waste one of conventional manpower planning. There is a further implication in this first assumption that early entry is the only or at least the normal route; provision of courses for

Supply side:
1 that entry to the system follows a period of formal training which is undertaken at the outset of a career
2 that participation in paid work is continuous over a working lifetime, and can be influenced by incentives of money and status available to a particular employer
3 that losses to the system will be due to retirements (which can be predictable), to job moves (which can be influenced), and to sickness (which will be minimal)

Demand side:
1 that jobs are discrete and non-substitutable so that demand for one grade cannot be filled from supply at another without unacceptable cost or quality implications
2 that the jobs are arranged in a hierarchy that corresponds with a subjective and objective notion of career
3 that the workload is best thought of as a series of these jobs such that each offers a standard amount of working time – full-time

Figure 4.1   Some assumptions of manpower planning

mature entrants, such as women whose childrearing responsibilities have lessened have not traditionally figured in mainstream manpower thinking. This brings us on to the possibility of re-entry which closely links with the second assumption, that of continuous participation.

Any realistic kind of planning for nursing has to take account of an episodic pattern of participation, where losses due to a career break and gains due to those returning after a career break will be substantial parts of the overall staffing equation. Furthermore, since commitments to home and family will at certain times in the life-course take a priority, the incentives that can be taken for granted for many men – their interest in promotion, their willingness to move and to move their families for career reasons – cannot be assumed to operate in the same way for women. Patterns of movement are thus not the simple matter set out in assumption number 3.

If the supply assumptions begin to disintegrate in this way, so too do those concerning demand. The reality of much nursing work in the hospital setting, as we shall see in the next chapter, is that it is done with a highly variable mix of trainees, trained and untrained staff. Whatever nurses themselves might wish and advocate, they are frequently regarded as substitutable one for another. This has an effect on hierarchies; to be sure there are pay grades and posts reflecting different qualifications gained. But the clinical career ladder that the nursing profession has long fought for still falls far short of full implementation. Looking at the third assumption, around 40 per cent of the nursing labour force works on a part-time basis, and, as we have seen above, those planning and managing the labour force tend to see this as a 'hassle' factor, rather than something that is integral to the planning process.[17]

Some might argue at this point that manpower models can be made more robust to accommodate what is simply an additional complexity. I would not agree; what is at issue here is that manpower planning has at its heart the notion of a male career path through the world of paid work, a model based on high added value through training, value that is to be nurtured and developed through a continuous, coherent, lifetime career passage. While individual women, in particular those who are single or without domestic commitments, can to some extent emulate this career path, the model has a logic which is gendered, and gendered male. Bringing women in not only makes the model more complex, but more awkward. This, as we have seen, is reflected in the day-to-day managerial thinking that regards women as a 'hassle', and only reluctantly makes arrangements to accommodate them. It is all but denied in the PAC's report on doctors, which tucks away in an appendix the statistics showing the substantially increasing proportions of women entering medicine, and suggests that the continuation of present trends will mean that women's careers will (rather conveniently) increasingly approximate to men's (House of Commons 1985: Appendix 1, B).

Nursing labours under a double disadvantage here. First, it is surrounded by manpower thinking to which it can relate only uneasily. Second, that very manpower thinking serves to direct attention away from how it is that nursing labour is treated – not as valued manpower at all, but, as we will see in the next section, as devalued womanpower.

3   Womanpower – an altogether different dynamic

A number of factors came together at around the same time that the PAC was meeting to prompt a much closer examination of the real dynamics of movement into and out of the nursing labour force. First was the determined effort from within nursing to effect a reform of the framework of nursing education. This is discussed more fully in Chapter 6, but here it is important to note that there was considerable consensus that such a reform would have to involve proper student status for learners, thus extricating them from their traditional place as part of the manpower equation in NHS nursing. The profession, if it wanted to change education, had to face head-on the question of what the student labour system currently meant, and what it would involve to eliminate it. Second, and arising in large part from the work that was carried out in this connection, there was a growing realization of an upcoming demographic crisis. Nursing took a very large proportion of 18-year-old females; the demographic dip that would hit particularly hard until the mid–1990s and remain depressed thereafter, was going to mean that the present supply strategy was under threat; certainly it could not continue unaltered if educational reform were to be implemented. Third, the links that had been forged between an independent research body, the Institute of Manpower Studies (IMS) and the nursing profession in support of the RCN's enquiry into nurse education,[18] were followed by a growing involvement of the IMS with research on nursing, at first through surveys of College membership,[19] then by means of investigations of the cost of nursing turnover (Buchan and Seccombe 1991a) and of a large-scale enquiry tracing career paths for nurses in Scotland (Waite *et al.* 1990).

All this created a novel information base about the nursing workforce, and began to suggest what its dynamics were. A reading of these several sources shows how fragmentary and inadequate are existing information sources for the job of providing a full picture of the dynamics of the nursing labour force. It also underlines the bankruptcy of the manpower model in what it offers as far as active management of a female labour force is concerned.

The nursing manpower model produced by management consultants Price Waterhouse for the UKCC in support of the Project 2000 reforms provides a useful starting point for this (see Fig. 4.2). It showed that in the mid-1980s the total nursing labour force in the NHS comprised over 500,000 in terms of whole-time equivalents, almost 60 per cent of whom were qualified, 23 per cent unqualified and 18 per cent learners. The consultants estimated that around 30,000 qualified recruits were needed each year to replace those who leave (leaving aside any increase in demand which might augment this figure). In practice, around 70 per cent of the replacements were found from newly qualified entrants, the other 30 per cent being those returning to nursing after a break. Nursing, the model clearly showed, was 'a high recruitment, high wastage profession where manpower replacement is student-led' (Price Waterhouse 1987: 8).[20] It was also massively dependent on the constant recruitment and replacement of young women.

If nurses wanted to improve training and remove students from the equation, the model had to be transformed to a low recruitment/low wastage one. Much of the campaigning for change at the time hinged on this. It was clear that it meant reducing all forms of wastage, concentrating on increasing the proportion of returners and diversifying sources of initial recruits. Few, however, stopped to ponder on how it was that such a system had come about, how such waste could be countenanced and what it meant for the young women who came forward for nursing. After all, the existing system stood the manpower model on its

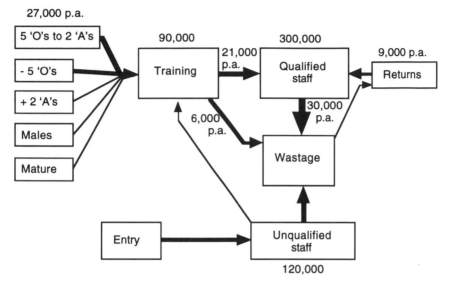

Figure 4.2   Simplified manpower model
Source: Price Waterhouse (1987: 9, vol. 1)

head; instead of carefully conserving and developing skills, it threw them away.

With this model in mind, a lot of the discontents that nurses express which we noted in Chapter 1, start to fall into place. The pattern at this point revealed that nurses were not valued for the skills they had learned, since their work was being organized on the principle that they were easily replaceable. There had been moves to encourage nurse returners, but this was a minor, not a major part of the recruitment strategy. Support for post-basic courses and continuing education was around, but was not treated in the same way as in medicine – after all, the assumption was that a nurse would leave. Lesley Mackay captured a number of aspects of this, as she concluded a chapter summarizing the hopes and aspirations of the nurses in her sample in these words:

The disposable workforce ethos – use-once-and-throw-away – is demeaning to the women who choose to take up nursing as a career. It also serves to reduce the prestige and status of nurses, nursing, and women. Thus nursing can easily be seen as a job at which women are only playing. At the same time the work of nurses can be trivialised if it is done by a perpetual stream of young learners. How then, can nursing be viewed as having a real contribution to make to the improvement of the health of patients? The past ease of replacement has meant that attempts to develop the skills and potential of the workforce are not made. What a waste!

(Mackay 1989: 92–3)

Has there been a change of heart since these findings were reported? Has the 'disposability ethos' been overturned in the light of the clear waste of womanpower that it entails? The answer to this is entangled with the government's response to the bid for reform of nurse education in Project 2000, which will be discussed more fully in Chapter 6.[21] A grudging acceptance of educational reform in the context of cost retrenchment, however, has had mixed effects. On the one hand, it has lowered turnover and encouraged more re-entry; on the other hand, it has also meant replacement of student labour in part by assistants without a full nurse training. There is nothing in all this to suggest a thoroughgoing admission of waste and a change of strategy as far as the devaluation of women and their work is concerned.

Yet it is possible to trace a growing acceptance, if not of the full implications for nurses and nursing of this important insight about the 'disposability ethos', then at least of the sheer wastefulness of constant replacement, in the way in which the IMS studies have developed.[22] Consideration is starting to be given to the needs of the young, often single and highly mobile component of the nursing labour force and the older, less mobile segment with domestic and childcare commitments; explorations have started to occur of the rates of promotion for those with children and of the limited career progression of part-timers. The detailed consideration that the team working on the Scottish data was able to give to the question of career breaks led them to a very direct challenge to the continuous career thinking that is part of conventional manpower planning. Nurses, with their vocational commitment, they argued, also need to be seen as having a 'cradle to grave' approach to their work – we should stop referring to the numbers 'leaving' each year, and start instead to manage the temporary career breaks that these losses actually signify (Waite *et al.* 1990: paras 12.1.1–12.1.3). Price Waterhouse (1988) too, moving on from their earlier study to consider issues of nursing morale, urged the more active management of a female labour force.

But there is a world of difference between advocating flexible hours, childcare, career break schemes and so on as measures for the minority or measures to meet a particular manpower crisis, and placing these at the centre of a planned system for the positive management of womanpower. What would a positively woman-friendly approach look like? It would look at flexible hours not in the sense of a few more part-time jobs, but of reorganizing work schedules and perhaps individualizing hours; it would carry out the kinds of cost–benefit studies of different forms of childcare

---

Will you explain to the Committee how annual intakes are set? How do you ensure that these figures will match the forecast level of demand?
The intake target is still set as has historically been the case between the Service and the university or college. While students are not part of the labour force any more, the contribution they make towards the end of their course frees staff for professional development which enhances the efficiency of the unit.

Are we to take it then that there is still no national picture of the overall staffing . . .
On the contrary, Madam Chair! That anomaly was rectified some years ago given our overall change of philosophy, and the annual Nursing Statistics Report, including appropriate regional and local breakdowns has been found to be a useful management tool.

Please explain to the Committee what this changed philosophy entails
First, and in line with our efficiency goal of maximum lifetime participation of all qualified nurses, the UKCC's registration statistics were considerably enhanced to give a full picture of employment status, location and intentions to return for those currently outside the labour force. The Research and Statistics Agency set up jointly by UKCC and Nursing Division is now recognized as a key information resource and has become self-funding . . .

Career progression for part-timers and for those returning after a career break were stumbling blocks in the past. Can you inform the Committee of developments here?
Certainly. Cost-benefit studies showing the way we were wasting trained staff by creating a part-time ghetto and by not providing clear career routes for any but the minority who had continuous full-time employment had a massive impact on general managers. Our six centrally funded Nursing Management Development Teams, set up in the late 1990s, with their remit to carry out demonstration projects and produce guidance materials were in great demand; from a position in the mid-1980s when nurse management was in the doldrums, things have turned right around. General managers were a little slow at first to see that the nursing contribution to corporate management was not the whole of the story, but the Management Development Teams showed their worth, demonstrating what active management of a female labour force meant. The work of XYZ Trust in transforming the patient day and linking this with individualized hours for staff means that the part-time ghetto is just not in the thinking of many of the provider units any more . . .

Figure 4.3 Public Accounts Committee, Minutes of Evidence, Year 2025

that took into the equation the real costs of turnover and failures to return.[23] It would work with a notion, as Waite *et al.* (1990) have begun to do, of lifetime participation and the management of career breaks to enhance this. Most important of all, a concept of the *extended nursing labour force* would need to take hold. This would mean prioritizing the production of good and routine data not only on those in work at any given time but also on those working elsewhere and those not working at all. Thus, the size of the pool of 'inactive nurses' would be a matter of knowledge not speculation, whereas at present we are still a long way from the kind of planning information that would show an annual picture of flows in and out of this pool nationally, regionally and locally.[24] The fictional exchanges between a PAC and DHSS officials which might occur some years from now which are set out in Fig. 4.3 will perhaps give some notion of what it would mean to take the masculine blinkers away from manpower in these kinds of ways.

Conclusion

This chapter began by exploring the differences in treatment by the PAC of nurses and doctors. The frameworks guiding the thinking of MPs led them to adopt a line of questioning that undermined the credibility of nurses and left them frustrated that the issues that they wanted to put on the agenda did not arrive there. I have tried to locate this in the partial vision that is represented by thinking about manpower and especially about the process of manpower planning. Two distinct aspects of this have been considered. First, because manpower thinking is orientated to a traditionally male career path and to the division of labour between men and women that this assumes, the project of 'adding women in' is contradictory. It is not just a matter of added complexity, for, as we have seen, at every turn, the assumptions of the model need to be modified. Thus, the issues concerning women's labour market participation, instead of being the central management challenge of the NHS, become a 'hassle', and nursing is a principal sufferer from this. Second, the hold of conventional thinking has for years obscured the actual treatment of nurses, drawing attention away from the constant recruitment model, which is not only straightforwardly wasteful of an increasingly costly resource, but devalues both nurses and the quality of the nursing they can deliver.

Gender makes multiple appearances on this particular stage. Harking back to the categories of the last chapter, gender is there on the surface in the strongly male-dominated arena in which the manpower debate takes place. Despite cross-party representation and a number of membership changes during the period of these reports on the professions, the PAC at no point had even one woman as a member. The health economists and statisticians who develop manpower models are also usually men. Gendered interaction and a gendered culture have not been explored directly in this chapter, though there is certainly scope in the verbatim exchanges reproduced in the PAC reports to consider the implications of the accepted adversarial style of parliamentary behaviour for the kinds of conclusions that can be produced. In the main, however, the chapter has been an exploration of organizational logic. Much as Acker, building on her theoretical discussion of the gendered character of jobs, hierarchies and bodies, critically explored job evaluation, so I have tried to explore manpower planning.

What's in a name? In this case it turns out to be a great deal. The practices described by manpower planning are the terms in which a discourse of public policy is conducted. It is a discourse which constitutes women's employment as a problem and directs attention away from the devaluing and demeaning dynamics of nursing work. Small wonder if nurses are silenced and diminished. As well as being silenced on the national stage in this way, nurses are also diminished and devalued more locally. This is discussed in the next chapter.

Notes

1 For a helpful account of the reform of the Select Committee structure in 1980, the revisions to the work of the Comptroller and Auditor General under the National Audit Act 1983, and the way these led to an increasing Parliamentary focus on management and expenditure in the NHS, see Harrison (1988: 91–7).

2 For another account of these two PAC reports, which includes some brief contrasts between the treatment of doctors and nurses, see Long and Mercer (1987). These authors suggest that the focus on staff utilization in the nursing report enabled the discussion to reach a higher level of technical sophistication. They also, however, suggest that the differences in treatment of the two staff groups reveal 'the extent to which medical dominance in the NHS can orient manpower investigations to a professional concern with the hospital career structure, while comparable debates in nursing are almost entirely ignored' (Long and Mercer 1987: 71). My argument, as will be seen, is not about medical dominance as such but about the congruence between assumptions in the medical model of profession and in the notion of manpower planning.

3 Medical manpower planning has long been a quite distinct, separate, self-contained and specialized function at DHSS level, with little attempt at integrating its activities with other health service manpower. I am grateful to J. Buchan for pointing this out.

4 See the account of this in Long and Mercer (1987: 65), where reactions from different sections of the medical profession are described as mixed but 'at times downright hostile'.

5 The significant changes to and tighter control of GP contracts which were to be outlined in the White Papers *Promoting Better Health* and *Working for Patients* (DHSS 1987b, Department of Health 1989) have been highlighted as key parts of a new era of control of medicine (Brown 1993). For a recent published discussion of doctor/manager power, see Harrison and Wistow (1993).

6 Members of the Committee had brought these issues up in questioning of officials. They had learned that there were over 25,000 entrants to nursing in England in 1985. Initially they were puzzled to be told that this was simply an aggregate of nursing schools who each set their own targets, but learning that these targets were negotiated with health authorities whose service depended on student contributions and that there was a regional review the topic was abandoned (House of Commons 1986: Minutes of Evidence, para. 427ff).

7 The comments of the MP were directed to the Chief Nursing Officer. She was in a difficult position; she had no objective evidence to counter the assertion that care had not deteriorated. She could hardly agree that nurses did not uphold their own code of practice in ensuring quality of care. In the event, her understandably circumspect answers served to leave the implied criticism of her profession intact (House of Commons 1986: Minutes of Evidence, paras 437–53).

8 Answers to such questions were just beginning to become available. Management consultants Price Waterhouse did a great deal to piece together the various components of cost and calculated for the UKCC that the cost of training a nurse was in the region of £13,000 (see Chapter 6). The question of lifetime participation, however, did not emerge as a possible way of thinking about nursing contributions until the work of Waite *et al.* in 1990. This will be discussed later in the chapter.

9 See note 3. The observation that the level of detail in official NHS statistics varied directly with the status of the staff group under consideration was made some years ago by Lesley Doyal (1979).

10 Rosemary White concludes her detailed historical investigation of debates about nursing policy with the observation that the Ministry has 'little regard for nurses and never appeared to see them as anything other than labour' (White 1985: 253). Robert Maxwell, Secretary to the King's Fund which sponsored her study, in pointing to this in the preface, provides a truly remarkable comment which serves not only to deflect attention from the question of why nurses should be ignored in this way, but to blame nurses for this and at the same time to warn them against any action to counter it! He states that it is 'disturbing' that nurses 'appear ... to have had a quite inadequate input to the shaping of health policy', goes on to urge them not to be defensive and expresses a hope that as their political sophistication increases they will not forget the patient.

11 The observation about this is worth quoting in more detail. Jane Robinson, after describing how, in her study with Phil Strong, nurses seemed unable to describe their innovations and doctors and general managers seemed ignorant of developments that had occurred on their own patch, went on:

> We suddenly realised that despite the impressive statistics (half a million workforce in the UK) nursing is relatively unimportant to government and to managers in comparison with medicine. It was medicine that the Griffiths reforms sought to control – nursing was merely caught in the crossfire!
>
> (Robinson 1992: 5)

The neglect of nursing goes on. John Brown (1993) has pointed out that the White Paper *Working for Patients* gives three mentions of nurses in a total of 102 pages.

12 In an article describing and introducing the approach of manpower planning for a nurse audience, Jim Buchan (1992: 38) acknowledges that the term 'manpower' is 'a singularly inappropriate label for an occupation that is predominately female'. Yet, while there are obvious alternatives – 'human resource planning', 'personnel planning', 'workforce planning' – he rejects them on the grounds first, that they do not have common currency and second, that their connotations are broader, less quantitative and less concerned with the fundamental business of matching supply and demand.

13 For an early and accessible account of what this might entail, see Shipp (1979). A considerable number of manpower planning enquiries have been carried out since the mid-1980s by regional and district health authorities, though these tend to remain in-house documents and are rarely referred to in any national-level debate.

14 The simple replacement of gender-biased terms by gender-neutral ones is not necessarily the answer. Where the masculinist assumptions remain intact, they can be even more difficult to spot in such sanitized language. The discussion of 'overgeneralization' as a sexist error in social research is relevant here (Eichler 1988).

15 Current approaches to long-term strategic planning in the NHS are conventionally dated back to the White Paper *Care in Action* in 1981 and to guidance issued in 1984. (See Long and Mercer 1987: ch. 3, and for a longer view Gray and Jenkins 1993).

16 For a parallel discussion of a 'climate hostile to women', and a view that a female labour force is a 'hassle', see Davies and Rosser (1986).

17 The convention of presenting NHS labour force statistics in whole-time equivalents is widespread. Useful as it is for many purposes, it does hide the extent of the part-time contribution, and the total size of the labour force to be managed.

18 See RCN (1985), and the details this report contains on statistical work carried out for it by researchers at the IMS and the University of York. A fuller account of this appears in Chapter 6.

19 Six surveys of RCN members were carried out between 1986 and 1991. They are described in five publications. These, in date order, are: Waite and Hutt (1987), Waite *et al.* (1989), Buchan *et al.* (1989), Buchan and Seccombe (1991b), Seccombe and Ball (1992).

20 The Price Waterhouse model is also described in full in a Project 2000 paper (UKCC 1987a) and in an article in the *Nursing Times* (Hanson and Patchett 1986). While it models nursing in the NHS it does not of course give a picture of the flows to and from other sectors of work, something that would be vital for effective management of the labour force as a whole.

21 The clinical grading structure agreement of 1988, involving the regrading of nurses throughout the NHS, is a further factor introducing change in the more recent period. This structure generated much unrest and challenge from nurses (Buchan *et al.* 1989). It has been suggested that it has raised the pay of

nurses *vis-à-vis* others and generated more scrutiny of what nurses do without in the end fully capturing the concept of clinical nursing and allowing it to flourish (J. Buchan, personal communication). From this point of view, therefore, the 'disposability ethos' remains intact.

22 There is a parallel here with the way that studies of women have been received across the academic disciplines. At first it was a matter of making women visible, adding on studies that covered women in a field that had ignored them. Later, things became more tricky. Adding women in was revealing the poverty and the partial character of the concepts and categories in use. A more radical adjustment was indicated, one more discomforting to the status quo.

23 For some important observations on how the hidden turnover costs for a nurse can amount to several thousands of pounds, see Buchan *et al.* (1988), and Buchan and Seccombe (1991a).

24 For a recent discussion of the problems of estimating the size of the pool of inactive nurses and a more pessimistic estimation than those in some previous work, see Waite *et al.* (1990: ch. 19).

five

PRACTICE: THE POLO MINT PROBLEM

Given the pressure on resources, it is ludicrous to suggest that jobs which do not require the clinical and technical expertise of professionals should nevertheless be done by professionals simply because they are professionals. The aim must be to have as much as possible done by non-professionals. . . . The way to raise clinical standards is to leave trained nurses more time to concentrate on clinical work by relieving them of the work which non-trained staff could do. And, having more non-trained staff means having fewer nurses.

(Eric Caines, letter to *The Guardian*, 11 May 1993)

It may appear that many nursing activities can be performed by untrained people . . . Nurses use (bathing, washing and other forms of personal care) . . . to perform other vital activities. Bathing is an ideal opportunity for observation of the skin and pressure areas. Counselling, reassurance and health education are carried out in a variety of settings when patients are relaxed and feel able to talk Replacing trained nurses with untrained ones wherever possible will save money in the short term, but will prevent trained nurses having the vital and regular informal contact with patients and will affect the quality of total and holistic care that nurses strive to deliver.

(Rosemary Gillespie, letter to *The Guardian*, 15 May 1993)

At first sight, what is at issue between the views expressed above seems straightforward enough. The first is the typical modern manager, questioning the professions and demanding that they prove their effectiveness and efficiency. The second offers the classic professional response, claiming that a complex form of expertise has not been understood and that autonomous practice is essential. Viewed through the gender lens, however, the picture is a little different. Eric Caines, who in May 1993 was the departing Personnel Director for the NHS, has granted in his comments that nurses have the clinical and technical expertise of a profession. He is, in effect, demanding that nurses take on the essence of the gendered model of professions described in Chapter 3 – the fleeting encounter, with backup support by others who have lesser and cheaper skills. Rosemary Gillespie, lecturer in nursing, is describing something quite different from this male-gendered model of profession: a model of nursing work as a sustained encounter, one that is more holistic and less hierarchical, and one that envisages multi-tasking – the simultaneous performance of activities some of which require considerable training and skill but others of which do not.

The reality for the vast majority of nurses, however, especially for those who work in hospital settings, is often neither of these. Nursing work, as we saw in the previous chapter, and as Eric Caines surely knew, has always been done by a variety of people, by no means all of whom are trained. And the vision that Rosemary Gillespie sets out, much favoured as it is by those in the 'new nursing' camp,[1] is far from a practical proposition in the busy ward staffed by a mix of students, temporary and untrained, as well as trained staff. The real dilemma is that qualified nurses find themselves in the main supervising and managing others who do most of the care delivery. In this situation, the practice of nursing, for the trained nurse, 'drops through the vacuum in the middle' (Pembrey 1985: 47). This is the Polo mint problem that gives the chapter its title. Much ink has been spilled in trying to define just what nursing is, and part of the difficulty, as we began to see in Chapter 3, is that it is defined in a residual way, as the work that medicine rejects or fails to see. Equally important, however, is the devaluation of the work; the workers who do it tend to be regarded as easily replaceable and interchangeable. There is a Catch 22 here; anybody can do nursing because we cannot define what is special about it, but we cannot demonstrate its specialness, because many different people are doing it.

Exploring the Polo mint problem is the main business of this chapter. Such an exploration will put us in a position to understand more about the dynamics of devaluation as they occur in relation to nursing work. This will give a better perspective on why it is that nursing seems so impossible to define, how it can come about that nurses profess to want autonomy but in practice produce hierarchy. We will begin with the realities of the

Polo mint problem as it manifests itself on the hospital ward. We will go on to examine one of its further manifestations, exploring how it contributes to an image of the nurse as apparently 'uncommitted' to her work, when from her own point of view, she is highly committed, perhaps even 'over-committed' to it.

1   The realities of ward nursing

'Patient care' encompasses a very wide variety of activities. Alongside, and closely connected with medical and surgical interventions are the needs for care of wounds, observation and monitoring of drug effects, co-ordination of investigative diagnostic techniques and of the therapies available from those designated as the professions allied to medicine. As well as this, help is needed with adjustment of and return to the normal activities of daily living. The maintenance of a physical environment in which all this can take place – in the case of in-patient care, somewhere in which food, linen, and other hotel-type services are secured to a given standard – is also crucial. At one end of the spectrum, nursing's responsibilities shade off into the medical and technical and encompass procedures that were indeed formerly the province of doctors. At the other end of the spectrum, these responsibilities shade off into domestic work. The work involves both strenuous physical labour and the management of emotions and psychological well-being. There is a component, increasingly present in the hospital and always there in the community setting, of health promotion and education, of teaching that will enable the patient to develop or regain a higher level of awareness, well-being and independent functioning.

Nursing is in the front line for these activities, and it is the nurse who is in closest contact with the patient or client. The nurse sees the delivery failures of others and faces the implications, often by intervening herself. One recent study has suggested that many nurses in ward settings spend around a quarter of their time on clerical/housekeeping tasks (Audit Commission 1991). A recent review of issues in nursing puts the point graphically, saying that particularly in general hospitals it has always been the case that nurses 'have done (and do) work which could be considered the province of cleaners, dieticians, porters, clerks, secretaries, ward housekeepers, receptionists and doctors' (Beardshaw and Robinson 1990: 8). The contrast with the male gendered profession of medicine is a stark one. The nurse is not engaged in the 'fleeting encounter', as described in Chapter 3, where the work has clear conceptual and practical boundaries; instead she is in a more sustained relationship with the patient or client and her work has a much more open-ended character. One of the dilemmas of 'being there' means that in the last resort she is not going to concern herself unduly with demarcation issues, she is going to do all that she can for the comfort and well-being of the patient.[2]

This crucially unbounded work of nursing is accomplished with a workforce that overall is around 60 per cent qualified, some with the three-year training and status of registered nurses, others with a two-year training as enrolled nurses. The remaining 40 per cent of the workforce is made up of around 25 per cent unqualified nurses and around 15 per cent of learners (Department of Health 1990). This represents a considerable improvement over time in the ratio of those qualified to others. The change has taken place over the last two decades, since in the early 1960s, less than half of the nursing labour force was qualified. It has been achieved by means of a decline in the proportion of students, and their replacement, first by a growth in the proportion of enrolled nurses, and more recently by a rise in the proportion of first level registered nurses.[3] Given, however, that available overall figures include those in senior managerial grades and those working in the community (a high proportion of whom are qualified), these will overestimate the likely proportions of qualified staff actually working on hospital wards. It is clear that variations by specialty area are immense, with qualified staff in some settings in a definite minority. None of these trends, until very recently at least, could be said to be a result of an explicit strategy on the part of the profession. Recent studies of staffing on hospital wards show that variations at ward level can be startling. A review of 39 wards in 10 hospitals in 1990 found the percentage of qualified staff on medical wards varied from a low of 38 per cent to a high of 72 per cent, that learners could be as much as half the staff or make no contribution at all, and that auxiliaries varied from 5 to 22 per cent (Audit Commission 1991). A plethora of other studies have documented a similar picture.[4]

Part of the reality of nursing work then, and a key aspect, as we shall see, in understanding it, is not only that it has an unbounded character but that it is done with a highly variable mix of staff, where the proportion of those fully trained can be less than half. Another part of this reality is the constant change in the individuals who are providing the care. The need for 24-hour cover obviously is a factor here, with three or perhaps two shifts needing to hand over to each other. Part-time working is another factor. Overall, nearly 40 per cent of nurses work part-time (around one-third of first level nurses, nearly half of enrolled nurses and as many as 60 per cent of unqualified nurses). But a further and crucial factor has been the student labour system.

Nurse education has long been organized on a block system – a block of formal teaching in school/college followed by a block of practical experience. Students have spent some six to eight weeks in a hospital ward or department, during which time they have been part of the ward labour force. The ward establishment figures have assumed their presence and the expectation of everyone on the ward has been that students are there to work as well as to learn. Students have quickly learnt that they are expected to 'pull their weight' and carry out their fair share of the work of the ward, and they discuss how important it is quickly to 'fit in' and to get to know the ways of each new ward setting that they pass through (Melia 1987). Wards thus experience a regular turnover of students and must accommodate this. Staffing establishments also are often student-driven. If the normal allocation of students is not met, and studies suggest that this can often be the case, numbers are made up by calling on agency and bank nurses, another source of variation and transience therefore in the nursing team (Proctor 1989). Melia's study of student nurses draws attention to yet another aspect of this. Students, she points out, are also used as an 'easily mobilized pool of labour', they are the obvious group to use if staff are needed elsewhere in the hospital. In this sense then, there are 'moves within moves' for the student group (Melia 1987: 109).

How can the work of nursing be accomplished with such a variable and transient labour force? The sister or charge nurse cannot know the level of skill and competence of each staff member, and the work therefore needs to be readily visible, as simple as possible and clearly supervisable. One solution is breaking it down into a series of tasks that have to be accomplished for all patients in a given period; allocating work for a group of patients to a small team which if possible includes a qualified nurse, achieves this. Newcomers can quickly be slotted in and they learn a routine which involves a round of backs, baths, bedpans or whatever, and the routine then determines what is to be done. Routine task allocation means that little additional instruction to staff is required, and it is possible to see at a glance how much progress has been made, and to reallocate staff where necessary.

Under this system, however, there is a sense in which the decisions about the nursing that is done are not actually taken by qualified nurses at all. The routine seems to take over. Susan Proctor's depth study observing work and interviewing nurses on three wards (medical, gynaecological and geriatric) is relevant here. She noted that the stated aim on all three of her study wards was to implement a system of individualized patient care,[5] and she demonstrated that the nurses themselves clearly identified goals of rehabilitation, patient autonomy and control, that were in line with individualized and not routine care. Her detailed accounts of day-to-day dilemmas and practices, however, show that despite the intentions of the nurses themselves and sometimes in the face of quite explicit instructions to the contrary, the organization of work as a routine prevailed. The transient nurses used the ward routine to identify the care needs of the patients; the qualified staff accepted this since it enabled the quick and efficient utilization of a transient workforce (Proctor 1989: 185)

It is important at this stage to tease out the implications of this way of working a little further. One key aspect, of course, concerns negative implications for the patient. Patients, though in general grateful for the care they receive and admiring of nurses, do perceive and criticize the task-orientated approach to which routinization gives rise and complain of the impersonality of the care that they receive. They comment on fragmentation in the shape of the confusing numbers of different nurses who attend to them and in particular, they suggest that communication suffers (see Pearson 1988). I shall be more concerned here, however, with the implications of this form of work organization for the nurse and for the ambivalent regard which attaches to nursing work itself. We will discuss in turn, the message about the nature of nursing work that is implied here, and the impact on the identity and confidence of the nurse.

Fragmenting of nursing work into a series of tasks that can be treated as routines, in effect presents nursing as an activity that consists of a large core of 'basic' tasks that can be accomplished (albeit under supervision) by people with little or no training, together with a number of more technical procedures that have to be the province of the trained. The qualified nurse, it is true, does carry out the more complex procedures. But routinization of the work ensures that much of the time she is either managing others or carrying out the same tasks in the same kind of way. Her own practice therefore cannot, as Proctor puts it, 'extend beyond that of the novice'. An important passage by this author captures the import of this in the following words:

> The current organisation of nursing work does not promote the utilization of nursing knowledge by qualified nurses to resolve the dilemmas and ambiguities inherent in patient care. . . . Qualified nurses, who potentially have the knowledge and authority required to change practice are removed from a confrontation of these problems by their role as managers of transient nurses to whom the task of implementation is delegated.
>
> (Proctor 1989: 187)

The use that is made of agency and bank nurses further confirms this overall point.[6] These are qualified nurses, often with considerable experience, who are usually either making a return to practice after a career break or looking for the flexibility of hours that this kind of contract can give in order to reconcile the demands of family life with their wish and need to work. The system, however, regards these nurses as interchangeable with students; their skill and perhaps also their years of experience cannot be recognized and utilized; like everyone else on the wards, in the last analysis they become 'pairs of hands' to get the work done.

The message of all of this is that, whatever the practical benefits on a day-to-day basis of this pattern of working, it affirms nursing as work that for the most part is not skilled. This serves, of course, in its turn to underline the kind of thinking that sees nursing as women's work, as something that 'comes naturally' and does not really need to be taught. Whatever might be said in the textbooks, whatever the potential of multi-tasking as described in the quotation at the head of this chapter, the practical business of coping with transience trivializes nursing work.

What does this mean for the nurse herself? In the first place a conflict is set up between nursing as it is taught and nursing as it is practised. The process of developing an individual care plan, of assessing, delivering and monitoring care, these are the core competencies of the nurse as set out in statutory rules and as explored in nursing textbooks. Yet they are not part of the day-to-day reality of practice. Reflectiveness, analytical ability and a search for individual and creative solutions, all emphasized in what the nurse learns formally, will get in the way of the daily routine and cannot therefore be encouraged. What is required is that the nurse acts in a reliable and disciplined way, if not carrying out explicit orders, then following set routines. A demeanour of deference rather than an independence of mind and a questioning stance is what is called forth by this form of work organization. If we add to this the widely reported complaint of work overload and the premium placed on speed and on getting through the work[7] (the kinds of discontents, in other words, that were outlined in Chapter 1), the exhaustion, the commitment to nursing yet frustration with the conditions under which it is done, begin to come into sharper focus. The system is one that undermines the confidence of the nurse, restricts the contribution that she can make, and sets up a constant questioning about the quality of the care that is being delivered.

Furthermore, this is true at whatever level one looks in the division of labour in the delivery of nursing care. Transience and the variable mix of staff with different levels of skill, experience and qualification means, as we have seen, that the staff nurse can feel frustrated at the amount of supervision and the lack of 'hands-on' care that is allocated to her; on some days, the enrolled nurse can find herself in the role but without the recognition or status of the staff nurse or sister. The student can feel she is 'used' as a pair of hands rather than being taught. The nursing auxiliary can claim that it is she who is doing the 'basic' nursing work. Guilt, anger, poor working relationships and low self-esteem are some of the likely consequences. In short, a close look at the reality of the organization of nursing work shows both how it devalues the work of nursing and how it undermines and demeans the nurse herself.

Let us pause for a moment to consider what is and what is not being said in this argument about the reality of nursing work. Nurses seem to profess autonomy but to practise hierarchy. Is it that they are 'their own worst enemies'? Are they really, as some would have us believe, rigid and authoritarian? Do they just feel more comfortable in subordination to each other and perhaps even in deference to doctors? Explanations like these direct attention away from dilemmas in the situation and towards inadequacies in the individual. Jane Salvage, in her pioneering book on the politics of nursing, warned that it was crucial for nurses not to fall into the trap of blaming individuals for faults in the system, but pointed out that this was what happened again and again. 'Instead of looking at the structure and its dynamics to understand and solve problems,' she said, 'the individual nurse at all levels of the hierarchy is blamed for her shortcomings' (Salvage 1985: 84). The stereotypes of gender offered by our cultural codes push us towards just such an assessment. If 'we know' that women are submissive, deferential to authority, lacking in confidence, we are not going to be surprised when a group of women workers exhibits these characteristics. We can all too easily let the argument rest there without going behind the gender stereotyping of individual attributes to explore the way in which gender has already shaped institutional structures[8] – producing in this case a system in which nurses confront the Polo mint problem. Wanting to practise nursing, they simply cannot do so – the form of work organiz-ation constantly pushes them to supervise nursing, but not to do it.

In the second part of this chapter, we will take a more direct and critical look at some of the stereotypes that arise from the reality of nursing work as it has just been described, namely those that suggest that nurses either are not or cannot be really 'committed' to their work and are not therefore interested in 'career progression'. The ground-work which has been laid in this chapter and indeed in Part One of this volume is crucial in enabling us to steer past these stereotypes towards a more adequate understanding of the many levels at which gender comes into play. The gender stereotype that has produced such negative images needs to be replaced by an understanding of the gendered struc-ture which has produced the Polo mint problem – an inability to practise nursing and an imperative to supervise it. The system that nurses enter is thus already gendered, and gendered in a way that works to their detriment.

2   The 'uncommitted nurse' and her 'unplanned career'

At first sight, there is a highly plausible initial picture of the nurse as fairly disaffected with the nature of the work which can be built up from the material available in recent large-scale surveys of motivation and morale in nursing. For one thing, nurses move jobs frequently. A look at the career histories of nurses in membership of the RCN in 1988, for example, revealed that over the previous decade approximately one-third had moved jobs in the course of any one year, and around half of the sample reported that they had given some thought to the possibility of moving in the last 12 months (Buchan *et al.* 1989). For another thing, and as we saw in Chapter 1, very many nurses are critical of the conditions under which they work, of the workload and the stress it generates, of the management of nursing and of the levels of pay compared with other work. These proportions, at around two-thirds, were high enough for management consultants Price Waterhouse to warn that the NHS should be worried about morale, about turnover and about potential losses of qualified staff (Price Waterhouse 1988). Yet the matter is not straight-forward; the survey researchers also point out that nurses display a strong vocational commitment to nursing and a frustration with circumstances which seem to conspire to stop them getting on with doing nursing, and making the contribution that they feel they have to offer.[9]

Let us take the case of nurses who move between jobs to gain additional training and qualifications. This is a longstanding pattern. As far back as 1960, it was observed that senior nurses changed jobs frequently and 'were unusually prone to seek postgraduate training' (Menzies 1960: 97). Recent RCN member surveys showed that over a quarter had actually considered undertaking more training in the last year, a figure that rose to 44 per cent amongst the under-25s (Buchan and Seccombe 1991b). How is the pattern to be interpreted? Are nurses 'migrant certificate gatherers'? This concept, though nowhere fully elaborated, has served to capture imaginations in nursing and has become rather well known.[10] It is alluded to in the important work of Lesley Hardy (1986) who compares career paths of senior women and men, finding that the women engage in a whole series of what amount to sideways moves early in their careers, adding qualifications in a number of areas in such a way that they stay on the same hierarchical level, or, having reached sister level, actually go back to staff nurse grade following a further qualification. She dubs this the 'lateral movement syndrome'. The men, by contrast, display a different pattern. They collect fewer qualifications and move fairly quickly though charge nurse to more senior nurse posts.[11]

Concepts such as these are a good example of the process we have seen Jane Salvage referring to above (page 96) as directing attention away from the system to the individual and as producing the result of blaming the individual, in this case the individual woman, for the faults in the system. Consider, for a moment just how negative the notion of a migrant certificate gatherer is. There is a strong implication that such a person is muddled in their thinking, is somewhat irresponsible in their behaviour and has not given proper thought to the matter of career progression. There is a hint perhaps, that this is a woman who is simply filling in time before marriage, or widening her prospects of meeting eligible partners. Then there is the word 'certificate', with its broad connotation of a low–level kind of qualification. There is something in this, in so far as the enormous variety of qualifications that nurses gain – registrations that enable them to practice as first level nurses in other areas of work, specialist qualifications enabling them to practise as midwife, district nurse or health visitor, advanced diplomas, specialist certificates indicating competence in a specialty – have not been clearly integrated into higher education, and the question of gaining educational currency for its qualifications is something that has long concerned the nursing profession. Yet, to sweep all these into the single term 'certificate', however, is surely to prejudge and dismiss just what should be investigated.

Is it significant that this certificate–gathering concept should emerge in a work area in which women predominate? A process of gaining additional knowledge in one's area of expertise, of committing oneself to the work required to gain a further qualification, were a man to be doing it, would be lauded as displaying career commitment and applauded for its demonstration of ambition. As it is, the notion of certificate gathering puts an opposite and negative connotation on such behaviour. We are back, once again, to the devaluation of the work of nursing and the devaluation of the nurse herself. A senior doctor, whose critical comments on the proposals for reform of basic education in Project 2000 will be examined in the next chapter, could not resist a jibe at nurses' propensity to collect further qualifications. He referred to 'the many RGNs who rush away from nursing to add further alphabets to their names' (Devlin 1987: 30). How irresponsible of women, in other words, to get themselves an education, and an inferior one at that, instead of remaining in their proper place!

Let us attempt to examine the same behaviour of certificate gathering from the standpoint of the woman who is a nurse.[12] Acquiring an initial registration puts her in a position to make the transition between nursing as a student and nursing as a staff nurse. The above analysis has suggested, however, that there is no clear transition to a practice role at this point. As a staff nurse, she will be called upon to carry out more complex procedures; beyond this, she will be part of a group of nurses, affected very much by the varying staffing levels on the ward, doing much as she did before, but this time with responsibility for supervising students. She will also sometimes be seen as the most senior person on the ward and will in effect find herself deputizing for the sister, and perhaps taking decisions about the transient staff among whom are part-time and bank nurses with a great deal more experience than she herself has. The position is not an enviable one.

After a time it will become apparent to the staff nurse that while she is consolidating her learning to a certain extent, the opportunities to deepen her practice, to extend it or to fill in what she might see as 'gaps' in her basic training are limited, given the daily reality of nursing work. Furthermore, there will be limited opportunities for her to put her learning into practice, to try out new ways of working or to use her initiative given the hierarchical orientation to which this form of work organization conduces. Learning, for her three years of training, has been equated with moving on (cf. Melia 1987:117). What then is more appropriate than once again to make a move?

An early 1980s study of nurses who had undertaken post-basic courses showed that around 70 per cent of them saw this extra study as a step towards promotion (Rogers 1983). Promotion opportunities, the recent study of Scotland's nurses has suggested, are indeed good, at least in the early stages. Around a third of the nurses in that study had reached sister grade before age 30 (Waite *et al.* 1990), though it also seems that levels of aspiration are high and that career bottlenecks are also likely to occur (Buchan *et al.* 1989).

Yet there are strong indications that nurses also make a distinction between career progression through promotion and personal development in a career. Reference to an opportunity to specialize, to explore a new subject area and (rather worryingly) a chance to fill a gap in their basic training appeared in the majority of cases for those doing post-basic courses in the early 1980s (Rogers 1983). A small-scale study, involving a number of in-depth interviews with nurses, centred deliberately loosely around what they saw as 'the next step' for them, gives some meaning to this.[13] Staff nurses in this study saw their main frustration, as will now be familiar, as shortage of time and staff and as not being able to do the job as they wanted to do it, as not being able to put into practice what they had learned and not being able to use their initiative. While some were looking early on to the responsibility of a sister post, others stressed that they needed first to broaden themselves and get 'good all-round experience'. It was important to move and not to 'become stale' or 'stagnate'. One said that she did not want to become a sister for the sake of it, and suggested that she was not ready, as she put it, to 'settle' into such a post. These nurses saw different possibilities in gaining midwifery, district nursing and health visiting qualifications, and in moving into different specialist areas where skills could be certified. In one of these latter cases, it was put to the nurse that what she proposed was a 'sideways move'; she rejected this: 'for me', she said firmly, 'it is an upwards move'.

Moving 'upwards' within the structure of nursing grades has long meant[14] moving into a post in nurse management, first as a senior nurse with oversight of the work of a number of hospital wards, thence in posts mirroring the levels of the NHS bureaucracy itself, at district, regional and national locations. The nurses in this same study reserved their strongest criticism for those who moved up the management ladder in this way. 'I came into nursing to nurse', they would say; and in their eyes going up the career ladder meant leaving the real business of nursing. Few had good words to say about what those in management actually managed to achieve by way of supporting the delivery of nursing care. In short, while they were undoubtedly thinking about their own career growth and career development, this required them to circumvent the conventional career ladder of senior managerial posts.

It is now possible to see 'certificate gatherers' in an altogether different light. These nurses are creating pathways of professional development *for themselves*. They are building a range of clinical experience, underpinning it by whatever qualifications are available, but acting without reference to the limited hierarchy that is open to them – and indeed are sometimes stepping *down* the hierarchy to achieve their purposes. It is their commitment, not their lack of commitment, that is producing this behaviour.

All this is not even to have mentioned the issue that frequently looms largest of all for the female nurse when she is thinking of her career, namely the way in which it can be reconciled with that of her partner and with her responsibilities, actual or in prospect, for childcare and care of other dependants. The anger and frustration that this can bring to nurses is something that has been clearly documented and was discussed in Chapter 1. A rapid process of gaining qualifications and experience can be a deliberate choice, an effort to set the seal on a future career once the years of childcare are over. In practice, however, they can find that it is nurses who work full-time, with no breaks or few breaks, who move up the career ladder, and who in turn, can all too easily look for something similar in those whom they promote. The strategy thus has no effect, or even has the very opposite effect from what was intended. On return after a career break, qualifications gained some years earlier easily can be swept aside as not relevant to current practice, and a willingness to work 'only' part-time can effectively close off opportunity to demonstrate potential and routes to advancement. Once again, stereotyping of women's attributes is substituting for a deeper analysis of the dynamics of the devaluation of women's work.[15]

It is important at this point to give some further consideration to men in nursing and the comparisons of their careers with those of women. Available studies regularly show that higher proportions of men have ambition for career progress than do women (see Davies and Conn 1994). We have seen too that samples drawn from those in senior positions show different patterns – more lateral movement among the women, and a more straightforward rise up the career ladder among the men (Hardy 1986; see also Hutt 1985, Davies and Rosser 1986). Hardy (1986) in particular has described a pattern where the careers of the senior men she studied were easily and immediately recognizable – involving as they did straightforward upward progression through posts of staff nurse, charge nurse and thence moves into nurse management or perhaps education. This pathway, she found, was accompanied by a strategic approach to qualifications, a firm sense of career direction aided by mentorship from those senior to them. The senior women, by contrast, had looked towards the more senior positions at a much later stage and when a mentor had taken an interest in them. She also comments, importantly, that the men's careers had built for them a positive and confident self-image, whereas the women's careers had not.

How are we to interpret what is apparently so clear a gender difference? The message cannot be the easy one that the men are committed to careers and the women are not. To leave it at this would be to hark back to the overly simple notion of gender as a pre-given personal attribute that was criticized in Part One, and to deny the very kind of analysis that this chapter has sought to provide. Instead, the message has to be an altogether more complex one, that while women and men acquire and act in terms of identities that are to some degree shaped by gender thinking, at the same time, that thinking has in addition served to devalue the work of nursing, to limit the opportunities for such work to develop and flourish and to make it difficult for women to reconcile work and family commitments in pursuit of a nursing career. Demonstrating a gender pattern in who is getting access to positions, therefore, may be only the tip of the iceberg. As well as asking about who is getting access to positions, we need to pay attention to the deeper frustrations about the practice of nursing and the possibilities of building a satisfactory career that have been discussed in this chapter, and to trace how it is that women, struggling to make sense of the frustration that they encounter and to find a way for themselves, can come to doubt the contribution they have to offer. But, of course, it is a great deal easier to look at the women, to see that their behaviour does not fit, and to blame them for it. Steering past stereotypes is an advanced exercise in navigation, to which we will need to return later in the book.

Conclusion

This chapter opened with an exploration of the nature of nursing work as it is carried out on hospital wards. The key to understanding this, it has been argued, is the 'Polo mint problem', the fact that the practitioner role is not there and that nursing must always be accomplished with a variable and transient labour force. *The day-to-day, and sometimes moment-to-moment, management of this labour force in a way that will produce safe practice and will get the work done comes to be the central task of nursing.* Practitioners, therefore, do not practise nursing but instead arrange for it to be done via their own labour and that of others. Subjectively, the work comes to feel like a series of expedients, of adjustments of workload and staff. When nurses exclaim in frustration that they cannot do the job for which they trained, when they exclaim in anger that they 'came into nursing to nurse', it is the unacknowledged character of this form of work organization that is at issue. But for the most part, nurses get on with the job in the circumstances in which they find themselves. They are known to make do and mend; they deliver nursing care whatever the resources available to them.

The Polo mint problem has already been identified in one way and another by a number of nurse researchers who have discussed questions of transience and of substitutability. Yet its significance and its ramifications are not widely understood either inside nursing or outside it. The first section of the chapter traced ways in which it both confirms the devalued status of the work – actively contributing to its trivialization – and also generates frustration, confusion and guilt on the part of nurses at all levels. The second part of the chapter suggested that by ignoring all of this, it is all too easy to confirm gender stereotypes of the nurse as somehow uninterested and uncommitted to a career or to tangle in unproductive ways with stereotypes about men and women. Acknowledging the Polo mint problem, by contrast, makes it possible to produce a very different argument, one that shows nurses as actively devising ways to realize their commitment to nursing and to develop their careers, in face of a system that provides no formally recognized and clear opportunities for this. Coping strategies here, however, as in the care delivery setting, are only partially understood and redound to the disadvantage of nurses who adopt them.

When gender stereotypes substitute for an analysis of gender in this way, there is a deeply ironic reversal; the problem of the lack of commitment of the NHS to nursing transmutes into the problem of the nurse as uncommitted to the NHS. The Polo mint problem and its associated pattern of 'careers by drift' indicates a two-fold form of failure emerging from our inability to understand gender and nursing. First, the system fails nurses, in so far as it fails to offer careers that are compatible with the lives that women lead and with the known variation in participation that women are likely to be able to offer over a working lifetime. We saw in Chapter 4 what some of the steps might be to rectify this; we have seen in this chapter how women's active attempts to create pathways for themselves can be interpreted in negative ways. Waste, frustration and demoralization are amongst the outcomes. Second, the system fails nursing, in so far as the conditions for its practice and its proper development have never been put in place. The long-running, often bitter and seemingly insoluble debates about non-nursing duties, about the position of the enrolled nurse, about the nature of training for an assistant to the registered nurse begin to take on new dimensions, once the lack of both conceptual and practical space to elaborate the role of the qualified nurse which has been traced in this chapter is acknowledged. The negative images that surround the nurse manager in this context also start to be seen in a different light. Nurse managers, day to day, can often do little more than make the Polo mint work, by redeploying staff, finding extra pairs of hands, or exhorting nurses to cope. To single them out for criticism as individuals or as a group is to fall into the trap of looking to individual solutions to a problem that is more than a matter of personality or style.[16]

Once again, and more importantly perhaps than in the last chapter, the importance of understanding the different levels at which gender operates is confirmed. The Polo mint problem can appear as something of nurses' own making, a pattern that arises from nurses' personalities or preferences. It needs, however, to be embedded in a deeper understanding of gender that equates nursing work with women's work, that fails to take nursing seriously. This has allowed nursing to be neglected, has failed to see the importance of disentangling learning from working, and has continued to treat that now very high proportion of the labour force who work part-time as if they are a temporary expedient, ignoring their experience, giving them little responsibility and taking no interest in the further development of their skills. Instead of coming to terms with the complex processes that devalue nursing we have been altogether too ready to look critically at the nurses themselves, as if they were the whole of the story, and as if, by dint of their own better strategies, they could singlehandedly change the terms and conditions of their work. This is a false hope, but it is one as we will see in the next chapter, that has been nowhere more actively pursued than in the context of nurse education.

Notes

1 'New nursing' will be discussed further in Chapter 7.
2 It is perhaps worth noting how 'strange' this perspective can be to those who do not share it. I was involved in a series of meetings with groups of nurses organized by consultants Price Waterhouse as part of the process of designing their study of recruitment and retention (Price Waterhouse 1988). Nurses described how they would come in early or stay late at the end of shift if the workload was such that it seemed to merit it. The consultant, new to the world of nursing, was amazed when he found that there was no reward in terms of pay or time in lieu. He kept on asking the group why they should do this. He remained mystified, bringing this up again later as the main and lasting impression he took away from the group session.
3 Many important data were gathered together in support of the mid-1980s enquiries into nurse education. Both the RCN (1985) and the UKCC (1986a) point to the inadequacies in published statistics on nursing. Work in support of the former by the IMS and the University of York is summarized in the report. For a brief indication of time trends in the skill mix in nursing see UKCC (1986a), Appendix D.II. A more recent account is set out in Beardshaw and Robinson (1990: 9).
4 The question of the 'skill mix' in nursing and its relationship to efficiency and effectiveness of care delivery came to the fore towards the end of the 1980s, when an initial review carried out by Nursing Division at Department level (Wright Warren 1986) was followed by a number of further enquiries. For a review see Gibbs *et al.* (1991).
5 Terms such as task allocation, patient allocation, individualized patient care, team nursing and primary nursing are not always used consistently. There is a brief discussion of this in Audit Commission (1991: ch. 1).
6 Although Proctor points to the use of agency and bank nurses as 'pairs of hands' she does not overtly link this with a strengthening of her overall argument.
7 See Clay (1987); see also reports by nurses of overload as a key problem as discussed in Chapter 1.
8 A fresh look at the classic argument produced by Isobel Menzies (1960) concerning routinization as a 'social defence system' against anxiety would be interesting in the light of the arguments here and of the feminist scholarship on psychoanalysis as outlined in Part One of this book. Menzies' argument contains a wealth of insights into the stressful character of nursing work, the nature and handling of responsibility and some perhaps contradictory remarks on the extent to which nurses are prepared to countenance change. The idea that the work itself is devalued does emerge in her account, but is not explored.
9 See Chapter 1. For an interesting study which struggles with the notion of commitment as masculine see Corley and Mauksch (1988). In an analysis that interestingly complements that developed here, the authors suggest that nurse commitment is romanticized, that this justifies neglect by others and that it reduces the pressure on others to ensure that they carry out their own tasks and responsibilities (see Chapter 7).

10 The term appears in the editorial introduction by Dingwall and McIntosh to a paper by Pape (1978) suggesting 'occupational touristry' among American nurses. For some thoughtful comments, not as critical as those included here and based on the student experience, see Melia (1987: 117–19).

11 This is discussed further below. See also Davies and Conn (1994).

12 For a methodological account that begins from the realization that much sociological analysis starts from 'within the gendered relations of ruling' where women are 'other' or 'object' instead of the subject of analysis, and an argument that we always therefore begin from the standpoint of women, see Smith (1987). There is still considerable debate, however, about the adequacy of standpoint versus other feminist approaches (see, for example, Harding 1986: ch. 6) and Dorothy Smith herself is quick to point out that an approach that proposes to start from the standpoint of women can be criticized in that issues of ethnicity and class remain to be tackled.

13 For a brief account of this study see Davies and Rosser (1986). Fuller details are contained in an unpublished report (Davies and Rosser, 1984).

14 An extended hierarchy of nursing officer grades, replacing the hospital and hospital group matron arrangement was introduced following what is known as the Salmon Report of 1966 (Ministry of Health 1966). This structure, revised with the different reorganizations of the NHS, was abandoned when general management came to the NHS in the mid-1980s (see Chapter 8). For an early discussion which highlights some of the gender issues see Carpenter (1977); for accounts of nursing in the new structures see Owens and Glennerster (1990), Strong and Robinson (1990).

15 This is a theme that frequently emerges in interviews with nurses, as we have already noted in Chapter 1. It was certainly present in the career interviews we carried out (see note 13), where one of the sisters, for example, was very angry. She had, she explained, decided to have her career first and then have children in her thirties. The result was that she had given 13 years to the NHS. Yet 'I feel strongly that my career is likely to come to an abrupt halt. I might not be able to pick it up again after having a family.' Lesley Mackay's (1989) interviews with much larger numbers of nurses bring out with clarity the sense of frustration and waste on the part of those nurses who find that the NHS makes only minimal adaptations to those who have had career breaks and those whose commitments mean that they can work less than full-time hours. To regard the woman here and those cited by Mackay as uncommitted to nursing is a tragic reversal of the reality that their choices are limited by the structures in which they find themselves.

16 For an attempt to explore apparently 'bad' management in nursing as a coping style that emerges in face of the gendered nature of nursing work see Davies (1992).

six

EDUCATIONAL REFORM: PUBLIC AFFIRMATION OF THE WORTH OF NURSING?

the process of moving to a Project 2000-style preparation for all nurses, is, as you recognise, not going to be accomplished overnight. There will undoubtedly need to be modifications in the light of experience. When Tony Newton met the Council last May, he stressed the importance that the Government placed on having well educated nurses, midwives and health visitors who will be able to meet the challenges of the next century. I assure you that the commitment given by Tony Newton remains.

(Kenneth Clarke, Minister of Health.
Letter to the UKCC, 18 May 1989)

In May 1988, there were scenes of jubilation at the annual conference of the RCN. Secretary of State John Moore was given a standing ovation when he announced the government's acceptance in principle of the recommendations for reform of basic nurse education that had become known as 'Project 2000'. It seemed that the awkward compromises that had dogged nursing from the days of Nightingale's reforms more than a century earlier, the bargain that had tied nurse education to service delivery, the slow process of gaining enough of a resource to teach and enough freedom to learn, the multitude of proposals for reform that had caused such bitter disputes and ended in inaction could now be set aside.[1] A new era was about to begin.

Was this really so? Is educational reform the big success story – where finally, after numerous attempts, the profession of nursing, united as

never before, won its case through rational argument, gained acknowledgement of the real significance of its work, secured the necessary resources, and in doing so overturned the historical basis of hospital care
delivery? Some certainly think so. Dolan, from a vantage point within
the RCN, has claimed that the achievement of any change by a profession in the late 1980s anti-professional political climate (something
that will be discussed further in Part Three) is noteworthy. In such a
context, he argues, it is hard to overestimate the success of educational
reform in nursing (Dolan 1993: 8–9). The view within the trade union
COHSE (Confederation of Health Service Employees), however, is a
very different one. The proposers of the reforms, it is pointed out, com-
promised at the very start, and the government did not commit itself on
key proposals; its pronouncements were masterpieces of 'flannel and
non-commitment' (Chapman 1989: 10). The small amount of money
assigned, the pulling back on numbers of courses to be approved, all
point to a set of reforms under the title of 'Project 2000' still remaining a
project – something the government can abandon if it suits them (Crail
1990).

This chapter weaves a way between these two positions, adding
gender into the warp and the weft. Nursing was able to mount and develop a campaign for change and to secure sufficient unity for this under
circumstances which, at the time, were not at all favourable; the changes
which were secured were important ones and ones which significantly
alter and potentially strengthen the position of nursing. But a close look
at reactions to the reform proposals in the policy arena, at the terms in
which the debate has been conducted and in particular at the process of
implementation, demonstrates that in this area, as in the others we have
examined, questions of the value of nursing as women's work and
doubts about the need for and worth of training women surface once
again.

The chapter falls into three main parts. First, we will consider the
context in which the campaign for educational reform took place, and
the form in which the case was put on to the negotiating table. This will
involve descriptive material that will be familiar to a nurse audience
though not to other readers. Second, we will consider some responses to
the reform proposals from within the medical profession. While only a
small volume of comment emerged into the public arena, the nature of
this comment and its hostility to nursing can be directly linked to some
of the themes in Part One of this volume. Third, we will consider how
the government's response evolved over a period of some five years,
and how costs and manpower issues and the 1980s agenda of NHS
reform were factors inextricably linked with educational reform in nursing. Once again, as in the previous chapters, we will see that the terms

of the debate provided a particularly restrictive framework as far as nurses and nursing were concerned.

1   Project 2000 in context

Nurse education in the early 1980s was a vast and complex patchwork of provision that was by no means easy for an outsider to describe or comprehend. Registration statistics for 1985 showed over 85,000 persons in training in that year in the UK as a whole, 91 per cent of whom were female. The majority of these, around three-quarters, were in training for three years to become registered general nurses, registered mental nurses, registered nurses in mental handicap or registered sick children's nurses (UKCC 1986a). Some were taking a two-year course to become enrolled nurses. This qualification too could be taken in specialist fields of general, mental and mental handicap nursing (Scotland, however, offered a generic training as enrolled nurse). These possibilities by no means exhausted the choices for a would-be nurse. While most trained in a health authority school, courses in universities and colleges had grown up over a period of a decade and more and offered combinations of registrations. Scotland, having amalgamated its educational institutions, started in 1982 to provide a somewhat wider 'common pathway' programme. Following initial registration, a nurse could go on to take further registrations in midwifery and in health visiting, or to participate in the wide array of courses of varying lengths in specialist clinical areas, in education and in management, some of which can also be recorded on the register.

The complexity of this pattern has roots historically in the way in which nurse education has evolved in close relationship to the hospital nursing service, offering at the outset more than 100 years ago, a docile and strictly disciplined labour force in return for the most minimal opportunities to obtain education and training. Periodic efforts at fundamental reform have been largely unsuccessful; instead, nurses have slowly won improvements – recognized qualifications for tutors, powers of inspection and a budget for schools, minimum entry criteria for students and so on. At the start of the NHS, the many often very small nurse training schools attached to individual hospitals and supplying them with a key source of recruits, were absorbed unchanged.[2] Successive reorganizations of the NHS and the grouping of hospitals had brought with them some amalgamation of what could be very small schools; over 600 schools in England in the early 1970s, for example, had reduced by the mid-1980s to less than 200, and both Scotland and Northern Ireland had managed to abandon schools in favour of a form of college structure by the mid-1970s. In essence, however, the tie to service cut nursing off from general educational developments and left it with a resource base and arrangements for educational delivery that severely limited its potential for development.

By the 1960s, however, some of the most energetic and committed had found ways out of the impasse. Shortened courses, integrated courses, degree courses in new associations with colleges and universities began to take shape. In these settings, pioneering thinking, new nursing text-books, nursing models and nursing research could begin to develop (Chapman 1985). Exciting as these developments were to those who could avail themselves of them, they also generated division and defensiveness. Did these 'university types' live in the real world at all, and were the models of nursing they advocated actually applicable in real life settings? Did they have any idea what it was like to have multiple student intakes through the year, to negotiate always from a point of weakness with service colleagues who harboured doubts about your clinical competence? The very ingenuity that nurses had employed in bypassing difficulties had become an important source of tension between nurses themselves.

A further factor entered the equation in the 1970s. The government-sponsored Committee on Nursing chaired by Asa Briggs reported in 1972 (Cmnd 5115). It offered a strong indictment of the overall neglect of nursing in the NHS; it argued for root and branch reform of the basis of education, and it proposed a new regulatory structure that would bring together the mix of panels, boards and councils that recognized and registered qualifications in nursing, midwifery and health visiting in all four parts of the UK. The delays and the divisions that were opened up by negotiations over the formation of an overarching regulatory structure were deep and damaging. Legislation in 1979 created a UK-wide Central Council for Nursing, Midwifery and Health Visiting (UKCC), together with a separate National Board for each country. Nine previous agencies were disbanded. The educational reforms that many had hoped for, however, had been shelved for almost a decade; to return to this issue was urgent. Yet the intervening period had been one that created bitterness and doubt.[3]

Where did this leave the profession at the start of the 1980s? The new UKCC was in an unenviable position. On the plus side, the legislative remit that had created it gave a new function concerned specifically with the improvement of nurse education. The Council had established new training rules that reflected the wish of nurses to do nursing – to assess the need for care, to carry it out and to monitor. It had weathered the stormy period of initial establishment and completed the practical business of setting up its own internal organization, bringing records and traditions from four countries together. It had dealt with assets and finance, not to mention consulting with the enlarged group of professions under its rubric on a wide array of matters relating to registration. On the minus side, the new structures, bringing together the four countries of the UK under the eye of a variety of watchful specialist interests, were as yet untried and untested, so that the relation between the Council and the Boards, on the one hand, and the Council and the professional associations and trade unions on the other, remained to be explored in practice. Educational reform was going to be the testbed to establish whether the new grouping of the nursing professions could work together in a constructive fashion. A growing impatience for educational reform in nursing,[4] together with a politico-economic climate of cost containment and suspicion of the professions added further to unease. My summary, after a first few weeks in post as Project Officer at the UKCC,[5] was that the brief was not only to create unity in a situation made more complex both by its neglect and by its rationalization; it was also 'do it all, do it fast, and do it cheap!'

The terms of reference of Project 2000 were 'to determine the education and training required in preparation for the professional practice of nursing, midwifery and health visiting in relation to the projected health care needs in the 1990s and beyond and to make recommendations' (UKCC 1986a: 3). Additional funding was secured and it was envisaged that the report would take up to two years to produce. Once agreed by Council, the report would need to go out for consultation with the profession, and modified if necessary would go to Ministers. In the event, six preliminary papers were distributed and discussed and reprinted in the nursing press.[6] It was decided that the timetable for the report should be rather shorter, and the main Project 2000 report was published in May 1986. While it was out for consultation, work commenced on exploring registration and curriculum issues and developing data on costings and on manpower. Management consultants Price Waterhouse were brought in to help with this latter task. Results of the cost and manpower exercise, an analysis of the consultation and modified proposals as agreed by the full Council went to Ministers in February 1987. Throughout this process, there was a sense that this was a 'last chance' for reform; for this reason Council did not feel it could remit the task to a small group, instead it fell to the whole of its Educational Policy Advisory Committee, which met sometimes for regular business and sometimes as the Project Group.[7]

What was the result? In the first place, the Project 2000 Report (UKCC 1986a) was not, as some expected, a detailed blueprint of what was to be taught, but a framework document, concerned with the broad approach that should be taken and with getting the conditions right for teaching and learning to take place. Fully half of its pages were concerned with the background and the rationale for change. There were several key components of this. First, it expressed the strong conviction that the time for tinkering was over. Improvement in basic nurse education had been hamstrung by its association with service delivery. That link had to be broken. What was new here was not the argument itself, but the convergence of interests between nurse managers and nurse education-ists. Faced with growing demands in the curriculum on the one hand, and a quickening pace and complexity of hospital work on the other, reconciliation of the two sets of needs was becoming harder and harder. They had to be uncoupled. Second, it was increasingly clear that a new nurse who had spent all her training time in hospital was not well placed to respond to the growing emphasis in the health planning process on prevention and on the increasing importance of care in the community. Pulling back from student labour in the hospitals would enable a broader-based programme to be devised. The report held out the prospect of a common foundation programme emphasizing health as well as disease, followed by specialist 'branches'. Third, it was hoped that the pattern would be simpler; a single registration noting the specialism would be possible, building on it would be a smoother and easier matter – it would thus rationalize an overlapping and confusing system. Fourth, an education-led system would be able to do much more to develop and extend the analytical abilities of the nurse, fostering confidence, enabling her to question her own practice in the new era of efficiency demands and to hold her own in a multidisciplinary team. Using students as labour, the report was saying, though not in so many words, had become a false economy. The new deal, in short, would be good for the health service as well as good for the nurse.

There was a further important dimension. Project 2000 was not only a new 'preparation for practice', but also a claim for a new practice. The nurse would be and should be not perpetually a manager of others who carried out the care, but herself at the heart of the delivery of nursing care. This responded to what has been described in Chapter 5 as the 'Polo mint problem' in nursing. That problem had begun to be named, particularly by advocates of practices associated with clinical nursing units,[8] but it was still a matter of finding words to express this. The Project 2000 team set out a vision of a practice-based division of labour, with the trained nurse as linchpin, supported by a non-nurse helper on the one hand and by specialist or advanced practitioners in the relevant clinical field on the other. They opted for the terms 'knowledgeable doer' and 'practitioner'. This was a formula that was to give rise to serious problems in nursing's own ranks.[9] And, as we will see below, while it attracted scorn and derision from some doctors, it was dealt with even more effectively in the main arena of costs and manpower by being discreetly ignored.

The published report contained 25 recommendations. In essence, they fell into three main groups, concerning the nature, philosophy and approach of the educational programme itself, the conditions – for students, for staff and for the institutions in which they were located – that would enable the new programme to be fully established and the measures (those at any rate that could be seen as within the remit of the statutory body), that would be necessary to put in place a single practitioner level of nurse at the centre of the delivery of nursing care. Under the first heading came the recommendations for a common foundation lasting up to two years of a three-year programme, to be followed by branches and by subsequent advanced courses and areas of work. Under the second heading came the all-important claim for supernumerary status for students and hence for training grants rather than salaries. Opportunities for staff development, organizational and budget conditions that would enable teachers to create and sustain the new educational programme also fit here. The third main focus covered recommendations for a single level of practice, a new set of competencies, a new helper, and cessation of training for a second level, together with opportunities for conversion for existing enrolled nurses. Much of the ensuing debate was conducted in a way that took recommendations one by one, ignoring the analysis in which they were set and the direct confrontations that they represented. These confrontations were two-fold. Project 2000 challenged both the longstanding arrangement that enabled nurse training to occur inside the health service and the fundamental concept of what a nurse was that had been supported by those arrangements.

2   Who wants an educated nurse?

In the six months following publication of the report in May 1986, Project 2000 received more attention and discussion in nursing than any other policy issue. A poll undertaken by the nursing press suggested that 88 per cent knew about the project by October 1986, and it was calculated that by the time the consultation process was over, between 30,000 and 50,000 nurses had taken an active part in debates about it. Not everyone was convinced about the whole package of proposals and there was some serious questioning of aspects of the report (UKCC 1986b). But the overall tenor of the profession's response was welcoming; the need to uncouple education from service, the paramount importance of achieving supernumerary status for students so that an education-led programme could be established and so that educational standards could be raised, was something to which the vast majority were sympathetic. There were concerns about how this could be done, whether it could be afforded, whether there was not a danger of moving too far away from the practical skills of nursing, but on the whole, the profession agreed that it wanted and deserved a better educated nurse and the way to achieve this was to free her from the necessity from the very outset of her training to be on the rota, delivering patient care in the hospital. Did outsiders feel the same way? Were they convinced by the diagnosis in the report? Did anyone outside nursing really want a better-educated nurse?[10] As we shall see, there were some at least in the medical profession who were prepared to say outright that they did not.

The group that formulated the Project 2000 proposals, as we have seen above, involved few outsiders of any sort. No doctors were included. A limited amount of informal contact with doctors took place while the project was under way, but on the whole interaction between the two professions was fairly minimal. Medical responses did emerge, however, in those early days, and we concentrate here on three in particular. First, there was the reaction of the British Medical Association (BMA). Records of discussions from two committees have been traced as appearing in print. Two further articles, one by a consultant physician and one by a consultant surgeon have been found, together with some observations from a medical journalist in the editorial columns of *The Lancet*. This is only a small volume of commentary, and cannot be taken as in any way representative of the views of the medical profession as a whole or indeed of any section of it.[11] Nevertheless, the hostility to nursing that emerges at this point, and the form that this hostility takes, is particularly instructive in the light of the arguments in Part One of this book about the gendered nature of the notion of profession itself.

Publication of the Project 2000 Report gave rise to considerable concern in some quarters of the BMA. Four months after its appearance (while nurses were busy trying to amass the support of their own profession for the proposals in their original or a revised form), the Central Committee for Hospital Medical Services (CCHMS) was sufficiently alarmed to resolve to seek meetings with the Chief Medical Officer at the Department of Health and with the RCN. The published record of their deliberations is brief, but conveys the strong feelings that were elicited (*British Medical Journal*, 13 December 1986: 1585). The Chairman set the tone; he had surmised from the list of names given that there was not a single practising clinical nurse on the Project Group. Dr Mary White followed up on this. Nursing, she stated, was essentially a practical skill, best learned through an apprenticeship, not in a technical college. The proposals, to her mind, were 'a disaster for nursing and for the enrolled nurse' whom she championed. The importance of nursing as a practical skill was echoed by others. Dr Appleyard pointed out that

Project 2000 altered the whole pattern of care in hospitals, that there were, therefore, implications for standards of medical care, and that the General Medical Council (GMC) and the Council of the BMA should be involved. Others counselled caution; nurses were leaving nursing, perhaps there were parts of this that could be supported.

Later, at the time that revised Project 2000 proposals (UKCC 1987b) were with the government and out for consultation in the NHS as a whole, the General Medical Services Committee (GMSC) drafted a formal statement.[12] Its tones were rather more measured. The Committee was concerned about the implications of reform for staffing and for costs. They felt that students would come to regret the exchange of salaries as health service employees for bursaries. They stated principled support for the 'knowledgeable doer', but added an immediate caveat. Would this new nurse be more interested in the 'technical' and the 'academic' than in the 'personal' and 'caring' aspects of nursing? Would she not therefore be 'over-trained'? The posing of the question is revealing in more than one respect; not only does it indicate that the efforts of nurses for decades to replace the term 'nurse training' by 'nurse education' were still ignored in this quarter, but it also suggests that even with a more limited vision of the enterprise as a training one, the doctors believed that training could be overly extended. There are distinct echoes here of the historical equation of nursing with the female sex, of the view that a good nurse is born and not made, that a good woman is a good nurse.[13]

Is this to read too much into a small caveat? Individually, as we shall see, doctors can be much less circumspect. Brendan Devlin (1987), a consultant surgeon, provides a particular case in point. He emphatically rejected what he dubbed the 'brave new world' of Project 2000. For him, the ideal was the enrolled nurse who was 'local, dedicated and long-serving'. Any talk of nurses as 'practitioners' was elitist nonsense, not, he felt, 'socially acceptable', either to doctors or to patients. His point was driven home by remarking on the composition of the Project team – there was not a practising clinical or community nurse among them, there was no manager, no representative of any other health care profession. This, in effect, was to disparage both the competence of nurse educators to pronounce on nurse education, and the value of that education itself. Not content with this, he further observed that it was small wonder that nursing students were confused when 'it is the house chat of junior doctors ... that much outdated clinical practice is taught in nursing schools' (Devlin 1987: 30). And he went on to add a dismissive reference to the many RGNs who 'rush away from nursing to add further alphabets to their names'. To talk of masculinity as based on a contempt for the qualities assigned to and associated with femininity, and to see this masculinity as celebrated through concepts of professionalism, as was done in an abstract way in Chapter 2, may have sounded somewhat extreme to some nursing ears. But surely contempt is not far from the surface in remarks such as these?

Dr Gibberd, a consultant physician, also rejected Project 2000, though on the face of it he was much more sympathetic. Stung by the UKCC circular to all doctors, put out in the midst of the health service consultation, he argued that Project 2000 was not, as the circular had tried to argue, the only option (Gibberd 1988). For him, the problems that nursing faced were not to do with education at all, but to do with unsocial hours, low pay, poor prospects and barriers to the nurse who wanted to take a career break and later return to practice. He could not see that learning on the job had disadvantages – staff who were committed to their work would want to impart their knowledge to others and would be better at it than specialist teachers, and, as for students being treated as 'pairs of hands' he simply denied that anyone thought this way. Nurses, he argued, needed a caring nature, but nursing was more than sympathy and sensitivity. How much more? In the end, the answer seemed to be 'not much'; for his solution was an 18-month, ward-based training, a 'non-academic course, run by nursing schools and cheap to organise'. This was a solution that in effect meant keeping things much as before, save that the period of preparation was to be cut in half![14]

From this point forward, the medical press remained surprisingly quiet about Project 2000. Four years on, however, medical journalist Malcolm Dean attended the RCN Congress and gave an account of his impressions to his doctor colleagues via the editorial pages of *The Lancet*. He gave a sympathetic account of what he dubbed the 'identity crisis' in nursing. Nurses resented being seen as exploited angels or sex kittens. They resented too the way in which the media regularly turned to doctors for comment on the health issues of the day. He agreed that altogether too little time was spent on examining the organization, management and future of nursing. He alerted his colleagues to the important changes that were under way; Project 2000, he thought, was reversing the old staffing ratios that had involved student service. Primary nursing whereby a nurse would be responsible for care from admission to discharge was getting under way, there was a realignment of tasks with nurses taking over some of the work of the doctor – including a limited prescribing role[15] and health care assistants taking over some of the routine work of the nurse. He declared himself broadly in favour of these realignments, and yet, echoing the themes of the nurse as bringing the practical and the personal he ended with his own clarification of the core of the difference between doctoring and nursing:

basically the heart of the doctor's world is 'science-based'; the essence of nursing is caring. The main aim of a doctor's training is to teach the skills of diagnosis: once you have got that right you have a lot of clues as to how treatment should proceed. The main aim of nursing is to improve a patient's comfort . . .

(Dean 1992: 1161)

This puts more overtly the themes of the several medical comments reviewed here. The work of the nurse, these doctors argue, is practical and personal; it is something that requires a fairly brief training, without a strong theory component. The doctors, even if their answer was not something nurses liked to hear, were facing directly the question 'what is a nurse?' The Project 2000 Report, and more particularly the debate and action which ensued in relation to the government, sidestepped this fundamental question. But the different answers of nurses and of the government ministers were never far below the surface.[16]

3   Implementing educational reform

Publication of the Project 2000 Report, members of the UKCC were fond of saying, was the start, not the end of a process of securing educational change. By the time it came to presenting proposals to government, it had to be possible to show that there was firm professional support from within but it also had to be possible to demonstrate that the changes to be made were feasible in terms of costs and manpower. The Council, in an unprecedented move, appointed management consultants to carry out work in this area. The difficulties that the consultants faced are an object lesson in the contradictions of devalued work and the challenge of trying to promote change.

   In the first place, high quality and reliable information about nursing had not been a priority in the NHS and was thus not available. On the question of the costs of nurse education, the absence of a clearly defined education budget meant that the consultants struggled to identify the various components and the channels through which monies were allocated. An early decision to send a questionnaire to all schools and colleges on this made clear that the situation was often equally opaque to those close to the ground. On manpower information they fared scarcely better. Case study work in four health authorities revealed that the notion of an overall nurse manpower system with a variable reliance on students and returners to replace the annual staff requirement that could be changed by a policy decision, was not part of routine thinking and hence not an information priority. Gross figures on joiners and leavers for example could be produced, but without information on where joiners came from (from training? from another job? from a career break?) or what leaving meant (leaving the employer, leaving the NHS?) or reasons for leaving (promotion? pregnancy? husband's job?), it was hard to use the figures in any meaningful way. Piecing together the different sources, getting informed and consensual estimates was often the best that could be done.

The manpower model that emerged from all this endorsed the claim of the original report. Nursing worked on a high recruitment/high waste model. It recruited large numbers of students, high proportions of whom left at different stages of the programme and in their subsequent work. Nursing did not focus its efforts (except when shortage threatened) on the question of returners. The 30,000 replacement required each year was achieved by 30 per cent returning to nursing and fully 70 per cent being newly qualified. By turning this around, by reducing the waste, it should be possible to reduce the numbers entering training, and with reduced numbers, more could be spent per entrant (Hanson and Patchett 1986, Price Waterhouse 1987, UKCC 1987a; see also Chapter 4, page 81).

Quantifying this further, however, required yet more information. What was the actual and preferred skill mix in different areas of nursing work? What was the real contribution to service that students made, and with what combinations of qualified and unqualified staff should it be replaced? These were questions that produced frustrations all round. On the 'what is' questions, information not only again proved scarce but showed that practice varied considerably. Skill mix was a result of local factors, hospital wards being staffed with whoever was available, custom and practice not being a priority for scrutiny. On the 'what should be' questions, the clear answers that the consultants needed were not forthcoming. The 'Polo mint' pattern as discussed in the last chapter, the way in which nursing was treated as a matter of staffing the wards with whoever was available, meant a firefighting management style, coping with crises rather than experimenting with different modes of care delivery (cf. Davies 1992). Detailed visions, demonstrations of alternatives with numbers attached and outcomes shown, were, not surprisingly, in short supply.

Authoritative talk around benefits of the new system foundered in much the same way. A considerable number of potential benefits for the new system had been identified in the original Project 2000 Report, but could evidence be produced in such a way that sums of money saved could be estimated? The team ranged far and wide to cull information about different practices and money-saving. In the end they suggested that with Project 2000 fully in place, as much as £80 million per annum might come from various types of benefit ranging from better organization and quality of care, rationalization of training, greater lifetime participation of nurses, reductions in wastage and so on. They themselves were cautious about this, never presenting costs net of benefits without also presenting gross costs alongside this. And, significantly perhaps, the whole debate came to be known in all quarters not as the costs, benefits and manpower issue, but as the issue of costs and manpower.

The results of all this work suggested that the net costs of educating a nurse currently amounted to a little over £13,000, a figure that with Project 2000 might rise to approximately £16,500 – all rather different from the £100,000 for a doctor (see Chapter 4). The costs to the Exchequer would turn on how many nurses one needed to educate. Assuming a 20 per cent service contribution from students and if, by management action in the NHS increasing the rate of return to nursing, cutting down on waste of trainees and trained staff, the annual demand for students came down from over 30,000 to 22,000, the gross costs in the year 2004 would be £400,000 million, that is £40 million greater than today. If one were to have faith in the benefits calculations, the costs would actually be lower than at present – although of course there were transition costs to be taken into account, so that the cost overall over the years would go up before it came down.[17]

Working closely with members of Council and exploring modifications to the initial proposals, the consultants were able to produce a set of calculations that could be put to the government and these were reflected in the Council's final proposals (UKCC 1987b). The consultants, rather than focusing on the devaluation of nurses and nursing, highlighted the demographic threat – falling birth rates meant that nursing could not continue to recruit such high numbers from the age group of 18-year-old young women, so that the status quo was not an option. There was no doubt, in the consultants' eyes, that the educational changes the Council wanted required a massive cultural change, a shift in the outlook of health authorities and a willingness to work to change the way in which nursing staff needs were assessed and nurses were managed. All turned on the political will in the NHS to make such radical changes. Here the consultants spoke of a 'significant risk' that the targets would not be achieved, but were encouraged by their calculations that were the management targets to be only half achieved, the ratio of qualified to unqualified would not deteriorate markedly. Implementation, they emphasized, was a major undertaking and were the change to go ahead, some means of supporting and co-ordinating activities would need to be found.

How was all this received in government circles? On the face of it, there was definite support for the concept of Project 2000. In announcing this publicly in May 1988 at the RCN annual conference, the Minister endorsed the structure of the new programme with its common foundation followed by specialism, and stated that a phased implementation would start if possible in the following year. He acknowledged that students needed to have a programme of clinical experience more closely aligned to their educational needs and that this meant removing them from the roster. He accepted too that a single level of nurse was 'the right way to go' (though adding that he had an overriding responsibility to ensure that health service staffing needs could be met). Nor was this mere words. The Department of Health had for some while itself been working on the costs of educational change in nursing. There had been discussion with the Treasury, with the result of broad endorsement for changes estimated to cost an additional £580 million over 14 years, assuming a 10-year implementation programme.[18] The complexity of the change process had been acknowledged. Things were to proceed somewhat differently in the different parts of the UK, but in the case of England, a Steering Group, chaired by the NHS Chief Executive was planned, together with an Implementation Group that would provide advice and guidance to health authorities, advise the Department on the feasibility of their plans for the Project and would ensure that the timetable was being met.[19] The whole process, it was felt, would be more speedily implemented if the monies were ringfenced and allocated centrally, rather than being added to the budgets of NHS regions.

This certainly seemed to be commitment on a large scale, justification for the celebrationist position rather than the cynical one outlined at the outset of this chapter. The text of the Minister's letter to the Council formally announcing acceptance of reform put matters in a different light. To be sure, it reiterated support for the new educational directions that were proposed. At its heart, however, lay a firm rejection of the manpower equation produced by Price Waterhouse. Those calculations, the letter stated bluntly, were 'not realistic'. The message was quite unambiguous: Price Waterhouse had envisaged that the nursing workforce in future would operate with a skill mix of somewhere between 64 per cent and 70 per cent of qualified staff (UKCC 1987b: 13); the official response was that 'a professionally qualified workforce of the size you envisage cannot now be achieved throughout the UK in the foreseeable future' (*Nursing Standard*, 20 May 1988: 4).[20] Nor was the government prepared to concede the cessation of EN training. This could possibly occur, but it would need to be subject to further work on manpower. Support workers too, it was emphasized, were of the utmost importance and wide recruitment was needed. In other words, Project 2000, seen strictly as an educational programme, was to go ahead. How and to what extent replacement of the student labour contribution would be achieved remained to be seen; all options were being kept open. The vision of qualified nurses not only planning but actually delivering the bulk of care remained just that. In practice, as we shall see below, educational changes were introduced 'as funds allow', and the division of labour in nursing work was to be subject, as a later Minister diplomatically put it, to a process of 'continual evolution'.

'... as funds allow'

For those in nursing education the announcement of the acceptance of Project 2000 was a great opportunity but also a daunting one. They had to produce not only a new curriculum, but a new philosophy underpinning it. New kinds of placement had to be developed outside the hospital, new thinking needed to surround the allocation of students to wards. The circumstances of timetabling were to be transformed. Alongside this they had to manage and maintain the old programmes and attend to the morale of students on them; they had to think about conversion courses for ENs and respond to developments both local and national on the nature of and training for a new support worker. Many were already embroiled in the process of amalgamations of schools and colleges and in some cases integration with or forms of joint working with higher education. In all this, far from separating from their service colleagues, they had to work ever more closely with them to ensure replacement staff were available as the students were withdrawn, and that numbers in training reflected the forecast needs of the service (for some discussion of teachers' perspectives, see Slevin and Buckenham 1992). To gain the additional funding for all of this, detailed plans had to be drawn up by Regions for the Implementation Group at the Department. The Implementation Group required a submission that on the one hand satisfied the requirements of the ENB and could pass its validation procedure, and that on the other offered a clearly costed and comprehensive manpower plan showing all the elements of cost that would be involved and claimed accordingly. For the first round, Regions were asked to put forward submissions on a timetable of just five months. Thirteen of the 23 received after this short timetable were judged educationally viable and all of these were given approval.

Thereafter, the uncertainty of funding made itself felt. In numerical terms, developments proceeded apace. Seventeen schemes were approved in the following financial year, 20 in the next and a further 14 in 1992–3. At the end of 1992, four years on from the announcement of acceptance, four out of five students were Project 2000 students, 17 colleges were still running the old style programmes (NAO 1992). In practice, however, the Implementation Group had not at any point been able to predict the level of funding that it would be in a position to allocate. This generated considerable tension and difficulty. For one thing, having invited two bids per region in the second round, having received 33 submissions, 24 of which were judged educationally acceptable, it funded only 17, and chose the least costly schemes rather than the first choices of the Regions. Proposers found that they were not looked on sympathetically if in the rush for funding and the complexity of the issue they had omitted items. There was confusion about how the costs of inflation would be handled, and the organizers of the first tranche of schemes, having costed five-year plans, found themselves at the end of their first three years with no guidance as to further funding. At all points, bids continued to be scrutinized individually and estimates pared down.

But it was not only a matter of the combination of speed and uncertainty in the funding timetable. The actual amounts available for replacement of the labour contribution of the traditional students, and the quality of the guidance concerning how this should be done were also crucial. These would set the tone for a new relation between those in education and those in the service and shape the context in which students would learn. The Project 2000 Report had set out its vision of a practice-based division of labour; Price Waterhouse had quantified this in terms of a 64–70 per cent qualified staff. The government had responded that this was unrealistic. The Implementation Group addressed the seeming impasse with a formula. It started with the total number of students to be replaced, adjusted this for assumed efficiency and other factors, and calculated a total sum based on the assumption of a 50/50 replacement with qualified and unqualified staff. The total sum was non-negotiable; the authorities were free to indicate that they would spend it with whatever ratios they chose. Alongside developing all aspects of the new teaching programmes, staff were required to decide quickly within a given budget, and with no guidance, how they would change skill mix. One study, which has traced events in detail in a single setting, documents the dissatisfaction and frustration that this situation produced. It notes the 'boxing and coxing' that went on; it concludes that there was simply not enough funding to employ qualified nurses in the numbers in which they were needed (Elkan et al. 1993).[21]

The National Audit Office, in its larger-scale enquiry evaluating Project 2000 implementation, acknowledges that the constraints of the public expenditure process had a deleterious effect on the Project 2000 planners (NAO 1992). It goes out of its way to applaud the commitment and hard work that the profession put in to produce submissions and it finds unacceptable the absence of a clear timetable for including the colleges that remain on the old programme. Nurses themselves put the criticisms rather more directly, pointing on the educational side in particular to the difficulty of presenting different programmes to students, to the confusion caused when planned initiatives could not go ahead and to the very negative impact on staff morale and especially on potential recruits (see, for example, Bolger 1990). The cry may well have gone up in some parts of Westminster and Whitehall and in the health authorities that 'the nurses are whingeing again'. But it is abundantly clear that 'as funds allow' was a formula that on the one hand, made the difficult business of developing and getting new educational programmes under way significantly more so, and on the other, left a vacuum where the debate about the required skill mix should be.

. . . 'continual evolution'

A year after the first Ministerial letter to the Council announcing principled support for nurse-education reform, a new Minister wrote again to the Council. The letter, received in May 1989,[22] was a further blow to the process of developing new educational programmes. The question of what help was going to be given towards the development of existing teaching staff to put them in a position to meet the new educational demands represented by a Project 2000 curriculum was still outstanding. The original report had not only envisaged moves to create new organizational entities within which there could be more staff specialization and access to the support of colleagues in higher education, but had also seen the need to start to move towards an all-graduate teaching staff. Minister Kenneth Clarke poured cold water on this. Earlier broad support for improving the educational position of teaching staff was reiterated but the positive tone of this was wiped out with failure to offer anything specific and the statement that 'it would be impractical and wrong to require an all-graduate teaching force at this time'.

The letter went further. The reforms associated with education in nursing, it stated, needed to be seen as in a process of 'continual evolution' as far as associated grades of staff were concerned. What did this mean? Taken in the light of the earlier letter which had stated so categorically that the proportion of qualified nurses that nursing envisaged could not be achieved, the Minister was trying to move things on. First, there was the matter of cessation of EN training. Here he kept his options open. Current ENs, he reiterated, had an important role still to play. He was prepared for health authorities to submit plans that linked the discontinuation of EN training to their bids for Project 2000 programmes, and he still held out the possibility that within five years the overall cessation of training might be agreed. Second, there was the question of the support worker. Even as the original Project 2000 Report had been published, moves had been made to try to develop this whole area.[23] Kenneth Clarke wanted to see definite progress on the matter; it was time for an agreed title and for vocational qualifications to be formally accepted. He pressed the UKCC to produce a framework paper on this. Specialist practitioners were dealt with in the same way. The ball was in the Council's court. The Minister reassured the Council that his commitment to well-educated nurses remained, although this would have to be reviewed 'in the light of experience'. The trade unions' accusations of 'flannel' (see page 107) do seem to have a point; each reassurance from the Minister was followed by a qualification.

'Continual evolution', meaning that the Minister was free to reassess at any point, was particularly important at the time. A review of the structure and functions of the statutory bodies for nursing was already under way, which could have changed their shape and remit considerably.[24] Even more importantly from a Ministerial point of view, the NHS reforms that were to bring the internal market to the NHS, to create new players in the shape of the Trusts and later to mean curtailment and eventual disappearance of the then regional tier of management, were already taking shape. The White Paper *Working for Patients* had been published four months previously (Department of Health 1989). Work to develop the implications of this for the totality of education and training associated with the NHS was being finalized. While it was not at all obvious how educational activity would fit with the growing emphasis on the separation of purchasers and providers and the creation of competition amongst the latter, separate funding, emanating from the centre, certainly ran counter to the overall tenor of the thinking. *Working for Patients; Education and Training; Working Paper 10* soon revealed what the overall pattern was to be. It was for employers locally to ensure that they had available the quantities of trained staff that they required. The amalgamated schools and colleges of nursing and midwifery, like service providers, would contract to provide the required trainings leading to qualifications at different levels, basic and more advanced. Nationally recognized training and qualifications structures were to be preserved, though the extension of National Vocational Qualifications and the principle of creating more accessibility and links and ladders between them were to be given every encouragement. The Project 2000 vision of a clearly demarcated and separate educational budget, managed by schools themselves, was being thoroughly overtaken by the new contract culture of the NHS.

Conclusion

Throughout the 1980s the nursing profession devoted considerable resources and energies to the quest for reform of its basic educational programmes, and deliberately placed this top of its public agenda. This was a matter of a fundamental change in the curriculum. But it was even more than this. On the one hand, it was a bid for a clear separation of education from service, an undoing of a historically unequal bargain in which 'neither the learners nor the teachers had the freedoms they required'. On the other hand, it was an ambitious bid to restructure the nursing labour force itself, a plan to abolish the 'Polo mint problem' described in Chapter 5, and to create what the Project 2000 Report called a practitioner-based division of labour. By the end of the decade, the first new programmes were running. Treasury approval for very considerable spending had been secured; monies had been found and the change programme was being spearheaded from the Department itself.

But nursing paid a price for all this. First there was the speed of development of the new programmes in the context of reorganizations and amalgamations of colleges and uncertainty about the future role and functions of the statutory bodies. The ENB was able, as implementation progressed, to provide a forum for support to nurse educationists, but the Minister's rejection of the recommendation for a move to an all-graduate teaching force was a blow to the concept of professional development for teachers – something that Project 2000 had regarded as a prerequisite.

Second, there is the question of the restructuring of the nursing labour force which has been on the agenda throughout. Holding on to its vision of a high proportion of qualified staff, nursing faced a war of attrition here. The government position was clearly stated at the outset – the skill mix that the nursing leadership wanted was unrealistic; hence agreement was withheld on cessation of EN training, and pressure was maintained on developing a framework for a new support worker. The onus then shifted to the Regions to produce individual plans for replacement staff and for numbers for admission to the new programme, plans that were scrutinized and in some instances pared down by the Department. There was no overt bargain struck at national level that nursing had to accept a restructuring in order to achieve educational change, it was all left to the strength of forces locally in the context of the speedy production of submissions for the new funding. What evidence is available suggests that the replacement formula has resulted in much continuing as before. The National Audit Office strongly criticizes the health authorities' bids for Project 2000 for failing to prioritize returners and to review skill mix. Elkan *et al.* (1993) describe a process of *ad hoc* decisions, of choices sometimes being put in a ward sister's court as to whether she wanted more qualified staff, but too few of them, or more unqualified staff and a reversion to task allocation for the qualified staff that remain![25] The process of implementation of Project 2000, in other words, has involved a new preparation at breakneck speed and a new practice not at all. The circumstances have certainly not been such that the Project 2000 message about shifting from a high recruitment/high wastage model, and valuing nurses rather than treating them as interchangeable pairs of hands has remained in view.

The events discussed in this chapter also demonstrate that educational reform in nursing has increasingly become bound up with the major NHS reforms which have been a key feature of the decade of the 1980s. Initially, this worked in nursing's favour. Project 2000's call for a nurse who was less hospital focused and able also to work in the community setting was attractive in the new climate. So, too, perhaps was its overt recognition that the training of health professionals needed to incorporate a preparedness to be more analytical which included questioning established practices for their efficiency and effectiveness.[26] NHS reforms, however, have meant yet more change in the organizational framework in which new programmes are delivered, change which is likely to tie education in new ways to local service demand. Uncoupling of student service has been accompanied by an attempt at any rate at a closer coupling of supply and demand – adding new opportunities and threats to which staff must adjust. The notions of competition and contracting, the extension of the purchaser/provider model from service delivery to educational delivery, are a long way from the ideas in the Project 2000 Report of giving educational establishments greater freedoms and ensuring that programmes are education- not service-driven.

The analysis of nursing that emerged from the effort to reform nurse education teetered on the very brink of confronting the gender dimensions which had produced it. It would have been a small step from the RCN report's stress on constant replacement, the UKCC's formulation of nursing as operating a high intake/high waste model and Price Waterhouse's figures demonstrating this, to suggest that it was an unequal and patriarchal bargain that first gave nurses a place for training in the hospitals. The relations that this entailed exploited and oppressed nurses, so that they have continued to be seen as pairs of hands, as the labour force that 'staffs' the hospital, and their efforts to develop nursing theories and nursing models have been ignored, doubted and even derided. Let us – just for a moment – imagine what the response to such an argument might have been in a culture that recognized its own deeply gendered nature, that acknowledged the import and heritage of the masculine vision as set out in Part One of this book. First there would be a clear acknowledgement of the historical dilemmas and difficulties faced. 'Yes,' nurses would have been told, 'our assumptions, our ways of acting, our frameworks of thinking put you in an impossible position, limiting the contribution that you can make.' Removing students from a service contribution would have been a *sine qua non*. But steps would then need to have been taken to identify the conditions that would enable teachers to develop programmes and practitioners to experiment with new forms of practice. On this model, it would be important that the replacement costs of the student contribution were entirely separate from the new sums to be devoted to nurse education, seen more as a one-off recompense or 'gender retribution' budget item, rather than, as now, integrated into the overall equation and part of the debate about whether change was worthwhile and could be afforded.

Was the acceptance of Project 2000 in the end, therefore, an affirmation of the worth of nursing? To the doctors, some of them at least, it was the reverse. Nurses were getting above their station. The politicians presented no such direct challenge, and by implication it seemed that the nurses' case had been accepted by them. The nature and level of the support that nurses received however, made one thing abundantly clear. Staffing the service takes precedence over educating the nurse. As one commentator wryly observed amidst all the excitement at the initial announcement of acceptance of Project 2000, 'what matters to health authorities in the 1990s is the supply of nurses – any nurses – to keep the hospital services running' (Dyson 1988: 15). It was not possible it seems, in the mid-1980s, to ignore nurses altogether in their claims for educational improvement, but it was possible selectively to hear what was being said, so that the most crucial issue of nursing policy, the question of who does what and who should do what in the nursing labour force, remained subject to local negotiation, to the constraints of providing 'pairs of hands'. Six years on, Project 2000 is neither the unqualified success that the optimists would have us believe, nor the 'success of the unqualified' that some cynics feared; certainly, however, it falls far short of the set of claims that had been initially proposed. Nursing education, by 1990, was on a new footing, but nursing practice remained much as it has always been.

This chapter completes the examination of some of the key policy debates in which the nursing profession has been recently engaged. It has become apparent that in the question of the numbers of nurses, of the organization of nursing work and now of nurse education, it is by no means easy to describe the social organization of nursing or to prescribe remedies for the tensions that have emerged. Too often, nurses appear as confused, and muddled – in need of an injection of 'rational' thinking that will yield clearer identification of tasks and skill boundaries; or unrealistic and elitist – behaving in a somewhat distasteful way in an apparent quest for power and status. This, I have in each case tried to suggest, is both because the 'disorders' of nursing are a product of deep and largely unacknowledged gender divisions and because the policy gaze that is turned on nursing is itself gendered and blind to the very gender dimensions it has produced.

It is now time to step back from the detail of these debates and to consider how an overall strategy might be conceived in order to move the argument on to new ground. Such a strategy, it will be argued, needs to go beyond the present parameters of profession and professionalization, acknowledging these as visions that are imbued with partial and masculinist ideals. Part Three will look again, with the help of some recent feminist scholarship, at nursing as the work of caring. It will also argue that, despite the contradictions that caring work encompasses, its fate, in the new contract culture of the NHS, may not be quite so bleak as one might at first imagine.

Notes

1 I have discussed the characteristics of the 'initial compromise' in nurse education elsewhere (Davies 1980). For brief notes on some 14 reports on nurse education from 1932 to the present day, see Dolan (1993: appendix 1).

2 This is not to say there was no debate around the reorganization of nursing in the post-war era. The Wood Report of 1947 recommended major reorganization. For a lively and critical account of the inquiries and discussions, see White (1985: ch. 2).

3 For an informative account of the context of the Briggs Report and the various negotiations that took place in the 1970s, see Dingwall *et al.* (1988: ch. 10).

4 The urgency and impatience about reform are witnessed in prior events. Both the UKCC and the ENB had issued consultation papers on reform. These had provoked a storm of controversy (see Davies 1985).

5 I took up post at the UKCC as Project Officer in September 1984 for a period of two years. The contract was subsequently extended, so that I left in April 1987.

6 The Project 2000 Report (UKCC 1986a) gives full details.

7 The Council's Educational Policy Advisory Committee at this time, and hence the Project Group, consisted of 19 members, together with a representative from the Health Departments. Meetings were attended by four professional officers from the UKCC, myself and the project assistant. Of the 19 members, the majority, 13, were in posts in nurse or midwifery education, and a further four were educationists from outside nursing. The other two were a Director of Nursing Services and a Nursing Advisor on the Health and Safety Executive in Scotland.

8 The relevant chapter in the Project 2000 Report opened with a quotation from the work of Sue Pembrey, herself closely associated with the Burford Community Hospital and Nursing Development Unit in Oxfordshire.

9 Midwives in particular took exception to the use of the concept of practitioner, which they felt had long reflected the conditions of their own

practice but not those of nurses. For an account of reactions to the report within the nursing professions see UKCC (1986b).

10 It should be noted that there were few, even in nursing itself, who at any point were prepared to suggest that the initial qualification for nursing should be a degree. The RCN favoured a move of educational programmes into the Higher Education sector, but others, including those on the UKCC remained very cautious about the feasibility of such a move. (For some comments, see Clay 1987.)

11 The question of medical responses to Project 2000 requires more detailed consideration than I am able to give it here. It is said, for example, that Tony Newton, as Minister, made it clear in visiting the UKCC in 1988, that all the Royal Colleges were against the reforms at that point. This is by no means the whole of the story, however, and for a very different and more sympathetic approach to examining the issues in nursing from those discussed in the text, see Delamothe (1988). This is one of a series of articles by the author in the journal that year on the subject of nursing grievances.

12 For a report on this, see Gaze (1988).

13 See Gamarnikow (1978) for a vivid account of the use of gender imagery to explain, justify and account for the relative position of doctors and nurses at the turn of the century.

14 Interestingly, a brief survey in the nursing press of reactions of health authority chairpersons, managers and doctors also singled out doctors' doubts about 'academic nurses' and 'too much theory' (Alleway 1987).

15 Nurses gained a right to prescribe a limited range of drugs and dressings under the Medicinal Products: Prescriptions by Nurses, etc. Act 1992. This came into operation in October 1993.

16 Some of the reactions of those in management were rather more positive. Alongside the views of Brendan Devlin and in the same issue of the *Nursing Times*, for example, came comments from Gillian Shephard, MP, who as chair of a health authority welcomed the wide-ranging nature of the Report, and declared that it was time for a thorough investigation of all aspects of nurse education and career structures, and a sympathetic hearing from General Manager Mike Schofield who, while recognizing the potential long-term economies, declared that it would cost and that this should not be fudged. The associations, the National Association of Health Authorities (NAHA) for example, and the Institute of Health Services Management (IHSM) were more cautious, giving support in principle but also stressing questions about costs and manpower. Regional Manager Catherine Hawkins emphasized the importance of putting the customer first, acknowledging that better education was desirable, but taking the position that the costs in time and energy should not be expended if other ways could be found (Hawkins 1986). This was a particular disappointment to those in nursing since this manager herself had a background in nursing. But there is no doubt that questions of cost and questions of manpower were the prisms through which Project 2000 was viewed.

17 The detailed findings (Price Waterhouse 1987) are summarized in UKCC (1987a).

18 The DHSS, for example, had put in considerable effort in costing proposals associated with an earlier set of educational reform proposals published by the ENB, and had involved a number of Regions in the exercise. How this later figure was arrived at and how it related to the Price Waterhouse calculations is not made clear by the NAO who cite it in their report (NAO 1992: para. 1.8).

19 The Steering Group held only one meeting. The work was done by the Implementation Group (NAO 1992: para. 2.6)

20 Though extensively quoted in this news item, the letter was not reprinted in full in the nursing press.

21 The Nottingham group has produced two reports on a study of implementation of Project 2000 (Elkan and Robinson 1991, Elkan *et al*. 1993). Other work includes a Department of Health funded study (see Jowett 1992, Jowett *et al*. 1992, 1994), a Northern Ireland study (O'Neill *et al*. 1993) and at least one other locally funded evaluation in England (Robinson 1991, Robinson, Jill 1992).

22 The Minister's letter was reproduced in full in *RCN Newsline*, 14(6), June 1989.

23 Investigation and enquiry into the question of a revised support worker role at Department level was seen as crucial to any staffing change associated with educational reform in nursing. See, for example, DHSS (1987a).

24 The statutory bodies for nursing, midwifery and health visiting were reorganized under new legislation in March 1992. Certain functions were transferred and the Central Council became a larger body with more direct, electoral representation of the profession whereas Boards became smaller with an emphasis on executive functions. For further details see UKCC Annual Report 1991–2.

25 Overall patterns of employment of nurses and the shape of the total nursing labour force began to change rapidly in the early 1990s. In the summer of 1993, for example, the RCN was reporting a sharp drop in total numbers of nurses in employment, and redundancies in nurse education across the UK (RCN, *Intercom*. No. 930, July 1993). By the end of the year, the College was citing figures showing a planned cut in student numbers of more than half between 1983 and 1997, and arguing that this represented a failure to plan properly for the nursing labour force (*The Guardian*, 21 December 1993).

26 Chapman (1989) points out that autonomous critical practitioners who can highlight deficiencies in care are hardly likely to be welcomed in the current climate.

part
three

BEYOND THE PARAMETERS OF PROFESSION

seven

PROFESSIONALISM AND THE CONUNDRUM OF CARE

The question we should ask is not 'is nursing a profession?' but 'should nursing want to be a profession, and if so, what do we mean by it? What are we hoping to achieve and is this the best way to go about it?'

(Salvage 1985: 92)

there is a great need to find better models for organizing caregiving work. To develop such models, it seems necessary to study not only the exploitative nature of women's traditional caregiving work, but also the positive qualities inherent in it as well as why they seem to get lost when professionalized . . .

(Waerness 1992: 209)

The question of whether nursing is or is not a profession appears with great regularity amongst the subjects to be considered by students of nursing. Lists of potential attributes of a profession are devised; they include the possession of a complex and valued knowledge that is inculcated through a lengthy, formal and systematic training, control over both education and work practice, self-regulation through a statutory body and an orientation to others that is cast in terms of an altruistic commitment to service rather than a hope of rewards in a marketplace. Attention might be drawn to the power and privilege that accompanies such characteristics, to the monopolistic position that a successful profession enjoys, to its power to shape and develop the direction of its work, to shed aspects of it, and to exclude competitors. The standard textbooks, by and large, however, do not debate the pros and cons of professionalism *per se* or question the justifiability of the power which professionalism brings. Energies are more often expended in arguing either that nursing is already a profession, or that it is vital that it should become one, in order to control its own work and to realize the unique function of the nurse in the process of health and healing (for something of an exception, see Jolley 1989).

Nor is this a mere student exercise. From the late nineteenth-century battles to create a register of qualified nurses to the late twentieth-century struggles to give full student status to new entrants and to create a research base for practice, nurse leaders have understood themselves to be engaged in a quest for full professional status. The zeal of exponents of primary nursing and clinical development opportunities, as well as continuing talk in the RCN of an all-qualified workforce attest to this. Alan Pearson, in his widely read and influential accounts of the Oxford and Burford clinical development units where what has come to be dubbed 'new nursing' (Salvage 1992) took important root, sees progress quite explicitly as a matter of 'shedding the shackles of bureaucracy and management' which have surrounded nursing, thereby enabling it to develop a more authentic, autonomous and essentially 'professional' practice (Pearson 1983: 5).

The attention that has been given to the gender dimensions of nursing in this book points to the need to examine this kind of thinking altogether more critically and more closely. If the model of professionalism is, as we have suggested, imbued with the mark of masculinity, and if nursing has been constructed as an adjunct to this masculinized model of profession, can it possibly represent a way forward for nursing? And if it cannot, then are we to say that some kind of a model of caring, imbued with the mark of femininity – and all the devaluations and disadvantages for survival in the public world that brings – is what nurses need to pursue?

The chapter will argue that thinking about professionalism is changing in a way which has a particular relevance for nurses. The new thinking, however, has not fully confronted gender and in particular it remains silent about the emotional aspects of nursing work and the caring work that nurses do. This understanding of professionalism, if it is to be helpful to nurses, needs to be informed by with a model of caring. And for this to occur we need a better understanding of what it is to care, and of the different contexts in which caring occurs. There are three main sections to the chapter: first, we will explore the attachment of nurses to the idea of professionalism, showing that the doubts that some are beginning to express, contribute to and link with 'new professionalism'. We will then consider the growing body of feminist research on caring work and tease out some of its potential. The production by the RCN of a series of stories, told in nurses' own words, about the nature and importance of nursing care provides a poignant demonstration in section three of the need to bring caring to the fore if 'new professionalism' is to mean something to nurses themselves and to offer a way forward in under-standing and supporting their day-to-day nursing experience.

1   Old professionalism – yardstick for nursing?

Is it possible for a nurse to argue against professionalism as the model for her work? At first sight the answer has to be no. It is not only that much that a student learns is couched in terms of learning to act in a properly 'professional way' in her encounters with patients and with colleagues and co-workers in health care; it is also that norms for 'professional conduct' are laid down formally and that the nurse is answerable ultimately to the Professional Conduct Committee of the UKCC which has powers to strike her off the Register and remove her source of livelihood in the practice of nursing if she acts in a way that is deemed unprofessional. If we distinguish, however, between a broad sense of professionalism as probity or integrity of personal conduct and pro-fessionalism/professionalization as a route taken collectively by members of an occupational group who refine and guard their knowledge base, set boundaries around who can enter and what the limits of practice will be, then there is something more to debate and to question.

Jane Salvage (1985), makes just this kind of a distinction, arguing that when leaders call for a 'professional nursing service', when they put forward visions of an all-qualified nursing labour force, it is not professionalism of individual behaviour, but professionalization of an occupation that is at stake. Her questions are of several kinds. First, there is the sheer unreality of a model of profession of this kind. The reality of the staffing of hospital wards, and indeed, we can say too of much community nursing care, is that it is not remotely approaching this; leaders, she says, are exhibiting the 'ostrich syndrome' in looking in this direction. Second, however, and much more importantly perhaps, since professionalizing entails the limiting of numbers, they are in danger of condoning the notion of nurses not only as highly skilled but also as a small and elite group. Such a group, of course, by definition does not deliver nursing care but manages it and/or provides technical backup through advanced skills. Her discussion (Salvage 1985: see esp. 95–101) throws down a number of challenges.

1 *Professionalism is divisive.* In failing to acknowledge that most basic nursing care inside and outside the hospitals is given by untrained

people and in identifying with doctors, it damages relationships and lessens the quality of care. Controlling access to knowledge has similar results.

2 *Professionalism seeks to impose a uniform view.* While all share the goal of good nursing care, interests do differ, questions of the exploitation of some groups over others – managers and students for example – get submerged.

3 *Professionalism denies the needs of its workers.* Service to patients is placed as the highest priority, yet there may be times when nurses need to assert their own day-to-day needs and not, for example, rule out completely the possibility of strike action.

4 *Professionalism emphasizes an individual approach.* It stresses individual responsibility for the personal delivery of high quality care; yet can staff be accountable for situations where they have little control? Is it right that the individual nurse should be disciplined for a personal failure when staffing levels are inadequate? Is it reasonable also to put the onus on the individual to keep up to date with developments in professional practice?

5 *Professionalism does not challenge the status quo.* Is more autonomy for the nurse automatically better for the patient? Should we be talking about more radical approaches to the fragmentation of health care, giving a basic training, for example, to more people?

6 *Professionalism does not give strong support to the NHS.* It directs attention to the needs of the professional group rather than to the needs of the health care system as a whole.

The doubts expressed here, about elitism, professional power, accountability and so on, are emerging with growing frequency amongst commentators on nursing.[1] They also, however, find an echo inside other professions, among the public at large and in academic studies of the subject. The years following the implementation of the NHS formed what was perhaps in retrospect the high point of public confidence in and respect for professions and their ability systematically to apply scientific and technical knowledge in the interests of the wider public good. Thereafter a critique began to emerge that questioned the efficacy of professional interventions in a number of spheres. It also pointed to the limited relevance of some of the solutions that professionals offered and to the motivation, which sometimes included self-interest, of individual professionals themselves. By the 1980s, what had mostly been left-leaning critics had been joined by free market conservatives in doubts about the solutions that professionals had to offer. Professions no longer enjoyed the unqualified support that they had once had.[2] As the next chapter will show, the Conservative governments of the 1980s, with their emphasis on control of expenditure and on value for money, were able to build on this and to mount a definite attack on the monopolistic tendencies and inward-looking character of professions in all areas of the public sector. For nurses in the 1990s to look to professionalism, is thus to look to a model of practice that is under severe attack. For this reason if for no other, it is wise to begin to cast the net rather more widely, giving attention, not to old-style professionalism as such, but to those who have seen the writing on the wall and are seeking to reshape it.

2   New professionalism – not enough

A clear agenda for the 'new professions' emerges from the study made by sociologist Margaret Stacey, drawing from her experience as a lay member of the General Medical Council (GMC), of the functioning of that regulatory body (Stacey 1992). Stacey mounts a strong argument that professionalism as evidenced by the behaviours of the GMC is an outdated nineteenth-century phenomenon – a set of 'collective illusions' that now needs urgently to be set aside. Doctors acting collectively have put 'profession before public' in their emphasis on the exclusive character of their knowledge, their insistence on unity and their preservation and enhancement of their own status. Factors such as these misguide doctors, keeping them on the terrain of restrictive and defensive practices, contributing to an inward-lookingness and arrogance, whereas the need is to rebuild from the ideals of service that were also implicated in the nineteenth-century ideal.

In particular, Stacey argues, doctors need to relinquish the outmoded idea that theirs is a one-to-one relationship with the patient. They must recognize the contribution of others (including the patient), to health and healing and make consequential adjustments to notions of clinical autonomy, of control over allied professions and of the exclusive right of doctors to sit in judgement over other doctors. At the level of practice, she goes on, change is already under way involving greater information sharing and collegiality with others (ibid.: 260). At the level of collective self-regulation, she offers a list of eight criteria for good practice, which include not only the familiar controls to ensure competence and qualifications to practise, but additional ones relating to the direct involvement of patients, subordinates and co-workers.[3] Development of these requires doctors to move towards a new professionalism which puts patients 'not necessarily first, but equal to and part of the professional interest' and means attending to lay conceptual frameworks as well as to those of medicine (ibid.: 260). It also means yielding to other health care workers, recognizing their different but essential input. Ultimately, she

suggests that new professionalism might well mean not separate regulatory bodies at all, but a single one for all those who work for health.
Stacey is able to cite an array of developments suggesting that medicine is
moving in the broad direction of new professionalism, but at the same
time, her brief outlines of new kinds of education, new forms of lay
involvement, changes in complaints procedures and mechanisms for
redress, demonstrate the far-reaching nature of a 'new professionalism'
that rebuilds on the older service ethic in this way.[4]

'New professionalism' is a notion that is now beginning to be fleshed
out by a variety of other authors also. Richard Hugman focuses on
nursing, the remedial therapies and social work, arguing that 'the
language of professionalism frequently serves to obscure the issue of
power' (Hugman 1991: 6). Like Stacey, he draws on the service ethic as a
mechanism through which the older, orthodox model of professionalism
might be criticized and transcended.[5] Where her 'new professionalism'
pulls back the power of medicine, seeking to insert it in a matrix of
influence of clients and other health workers, however, his concept of
'democratic professionalism' holds out the prospect of a structure that
further empowers both users and the members of professions that often
experience themselves to be weak in the context of the hierarchies and
controls they face. 'Democratic professionalism', in Hugman's vision,
means creating the kinds of partnerships and participation at the level of
service delivery that are already visible in relation to anti-racist and
anti-sexist practice in social work (see, for example, Dominelli 1988,
Dominelli and McLeod 1989). It also means creating new mechanisms at
policy-making levels that bring service users into direct participation
both in the policy-forming structures of the NHS and in the professional
associations and trade unions at the points where the nature of the service
and the means for its realization are being debated. The possibility that
allied more closely with users, each of these health and welfare
professions might come together to share experience and to start to draw
new boundaries between themselves is suggested.

By 1993, sufficient thinking of this sort was available to make it
possible to produce a fairly lengthy collection of readings for health and
welfare professionals based around the notion of a revised professional
practice. Professional knowledge, the editors argued, was not something
fixed and impersonal, to be inculcated as a set of abstract principles;
practitioners needed to be aware of and use their own humanity and
experience, they needed to respect the diversity of their clients, to
recognize the need to empower them and to engage in teamworking with
colleagues. For those working in the helping professions in health and
welfare, they suggested, the relationship with the user could actually be
more important than their role as expert (Walmsley et al. 1993: 6). The

message was underlined by including readings authored by users (including the perspective of a practitioner-turned-user), by attending to practitioner unease with traditional care delivery and by including a discussion that replaced the usual emphasis on professional detachment with the idea of 'meaningful distances' in professional health care (Purtilo 1993). Jan Williams sets the tone for the whole volume in her discussion of expertise and experience. She explains:

> Instead of a one-way transmission of knowledge from professional to client, there is a two-way transaction, building on existing knowledge and experience of the client, according to the client's perceived needs and the professional's response to these.... No longer is the professional seeking to impose her view.... Her role has changed from one of controlling to one of supporting and enabling, helping the client to draw on and think through his own experiences, and sharing her expert knowledge to help him develop his understanding.
>
> (Williams 1993: 11–12)

Underpinning much of this thinking is the concept, first developed a decade ago, of the 'reflective practitioner' (Schön 1983).[6] Professional practice, Schön argued, is not a matter of straightforward rational analysis, of 'instrumental problem-solving made rigorous by the application of scientific theory and techniques' (ibid.: 21); instead it involves a process of situated reflection on expertise and experience, which attends to the uniqueness and the uncertainty of the specific situation, and which may be as much about finding the problem as with solving the problem found. This reflection-in-action, he maintains, is actually the core of professional practice, even though it is rarely accepted, even by those who use it, as a legitimate form of professional knowing. The dilemma is that we are 'bound to an epistemology of practice which leaves us at a loss to explain, or even to describe, the competencies to which we now give overriding importance' (ibid.: 20).

Why should this be? Valorizing abstract principles, orderly and codifiable knowledge and above all emphasizing technical rationality in this way, Schön argues, reflects the triumph of scientific thought, the extinguishing of religion, mysticism and metaphysics and the ascendancy of positivist thinking in Western ideas and institutions. The move of professions into the universities meant acceptance of this form of thought and of a hierarchy which elevates research over practical problem-solving, downplaying the complexity and uniqueness of specific instances. It favours rigour over relevance and reflects this in curricula that emphasize the core disciplines, seeing applications and skills and attitudes as an 'ambiguous secondary kind of knowledge'. Schön's account of this broad historic process has striking parallels with the account of gendering set out in Part One; the technical rationality that masks reflective practice is the same masculinist project – of mastery of knowledge and of control and domination over others and over an environment – that was described earlier. In these terms, his discussion of reflection-in-action may be seen as describing the limits of the cultural code of masculinity, its unreality as a prescription for effective behaviour on the part of embodied individuals. It thus enables us to begin to speak more critically and less apologetically of the theory/practice gap to which nurses often refer, and of the way that this is sustained by the hierarchical practices of knowledge creation and transmission with which professionals are involved.

But there are at least two important silences in Schön's account. In the first place, he fails to see the gendered division of labour that helps sustain the elite professions through the work of women dealing with the local, the applied and the human dimensions of professional practice, and the acute dilemmas that this adjunct work produces for women who wish to appropriate the label 'professional' for the work that they do. In the second place, the concept of reflective practice emphasizes reflection as an act for the most part of the practitioner alone. For this reason, we can say that Schön fails fully to confront the engagement of the practitioner with the client, hence ignoring the always specific and embodied character of the contribution the professional makes, the commitment to and respect for the client and for co-workers, all with their histories and identities which are to be brought into play if the full pattern of experience and expertise is to be acknowledged and utilized. In terms of the model set out in Part One (page 27), Schön has effectively challenged its cognitive elements (knowledge as mastery) but has retained altogether too much of the masculine notion of self and the distant, emotionally controlled and controlling instrumental actor for him to have provided a satisfactory model for nursing care. We need therefore to examine *both* the professional *and* the caring side of professional practice and it is to the question of conceptualizing care, especially nursing care, that we now turn.

3   Caregiving, carework and professional care

Caring, as Hilary Graham (1983) ably demonstrated in a ground-breaking article a decade ago, is something that slips through the conceptual nets offered by the academic disciplines of the social sciences. Its fusion of 'labour and love' is frustratingly diffuse, hard to capture by means of the usual apparatus of definition and measurement in the disciplines of psychology, sociology and social policy. Practical job analysis techniques such as are employed in organizational settings, with their minute breakdowns of tasks, cannot encompass it – since a moment's reflection suggests that all kinds of specific activities can be carried out in the name of care for the other, including apparently no activities at all. Caring can mean just 'being there' for someone, not necessarily listening, not necessarily even being physically present but being known to be available, checking the situation out from time to time and being ready to respond if asked. Caring in this broad sense can be defined as *attending, physically, mentally and emotionally to the needs of another and giving a commitment to the nurturance, growth and healing of that other.* Caring does not involve specific tasks; instead it involves the creation of a sustained relationship with the other, an ability to reflect on the specifics of that person's history, and an ongoing process of dialogue through which assessments and interventions can be tried, monitored for relevance and adopted or adapted as necessary. It is this business of 'attending' to another, the close observation that a carer undertakes, that attunes her or him to minute differences that are not necessarily available to the more casual or sporadic observer. In the public world of paid health care, the nurse is often, though not always, structurally placed to achieve this, whereas the doctor is rarely so placed.[7]

Our understanding of caring, particularly within British scholarship in the last decade, has been filtered through studies of what I shall here refer to as 'caregiving', the unpaid caring that women do in the home, much more than through studies of 'carework' or 'professional care', forms of paid caring that is done in the public arena of hospital and community care settings.[8] An important corpus of feminist scholarship on caregiving has now been built up largely through in-depth interviews with women who are caring for elderly parents and sick and disabled children.[9] This work has demonstrated that carers often find it difficult to put into words what it is that they do; they would comment that it was 'natural' that they should care, that they just 'got on with it', sometimes cheerfully, sometimes with resentment. The researchers were able, however, to document the wide array of tasks that carers carried out for those for whom they cared, the hard daily grind of physical labour that was often involved, the lengthy hours spent with the cared for and the emotional turmoils and moral debates about love, duty and guilt that the work as a carer can evoke. Their commentaries emphasize the importance of bringing previously hidden and taken for granted aspects of women's lives as carers into view; they ask about the consequences for women who do this work, and the opportunity costs of caregiving. This work has been particularly important in practical social policy terms in introducing discussions of respite care, support and payment for carers, and in broader political terms in uncovering and questioning the personal self-sacrifice that is often involved when women take on unpaid care in the home and in raising broader issues of social justice and equality between the sexes.

Some writers have expressed concern about a possible overemphasis in these studies on the oppressive side of caring, and an underplaying of the rewards of care. Whatever the merits and demerits of such an argument,[10] we need to note that work which questions the family as the ideal model for care, and acknowledges that there are negative aspects of caregiving in a domestic setting can help to release us to consider forms of paid caregiving in a new light. Paid caregiving can thus be seen not as a poor and somehow always unauthentic substitute for 'real care', but as an activity that has the potential, through appropriate training, organization and support, to overcome some of the tensions and dilemmas of home-based caregiving. Idealizing care by women in the home, in other words, has guaranteed its underanalysis; looking at it more closely and critically is a step on the road to conceptualizing care more adequately and identifying the kinds of care and of caring work that we need to sustain and support in the public arena.

The care that women give in the home and family setting is governed by values of love and spontaneity, is carried out in isolation from others, is bereft of validation by any source apart from the care recipient. It is rare in this context that anyone puts into words the skills and experience that are brought to bear and distinguishes these from the specifics of the setting and the personalities involved.[11] Arlene Kaplan Daniels is one writer who has emphasized and expanded on this in an important way, making links between domestic caregiving and paid carework. She suggests that as far as women's paid work is concerned, the closer it is to the activities of nurturing, comforting, encouraging, and facilitating interaction – features encompassed by the definition of caring given above – the more likely it is to be seen as natural or the expression of women's style in general (Daniels 1987: 408). She then sets out four specific areas of skill that are involved. There is the skill of attending to how a setting is affecting all others in it; this involves the ability to take the role of the other and to feel some of the same feelings. There is the focusing of attention, through a process she describes as 'ruminating about the past and planning for the future'. There is a process to do with assessing the reasonableness of preliminary judgements that works through checking the behaviour of all present, noting and acting on an observation that someone is ill at ease. Finally, there is the matter of creating a comfortable ambience, one of warmth, sympathy and concern for others. These skills, of 'making community',[12] she claims, are routinely required, not only in the domestic sphere but also very frequently in the public world of work and politics – particularly where service work and teamworking are the order of the day. As interpersonal skills they are sometimes recognized and rewarded when men display them; but the pervasiveness of gender thinking means they are taken for granted and are resistant to recognition and reward when they are exhibited by women.

What happens when the unpaid caregiving described above becomes 'carework', the paid work of public caregiving? The jobs of care assistants of various kinds in the home or in residential care, of home helps, of domestic servants, childminders and so on have a number of obvious characteristics. They remain largely women's work, they exist outside any sustained training framework, they retain a low status and attract low rewards. All this is consistent with a blindness to the skill base which is involved. Equally important, however, is the conflict that such work sets up when incorporated into a regular bureaucratic control system. This has been described particularly vividly in the case of home helps whose work is organized in such a way as to allow them to give flexible and versatile services to a small number of clients in their own homes over a long period. Home helps exhibit strong personal attachment to the clients, and this is the feature that they most enjoy and see as integral to the work. They can be acutely aware, however, that the values that they bring to their work and the experience and skill that they draw upon do not strictly 'make sense' in the public sphere in which they operate, as the following passage vividly shows:

> These middle-aged and elderly women argued that their experiences as housewives in their own families for many years was the most important training for being able to do a good job as a home help. Even those who had had special formal training for this occupation doubted it had any value, apart from heightening the status of their job. Working on the basis of their competence as housewives, however, often meant they had to break the official job instructions. Often they had to work for more hours than they were paid, and sometimes they even had to do things that were directly forbidden according to the rules. They also expressed a very clear opinion about the negative aspects of their job. The isolated working situation, which meant that they had no colleagues to share problems and experiences with, and the lack of influence compared to the more professionalized working groups in the social services, were regarded as very negative features of their work-role. They also had a very clear understanding that their conduct as employees in many ways could be evaluated as foolish according to the general norms for rational behaviour on the labour market.
>
> (Waerness 1992: 221–2)

The work of Norwegian sociologist Kari Waerness, first published in the early 1980s,[13] provides several important links in the chain of understanding carework. Waerness insists that a fundamental shift in approach is required if we are to bring this work into focus at all, a shift that goes against the mainstream of thinking in the social sciences. The first step is to work with a more rounded notion of the individual as a 'sentient' being, who blends thought and emotion, who not only takes a cognitive, instrumental approach, calculating likely outcomes on the basis of systematic knowledge and the rules which can be derived from this, but also takes account of the particularities of persons and the feelings of all concerned. In an argument echoing aspects of that of Donald Schön in the previous section, Waerness identifies the limited nature of scientific rationality and its embeddedness in a masculinist thinking that stresses a cognitive solution to problems via mastery of knowledge and control of its applications. From this perspective it is possible to begin to lay bare what she calls a 'rationality of caring', an approach that is not driven by blind emotion and sentiment, but which has a describable logic of its own. To operate within a 'rationality of caring' means acknowledging that caring work cannot be entirely contained within and governed by scientific knowledge, accepting that emotions and commitments are part and parcel of the process of effective caregiving and recognizing that flexibility, adaptability and hence uncertainty are entailed by this work. These are recurrent themes in the remainder of the chapter.

Where then does professional care, public caregiving that is preceded by systematic formal training fit into all of this? Waerness, as the quotation at the outset of this chapter shows, provides a pessimistic comment, suggesting that caring values tend to get lost when brought into the public arena and professionalized. She cites empirical work that suggests that formal training suppresses the values of caring and promotes not flexibility but rigidity, and she observes:

> [B]ecause the head–heart duality is accepted in all sciences, it seems probable that any kind of formal education based on scientific knowledge will to some degree promote a more instrumental attitude towards work, at the expense of the expressive.

> (ibid.: 223)

She sees nursing as a particular case in point. Its leaders everywhere favour the development of formally acquired knowledge as a route to greater status, but, she comments:

> 'nursing science' is . . . not a solution to the problems of strengthening the values inherent in the rationality of caring, at least as long as

this science is based in the generally accepted notions of scientific knowledge and learning.

(Waerness 1992: 224)

Nurses do not simply attempt to take on the mantle of old professionalism, however, they also frequently face the issues of reconciling professionalism and caring as dilemmas of daily practice. There is plenty of evidence for this. It is there, for example, in the frustrations of nurses who say that the system does not allow them to nurse, and in the striving to provide individualized care set out in Chapter 5. It is apparent in the way that nursing seems so resistant to clear definition, and in discussions that refer to the 'science and art' of nursing, in the unease yet fascination with books and articles that propose that nursing is 'a form of loving'.[14] The discrepancy between the recordable and recorded tasks of nursing care and the apparently unrecordable and hence not entirely legitimate delivery of 'tender, loving care' is a repeated theme of empirical studies.[15]

The commitment to care that nurses bring, because it is not at all well articulated or understood, and because it is simultaneously romanticized and trivialized by others, can serve to lock nurses into a spiral of resentment and to cut them off from co-workers. Corley and Mauksch (1988) explain how this works. The assumption by co-workers that nurses will care about the patient absolves others (particularly doctors) from identifying with the patient, and protects them from feelings of guilt and failure. This means that others can neglect their work, effectively 'dumping on' nurses who are unlikely to resist, and who are thus placed in an unenviable position of responsibility without power. Some of the 'silent frustration' of nurses alluded to at the very outset of this book comes into better focus when we see that the vocabulary of professionalism and the strategies of knowledge creation that it entails leave no place to discuss the contradiction of care, and the paradox of daily experience. In facing these dilemmas, professional nurses are in the same position as the home helps described earlier – there are no acceptable words for the logic of caring that they are trying to put into practice, the work has not been and cannot be conceptualized without a revolution in the frameworks on offer. This is not simply a matter only of finding words to express negative feelings. We will see in the next section that when nurses themselves recount their most positive experiences in their work, their words continue to fall outside the professional frame.

4 'The value of nursing': the voices of nurses on professional care

In 1992, the seventy-fifth anniversary year of the RCN, the College took as the focus of its campaigning the question of the worth and the value of nursing. One result was an exercise inviting its members to write in with events and incidents demonstrating what it was for them that was unique and worthwhile about nursing practice.[16] A publication was subsequently drawn up which presented 50 of these accounts, interspersed with a commentary from the College (RCN 1992). The dilemma, the College argued, was that good nursing was rather like invisible mending – much of it could not be seen. An insider view, therefore, was necessary to clarify for others just what nursing truly entailed. What is striking in the context of the present discussion is the way in which the stories themselves reflect, in their very different words, the same themes that have emerged from the academic work discussed above. New professionalism's reflective practice is clearly in evidence together with the values and the skills that are present in caregiving, carework and professional care as described above.

That nurses can and do take pride in technical knowledge is evidenced a number of times in the RCN publication – in the case, for example, of the nurse who clearly had more experience in coronary care than her medical colleagues, or in the case of the nurse who was able to diagnose porphyria, and in the incident where the nurse recognized the significance of repeated swallowing in a barely conscious patient. Yet there are few cases here which could be classed in a clear way as celebration of mastery of the principles of textbook knowledge; instead they are about weighing this knowledge against an understanding of the full circumstances of a patient, continuing to observe and puzzle when something is not quite as expected. The case of the man whose symptoms did not make sense until the junior nurse saw him taking the anti-inflammatory drugs that he had not thought to mention is a case in point. Nurses remember with pride spotting something that others might have missed; in some instances this comes as a result of years of experience, in several it is a result of patient, minute and detailed observation that takes place in the sustainedly close relationship that the nurse has with the patient.

Emotional commitment to patients, caring about outcomes, building a relationship so as to learn more about the person and hence adjust the environment and the care plan accordingly are repeated themes. The commentary refers to the way in which nurses need both technical and interpersonal skills and will make an emotional commitment. It also notes that the nurse takes 'the risk of coming very close to the patient', explaining that this can entail forming 'an intimate but not intrusive relationship, using touch, massage, and gentle encouragement to help patients find new hope or the comfort in distress' (ibid.: 2). Why the term risk? This is not explained, but refers, I would suggest to the crossing of the boundary between the rational action that is appropriate for the public domain and the intimacy which our gendered thinking reserves for the private and domestic one.

The skills of 'making community' are very much in evidence. The sheer impossibility of rigid job demarcations when the paramount issue is to remain alert to the needs of the patient, the client or the relatives and to find appropriate ways to meet these, comes out in a wide array of incidents. It is there, for example, in the evident pride of the nurse who performed last offices for a Jewish woman on a Friday when the Rabbi was not available and was then asked days later by the Orthodox Jewish family to do the same for her husband. It is present, too, in a number of cases where nurses who deal with clients with learning disabilities devise and take part in initiating innovative routines for daily living that will provide a framework and give a sense of progress for all concerned. The role of the nurse, the commentary explains, has to be infinitely flexible 'because the primary task is to act in the interests of the patient according to the nurse's professional judgement' (ibid.: 25). Yet, it is rather more than this. Because nurses in these examples are attending to the whole situation and the resources it offers, because they are prepared themselves to become engaged and to seek to engage others, they are fusing reflective practice with the skills of community that were outlined earlier.

Four examples are given below as demonstrations of these themes. The first underlines not only the paramount importance assigned to the active management of feeling states (of the nurses as well as the patients), but also the deliberate effort to hand control to the patient and to cope with the uncertainty that ensues. The second, while not describing any particular incident, reflects in a very practical and straightforward way on the matter of experience and knowledge and the way the two interact with on-the-spot observation in the care of elderly people. The third exemplifies the 'risk' of coming close to the patient, making a calming physical contact, something, the nurse observes, that was not part of the formal programme of teaching and learning, whereas the fourth, a good example of reflection-in-action, shows how such reflection encompasses a whole series of social judgements alongside the technical ones.

I was a student nurse and I was being taught by the enrolled nurse how to pass a nasogastric tube on a patient. The lady we were working on was quite poorly. She had lung cancer and had had fluid drained from her pleural cavity twice that week. . . . The enrolled nurse explained to her exactly what we were going to do and how much better she would feel. He was quite clear about how unpleasant the tube could be when it was going over the back of her throat. He then explained it again to me and she watched like a hawk, holding the tube he had given her in her hand. After all the preparation, he proceeded to put the tube up to her nose, and lifted her two hands and wrapped them round his. 'At any time when you want, you can stop this,' he said. So she did, three seconds later. The second time, he was just as patient. Eventually, with tears pouring down her face, she pushed at his hand to 'help' the tube going right down her throat. After she was all tidied up and settled, and some of the bile had been drained off, we all held hands for a second, and he made her laugh by inviting her to help with the intubation of any other patient who might need it. (Student nurse)

When you look after old people who have Alzheimer's disease, it is sometimes possible to tell that there is something wrong with them, even if there is no measurable change in their condition. It may be a tiny change in appetite or wakefulness that is too minute to be worth reporting, a change in temperament, or bowel habit, that is still within the normal range, but you know that there is something wrong. They can be quite clearly 'coming down with something'. It's not just a hunch, but if you know the patient and keep a close eye on them you can predict what is going to happen. That's why it's good to have an experienced nurse looking after old people. (Care of the elderly nurse)

Bill had Huntington's Chorea and he used to stagger about all over the place with his arms flailing. . . . On one occasion he inadvertently struck one of the patients who responded by hitting back and there was a tussle which the nurses had to sort out. I took him to the day room with me. He was clearly quite distressed. . . . I managed to persuade him to lie down on the sofa. He was still moving about a lot in his agitation. I got him to curl round one of the cushions and sat very close to him rubbing the back of his neck and stroking his hair at the base of his skull. I had seen his wife doing this before and it seemed a natural and comforting thing to do and before long he had dropped off to sleep. It is not something they taught me at the school of nursing but it felt right and it worked. (Mental health nurse)

We had a drunk in one night who was shouting and bawling in pain. He was a biker who had come off his bike when it had hit a wall. You know how sometimes you feel about drunks – he was making all this row while the quiet ones lie still and bleed to death – nevertheless there was something about the abrasions on his face that made me think he must have had a real bump on the head, so I held his head and neck still while the other staff got the clothes off him and splinted the broken legs. Even in X-ray he was cursing and trying to sit up. We put on the lead aprons and held him down. He was known locally as a drug abuser and we wondered if he really only wanted some pethidine. I made sure he had some anyway. The relief was instantaneous, too quick, still I'm glad we got it for him. It quietened him down and it turned out that he had fractured his neck, one sudden false move would have paralysed him. (Accident and emergency charge nurse)

(RCN 1992: various pages)

Taking these descriptions of professional care together with the earlier discussions of caregiving, we can see a number of common themes. First, it is clear that professional caring stands in a complex relation to scientific knowledge. It is not a matter, as in the home helps example (see page 143), of a fairly complete dismissal of the value of formal knowledge and training, nor does it mean giving it, as in the traditional professional model, clear epistemological priority. Instead, formal knowledge is put *alongside* other knowledges, leaving a considerable place for adjustment and negotiation in the light of a carefully acquired and detailed knowledge of persons and situations. Second, these professional carers see emotions and commitment as part and parcel of the process of effective caregiving, and not as something that must somehow be purged when caregiving enters the realms of the public and the paid. The fusion of 'caring for' and 'caring about' that characterizes homebased care of kin (Graham 1983) in their eyes quite clearly has more to offer to a sustained caring relationship that will bring about healing than has the professional detachment stance that is associated with the fleeting diagnostic encounter of medicine. Moreover, it is not only the one-to-one relationship that is at issue here, the aim can often be seen as deliberately enhancing the quality of involvement and commitment of all those delivering and receiving care. We noted above the way in which Daniels (1987) offered a glimpse of the skills that are involved in the active management of an emotional climate, skills of making provisional interpretations, checking out their relevance, remaining alert to and attending to discordances. Third, the necessary uncertainty that all the above elements of caregiving work entail is very much apparent. If the rules deriving from abstract knowledge cannot be applied in a clearcut way, if attending to emotions and feeling states is an inexact process, if listening to the client and being prepared to act on that listening is crucial, then nurses have to be flexible and adaptable. Predictability and hence hierarchical control over the work is much reduced.

We can regard what is at stake here as an act of *dislodging the gendered model of profession*, the model that arose from a masculine notion of self and a set of cognitive and relational styles that attended to this. The caring practitioner model that is beginning to emerge goes beyond the gendered thinking outlined in Part One in a number of respects. Specifically, the new practitioner is:

- neither distant nor involved but *engaged*;
- neither autonomous nor passive/dependent but *interdependent*;

- neither self-orientated nor self-effacing but accepting of an *embodied use of self* as part of the therapeutic encounter;
- neither instrumental nor passive but a *creator of an active community* in which a solution can be negotiated;
- neither the master/possessor of knowledge nor the user of experience but a *reflective user of experience and expertise.*

Crucially important as it is, only the last item in this list echoes the reflective practice concept and the shift from Schön, the augmentation of his contribution, is apparent in the other items. These recognize the power of emotional engagement and commitment of the parties to a healing relationship, and accept that there will be contributions that can flow from the 'embodiedness' of participants, that is, that factors such as their age, sex and ethnicity may have a part to play irrespective of place in the hierarchy or level of formal knowledge. Particularly important here, however, are the alternative assumptions about self and world that are present, the move beyond gendering and the power/passivity dichotomy that this invokes. The reflective practitioner, as noted earlier in this chapter, has stepped aside from instrumentality in the use of knowledge, but remains strongly agentic, committed to action, to making a difference in a world of hostile (or at least potentially recalcitrant) strangers. The caring practitioner, by contrast, exhibits the humility of interdependence, recognizes the potential contribution of others and seeks to enhance it in a world regarded as more co-operative. [17]

It is very clear from this that to bring the terms profession and care together is more than a step in semantics. Much work is already under way, at both a theoretical and practical level, to further clarify and develop this. Still more needs to be done to explore the nature of professional care and to codify our understanding in such a way that we can legitimize and hence embed caring values in nursing practice. Only by deepening our understanding in this way will we be able to support and foster professional care within organizational settings. Already the difficulties and dangers of burnout in caring work are much discussed and the notion of a 'meaningful distance' that avoids overidentification on the one hand and overinvolvement on the other has come into play (Purtilo 1993). The issue of working across hierarchical boundaries, finding ways to foster, acknowledge and support the contribution, for example, that an older married woman nursing assistant or domestic can and often does make to the care of a patient (see James 1989, 1992, Diamond 1990, Hart 1991) poses significant challenges to current thinking about status and work organization. Here, as James has suggested, an 'inverse law' of status and skill can sometimes be in operation (James 1992).

Nursing has been the focus for some of the recent developments in understanding of caring and nurses themselves have contributed to the ideas that are now emerging in this field. The work of Nicky James (1989, 1991, 1992) has already been cited. She has been able to set a systematic comparison of domestic caregiving and paid emotional labour both in a broad sociological context of arguments about the separation of rationality and emotion and in the immediate context of the delivery of nursing care in a hospice setting. Pam Smith (1992) builds on this in relation to the needs of nursing students to be able to confront and develop the kinds of themes which have been explored in this chapter. She argues that the values of connection and involvement that are expressed within nursing care, and the emotional labour that nurses do, need both to be taught in an explicit way and to be underpinned organizationally if nurse and patient are to be protected. There is also the work of Patricia Benner and Judith Wrubel in the USA, a *tour de force* in its discussion of the philosophical roots of caring, its practical and inspirational discussion of the nature of nursing and its confrontation with the concept of caring as a 'cultural embarrassment' which has to be overcome. As those authors ruefully but accurately observe, we know a lot about controlling and disciplining a recalcitrant labour force, but in all the management literature on motivating employees there is 'little sage advice on how to enable highly motivated and dedicated workers to perform at the level they want to perform' (Benner and Wrubel 1989: 383).

Conclusion

This chapter has reviewed two ongoing debates that are of central significance to the future of nursing, one concerned with 'new professionalism' and reflective practice, the other concerned with the conceptualization of the work of caring in the many different settings in which it takes place. I have argued that both are necessary if nurses are to come to stand in a more confident relation to the work that they do, and that 'new professionalism' can ultimately only represent a way forward for nursing if it acknowledges, directly or indirectly, the cultural baggage of masculinity that the old model of professionalism has contained and offers a resolution of its limited and blinkered character.

To argue that there is something to be gained for nursing from focusing on unpaid and lowpaid carework which so often falls to women – activities such as childcare, eldercare, residential care, home help and so on – may seem anathema to many in the nursing profession. After all, has nursing not advanced precisely by distinguishing the work of the trained and untrained, distancing 'professional nursing' from the 'nursing' that is done at home? Other dangers too seem readily apparent; that there will be few incentives and few spaces in a world gendered masculine for a new approach to be heard, that such an approach will be misunderstood, that it will take nurses away from the very actions and activities that grant occupations the status they need, that it will indeed lock nursing further into the devaluation it already experiences by association with women's work. My answer to this has two parts. First, an advance into old professionalism is an advance into a cul de sac. There is too much in the model that is directly antithetical to what nurses wish to do. Nurses would be better engaged in joining the growing army of those who wish to build a new professionalism from the ashes of the old. Second, while work on the 'rationality of caring' is not yet far advanced, its outlines are sufficiently clear to see that it offers a real potential to reflect back to nurses their subjective understanding of their work, to legitimize the work that nurses do and to give them a new confidence in policy settings in place of the repeated silencing we have seen in Part Two of this book. The escape from gendered discourse in which nurses need to take an even greater part makes it possible simultaneously to revalorize care and to revalorize nursing. Putting caring into words, necessary as it is, however, is only a prelude to putting caring into action. The next step, therefore, is to consider how this new thinking will fare in relation to the changes that have been put in place in the NHS in recent years.

Notes

1 See, for example, the discussion of the future of nursing as an occupation and the proposal for a craft model in Melia (1987: 181ff), the critique of recent trends in nursing in K. Robinson (1992), and discussions of different segments including a professionalizing segment in White (1985) and in Dingwall *et al.* (1988).
2 The critical sociological literature on the professions is now voluminous and its support for professionalism has waxed and waned over the years (Stacey 1992). Two American accounts that focus in particular on the turn towards criticism from the late 1960s onwards and link particularly well to the themes of this chapter are Schön (1983) and Hoffman (1989).
3 Stacey's eight criteria to judge whether a medical profession is well regulated are as follows:
  1 that the profession ensures that only appropriately qualified doctors are admitted to practice;
  2 that those continuing in practice are competent;
  3 that they work conscientiously;
  4 that those allowed to practise do not exploit their patients economically, socially or sexually;
  5 that those allowed to practise do not exploit their colleagues or subordinates;

6 that patients or their representatives have ready access to the regulatory body in case of the alleged failure of a practitioner in any of these respects;

7 that patients or their representatives should receive equitable and adequate compensation for any damage resulting from medical accident or misdemeanour;

8 that practitioners are afforded appropriate protection against wrongful actions of patients, employers, colleagues or others.

(Stacey 1992: 253)

4 Stacey draws attention to the arguments of Watkins (1987), himself a public health doctor, who suggests that doctors by their refusal to share power create the hostility and opposition which they fear and hence demand loyalty and discipline within their ranks. These references to a hostile world, to conformity and control, are strikingly reminiscent of the presentation of the cultural code of masculinity outlined in Part One of this book.

5 Hugman's overall thesis concerns the nature of power in the caring professions and gives strong emphasis to gender and to racism in the context of a comparative analysis of professions in nursing, remedial therapies and social work. In doing this, his work breaks new ground and deserves more consideration than it has received. Though this is not the place to provide it, a more explicit comparison of his approach with that in this chapter might be rewarding. It might start perhaps with the suggestion that where he is concerned centrally to problematize power and secondarily to problematize care, my priorities are the reverse.

6 The idea of reflective practice has recently begun to take root in nursing; see, for example, Clarke (1986), Saylor (1990), Newell (1992) and Greenwood (1993). I am grateful to Mary Jenkins for drawing my attention back to the relevance of Schön, whose work she discusses in relation to professional practice in occupational therapy (Jenkins 1994).

7 Literature on the concept of caring is now growing rapidly. For further discussions see, for example, Mayeroff (1972), Ungerson (1983, 1990), Dalley (1988), Graham (1993). A review and attempt at codification of much of the British work is contained in Thomas (1993); a good indication of differences of approach in the USA can be gleaned from the introductory chapter in Abel and Nelson (1990). For a recent extended set of discussions in the nursing context, see James (1989, 1991, 1992) and also a special issue of *Advances in Nursing Science*, **13**(1), 1990. Caring also features in nursing in texts on ethics, see Brown *et al.* (1987: ch. 3).

8 The distinctions used here – caregiving, carework and professional care – are a device for drawing links between caring work in different settings. Terminology currently varies and there is as yet no agreed classification of carework though several authors have made suggestions (see, for example, Abel and Nelson 1990, Waerness 1992, Thomas 1993). It may well be useful to extend existing schemes to consider commercialized care, where nurses have paid particular attention to the work of Hochschild (1983) and to service work and its sexualization (Adkins 1992).

9 See Burton (1975), Glendinning (1983), Ungerson (1987), Lewis and

Meredith (1988). The British tradition, unlike for example the Scandinavian one, has not considered childcare as part of caregiving. To do so raises new issues (Ungerson 1990), including issues of whether there is a specific 'maternal thinking' guiding caring action (Ruddick 1990).

10 For a discussion in the context of the USA, see the introductory essay in Abel and Nelson (1990); for some important observations relating directly to nursing in Britain, see James (1989, 1991, 1992).

11 Ungerson (1987: 104ff) contrasts the attitudes of men and women carers. In particular, she cites the example of a man caring for his wife who comments that he now has new skills to offer in the marketplace (p. 104). No women are cited as offering similar observations.

12 Reference to 'making community' in this way seems to express in different words what was referred to in Part One of this book as the culturally suppressed values of the feminine, the acknowledgement of interdependence, vulnerability and the need for support. For an account stressing unacknowledged skills and relating this to the rationality/ emotions debate see especially James (1989).

13 All page references to Waerness in this book refer to the 1992 edition of an edited collection that contains her article. It was first published in 1984.

14 The notion that nursing is a 'form of loving' appears in Jourard (1971) cited in Williams (1993: 13). In my time at the UKCC, a book entitled *Moderated Love* (Campbell 1984) caused much discussion in nursing circles.

15 For a discussion by a sociologist participant observer working as a nursing assistant, see Diamond (1990). See also Stacey (1981: 185–6) and Campbell (1988).

16 I am grateful to Christine Hancock for first drawing my attention to this. She points out that the impetus for it came in some measure from the work of Benner and Wrubel (1989), which is discussed further below.

17 This is not to imply that power is absent from the caring relationship or that enabling and empowering patients and clients is a simple 'handover' process. Hugman (1991) has a valuable discussion of power and caring. A critical examination of the much used term 'empowerment' can be found in Gomm (1993).

eight

MANAGING TO CARE IN THE NEW NHS

The transfer, during the last decade or two, of managerialism from private sector corporations to welfare state services represents an injection of an ideological 'foreign body' into a sector previously characterised by quite different traditions of thought. . .

(Pollitt 1990: 11)

At any time during the first 25 years of the NHS, an invitation to attend a conference entitled 'The Business of Health Care' would have given its recipient a brief moment for pause. 'Business' being a loose kind of metaphor, it would not have been clear exactly what was planned. In more recent years, however, that same title would have held no such ambiguity. We would immediately understand 'The Business of Health Care' to mean treating health care as a business – we would expect sessions on corporate strategy, on quality and customer satisfaction, on the purchasing role, on marketing and so on. For large parts of the programme, the language might be entirely generic; it would not be obvious at all that the product under discussion was to be health care. Such is the impact of what has become known in the last decade or so as 'new managerialism' in the NHS.

It is the aim of this chapter to explore this changed and still changing culture of the contemporary NHS with its insistent emphasis on marketplaces and managers. At first sight, it seems that nurses cannot but be deeply pessimistic about the 'ideological foreign body' of managerialism, particularly in the context of a discussion of the nature and importance of caring such as was conducted in the last chapter. Does caring not amount to nurses asking for a blank cheque to be written on the NHS account? And what of those who have taken up posts as executive nurses in the new NHS Trusts – have they simply deserted nursing to follow a career in management, or is it possible that they and others, in the new purchasing roles, for example, could now create the contexts for nurses to advocate and practise nursing care?

The chapter begins with a brief account of some of the elements of NHS reform as they emerged in the course of the three Conservative administrations of the 1980s, and as a fourth began its life at the start of the 1990s. It draws attention to the ways in which new managerialism has been constructed and criticized and to the virtual absence of any account of nursing in all of this. It is the absence of any sustained reference to nursing that provides the clue, in the context of the analysis of gender that has been developed in the course of this book, to seeing that managerialism has important continuities with the professionalism and bureaucracy that on the surface it seeks to challenge. New routes for nursing in the current managerial era, the alliances that it might form in face of the apparent 'clash of masculinities' that current policy presents are then considered.

At one level, this chapter can be read as a guide to a set of changes which many in the nursing profession are still inclined to regard as one more reorganization, of no real concern to them in their daily practice of delivery of nursing care. At another level, the chapter explores what it means to begin to develop and apply the gender analysis of Part One to the specific historical situation in which we find ourselves. In this chapter, with its close and detailed attention to contemporary policy development, it is quite clear that a unitary notion of a masculine vision will no longer do; we must deal with diverse and competing emphases in masculinity, and with the questions that these prompt and the efforts at criticism and change that ensue. In this context, I shall argue that there is an important new place for nursing to build alliances with those who are uneasy about the directions of health care reform and who are starting to restate notions of 'public service', of 'health' and of 'care'.

1   The road to NHS reform

Health service reform in the UK took shape in the decade of the 1980s over three terms of Conservative government under the premiership of Margaret Thatcher. What was at stake was not just change in the NHS, but – in the context of a continuing economic crisis and of ever more confident New Right philosophies – a rethinking of the nature of welfare responsibilities and of the very legitimacy of the public sector and the way it had taken shape in the post-war era.[1] In an unprecedented series of policy changes, nationalized industries and public utilities were transferred to private hands, whole areas of civil service activity became the responsibility of new executive agencies, work done in-house in local government and health was put in a variety of ways to the test of the market. No area of public life was exempt from scrutiny; over time, the conviction grew rather than diminished that government was 'too big, too expensive and too inhibiting of individual enterprise' (Pollitt 1990: 48).

At first, the NHS seemed the most resistant of all public institutions to change. It was protected by its popularity on the one hand and by the strength and intransigence of medical power on the other. Talk of a different funding base, of expanded private practice or a public/private mix for health care gave rise to loud rebuttals; and the government frequently found itself sorely embarrassed by the protest and publicity that its policy ideas attracted.[2] Again and again, however, the storms were ridden. One after another, in the course of the 1980s, important mechanisms of managerial change were put in place in the NHS. One way to evaluate these is to consider the steps taken in each of the three administrations of the 1980s. Just how far and in what directions have the existing bureaucratic and professional frameworks been transformed? And to what extent does that transformation give any potential that a nursing voice might be better heard?

The new Conservative government of 1979 had no choice but to give early attention to the NHS. Two months after it took office, the Royal Commission on the NHS (1979) delivered its report. Although the Commission had plenty of recommendations, it was not suggesting fundamental change. The NHS had already been through a protracted period of uncertainty; it was grappling, rather later than other parts of the public sector, with the mechanics of long-term strategic planning and priority setting. It was not, in the Commissioners' words, 'suffering from a mortal disease susceptible only to heroic surgery' (para. 22.4), so that in the main it was small steps and continuing vigilance which were needed. This, as one of its close observers has pointed out, was not a message likely to have thoroughgoing appeal to the government:

> Because of its size and cost, its dominance by authoritarian professions, its lack of clear lines of accountability, its sharply demarcated separation from the private sector, and its overwhelming reliance on Treasury funding, the NHS was almost bound to be a key target for the reforming zeal of a government bent on rolling back the frontiers of the state.
>
> (Butler 1993: 55)

The consultation paper which quickly followed showed little in the way of this reforming zeal. It signalled the government's intention to streamline the cumbersome management arrangements of 1974 by removing one tier of administration. It promised further study to simplify arrangements for planning and professional advice. It spoke in broad terms of more delegation and of a shift of decisions to the local level and it made changes to the composition of the new single tier of district health authorities (DHSS 1979). There was little on the face of it that could be called really radical in this set of changes; the government was careful not to challenge the medical profession and it had very deliberately left intact the consensus management structures that had been put in place in 1974 that many now agree represented the apotheosis of professional control of the service and involved cumbersome processes of consultation.[3]

Alongside this, however, came a veritable 'spate of initiatives' (Harrison *et al.* 1992: 43). Limits were set on the NHS budget, the device of securing efficiency savings through short, sharp investigations was taken over from the civil service to the NHS,[4] first steps were taken towards demonstration projects that would identify clinical budgets. All these gave a message to the Service that it would have to think about getting more for less and take much more account of value for money. Early in 1982, an entirely new performance review process, whereby Districts would meet annually with Regions and regional staff would then meet with Ministers to give an account of their performance and achievement in key priority areas was put in place. By September 1983, a first package of some 70 indicators was available. And there was more; NHS land and property came up for consideration as to active asset management, audit arrangements were examined with a view to focusing these not only on following proper procedures but also on ensuring greater efficiency of resource use. Numerical limitations on manpower were imposed early in 1983, and shortly after that it was made clear that GPs' prescribing patterns were to be reviewed. In the autumn of the same year came the requirement that laundry, domestic and catering work, all part and parcel of the NHS as it had been understood since 1948, were to be put out to compulsory competitive tender.

It is quite apparent that much of what was done in this period was reactive. The government had not taken office with an explicit radical health manifesto (Jobling 1989), and, as we have seen, was forced to take some action on the NHS at a very early stage. It was facing an altogether more effective Select Committee structure, which meant that awkward questions about costs, manpower and management of the NHS were frequently on the agenda in the House of Commons in such a way that it continually found itself on the defensive (see Harrison 1988: ch. 5).

Opposition MPs and organized interest groups were also keeping up the questioning as to just what the government's long-term intentions were. It was very clear that the NHS, for all its faults, had considerable public support. Major change was daunting both as a political and as a practical prospect.

It was the embarrassment of escalating manpower numbers at a time of financial stringency that led in the end to what was the central change of the period. An initial plan to seek advice from the private sector on manpower control became transmuted into not a manpower inquiry but a much wider management inquiry.[5] A group of four leading business people, chaired by Roy (later Sir Roy) Griffiths of the supermarket chain of J. Sainsbury, formed the Management Inquiry Team.[6] The plan, as the press release explained, was not to go for the usual public sector strategy – a lengthy investigation, a report, a consultation on the report – but to go 'straight for management action, with the minimum of fuss and formality' (Harrison 1988: 60).

For the Griffiths team, with its business eyes, there were four main weaknesses in the then current organizational arrangements of the NHS. These were a lack of clear overall accountability, a weak implementation machinery, no strong orientation to performance and to outcome measurement and a failure to be concerned in a central way with the needs of the consumer (Griffiths 1983). Harrison has pointed out that a very similar set of features – which he labels pluralism, reactivism, incrementalism and introversion – emerge from much of the social scientific research on NHS organization in the previous decade (Harrison 1988: ch. 4). At the heart of the Griffiths solution lay the creation of a role of general manager, at Region, District and Unit levels. General management was to bring a firm action orientation, locating responsibility for performance in a single individual and replacing the multidisciplinary consensus managerial teams. To encourage a culture change, general managers were to be recruited from outside the Service as well as from within. Three-year contracts, individual performance review, performance-related pay were added to the armoury whereby pressure could be exerted on the manager from the centre. Allied to this was streamlining at the centre. A Supervisory Board to establish objectives and priorities and a Management Board, headed by a chief executive to oversee implementation were suggested. Work in hand on management budgeting and the annual review process was endorsed and strengthened. Only on the question of how to achieve a greater emphasis on the consumer were no specific mechanisms put forward.

Events moved rapidly. Changes at the centre were put in train immediately; consultation on other arrangements was brief, and notwithstanding the negative reactions of doctors and particularly of nurses

(Cox 1992: 26–7), the critical stance of the House of Commons Social Services Committee, and the upheavals that reorganization represented, general managers were on the NHS scene by the end of 1985, less than a year from the time that the Griffiths Report had been made public.

At the time, there were different views as to what was at stake in all this change. For Klein, writing at the start of Margaret Thatcher's second term, the set of measures up to and including the Griffiths reorganization represented a clear series of failures and retreats by a government ideologically committed to a much more fundamental change. Discussions about an alternative funding base for the Service, for example, had come to naught; plans for hotel charges had been dropped, private medicine did not expand and overall public expenditure on health care, far from diminishing, actually increased. The government's preoccupation with savings and value for money, furthermore, led it in the direction of more involvement and tighter control, not the decentralization that it had signalled in its White Paper. Party ideology, Klein concluded, was not a good guide to practice and had had to be abandoned in the face of constraints which included the power of the medical profession and popular support for the NHS (Klein 1984). I myself, writing a little later in the second term, took a different view. I saw in these same measures the groundwork for a change of culture, a shift involving not only a more assertive managerialism and an emphasis on performance, but also another step towards new thinking about buying and selling that was to create a climate for a plurality of providers and, in effect, for the ideas of an internal market which were not to surface fully until the third term. This was not to say that there was a hidden plan available from the start, but rather that there was a broad direction, based on a belief in the fundamental unsoundness of public sector organization and the superiority and discipline of markets/entrepreneurship and competition, which was pursued with considerable determination and against all opposition (Davies 1987).[7]

General management, however, did not represent a massive influx of business-trained entrepreneurs, nor did it mean a once and for all diminution of the power of the medical profession. In terms of NHS traditions, however, general managers had a quite unprecedented and startlingly broad brief to make things happen and to design their own structural arrangements (Strong and Robinson 1990: 23–4). Their arrival – particularly in a context where the government felt constrained to keep as tight a control as possible on expenditure and continued to explore ways of bringing the discipline of business into the activities of the public sector as a whole. keeping up its stream of initiatives (Davies 1987: 309–12) – consolidated and made quite clear the injection of new managerialism into the NHS. Harrison *et al.* (1992) have reviewed the results of more than 20 empirical studies of the Griffiths changes that were under way in the latter years of the 1980s. The picture they draw is a complex one. It makes clear that business thinking is not easily reconciled with the delicate politics of health care, notes the problems arising from the absence of any clear direction, save a financial one, from the centre, and judges general managers as 'singularly unsuccessful' in confronting doctors. Yet if a new culture had not altogether taken over in the first few years, it was clearly much in evidence; the old pattern, that Harrison (1988) had characterized of the manager as 'diplomat', consulting all interests, building a consensus, had gone. The new assertive, finance-driven style might not be universally accepted, as the cynical remarks about managers as mouthpieces of the government, as being put in place to manage cuts and, in the words of one consultant geriatrician, as having 'cash register eyeballs' (Harrison *et al.* 1992: 59) all suggest, but it was clearly having an impact. Butler (1993: 56), writing from a vantage point after the most recent stage of reform, sees the foundations of a strong and centralized management culture of command and obedience as having been laid by the Griffiths reforms and as having effectively created the climate for the next stage, that of the internal market.

The Tory manifesto which preceded what was to be Margaret Thatcher's third and final term in office, contained no hint of further organizational reform for the NHS. It seems that it was the political storm over underfunding, closures and cuts that catapulted the Prime Minister into announcing the existence of a government working party reviewing the NHS. By now, any such review could capitalize on the experience of income generation schemes, of buying and selling assets and of contracting for services (in some cases clinical services that had been undertaken by some of the general managers), could draw upon a decade of academic writing and think-tank speculation about how competition might be introduced into health care, and on efforts elsewhere in the public sector (Butler 1993, Allsop and May 1993). The publication in January 1989 of *Working for Patients* (Secretaries of State for Health 1989a), made clear a belief that the performance and efficiency orientation of managers alone was not enough. What had to be added was the discipline of competition.

The essence of the White Paper and of the Health and Community Care Act 1990 that followed was that it created the 'purchaser/provider split', giving managers, while still significantly controlled from the centre, the marketplace in which they were to manage. On the purchaser side, the existing regional, district and family practitioner bodies remained, but their functions and structures were transformed. District Health Authorities (DHAs) now had the responsibility to commission and purchase health care for their local residents, making contractual arrangements for the provision of this care, specifying the volume, costs and quality of provision. Their management bodies were to be 'reduced in size, and reformed on business lines, with executive and non-executive directors' (Secretaries of State for Health 1989a: 5). Alongside them, was to be a new group of purchasers, general practitioner fundholders (GPFH). These were groups of GPs from the larger practices, who would apply to the Region for their own budgets to purchase hospital care for their patients, budgets that would then be deducted from DHA funding. GPFHs thus were to become significant players in the market and were also given considerable freedoms in the deployment of their budgets. On the provider side, again there were old and new institutions. The new were the NHS Trusts. These were to be directly accountable to the Secretary of State, bypassing the monitoring and planning machinery at District and Region. They were to have self-governing status and to be self-contained financially. They had new freedoms, to borrow funds, to employ staff directly and thus shape job descriptions and pay. Those providers who did not apply for Trust status remained as directly managed units (DMUs), who nevertheless would contract with DHAs, competing with Trusts as alternative providers. In this case, the purchaser/provider split was somewhat blurred, since DMU staff remained employees of the purchasing authority and continued to be managerially accountable to it. Private sector health care bodies also fitted into the scheme both as purchasers and providers (see Tilley 1993).

Before the year was out, a further White Paper had been published on community care (Secretaries of State for Health 1989b). The language of *Caring for People* was rather different; social services authorities were to be 'enabling agencies', who would seek to create a 'mixed economy of care', maximizing the use of private and voluntary providers in the fields of care for the elderly, those with mental illnesses, mental handicap and physical or sensory disabilities. More was said about the need for authorities to develop planning and to monitor, but contracting was clearly meant to evolve and the purchaser/provider split and complementarity with the earlier White Paper was deliberately underlined.[8] In short, events of the 1980s had seemed to show that it was impossible to move the NHS out into the marketplace. The solution, given an overriding faith in the discipline of the market, was to bring the market to the NHS. *Working for Patients*, it has been observed, 'finally marked the break with the service structures erected by Bevan and Beveridge' (Butler 1993: 56).

What has happened since 1990? There has been a wealth of writing in abstract terms about the fundamental nature of markets and the theoretical limits and possibilities of market transactions, and in more practical terms about the mechanisms that have been put in place, the unanticipated consequences of these and the consequent adjustments. Some writers remain strongly in favour of markets, others are equally resolute anti-marketeers. In some ways, it is still too early for reliable judgements about the functioning of the new system; certainly it has brought a constant stream of guidance and regulatory action from the centre such that there is a growing recognition that competition, in a field as sensitive as health care, is likely to need a severe dose of regulation and management if political embarrassments are not to follow (Hughes 1993). 'The NHS', as a recent observer has ruefully pointed out, 'has been launched on a huge experiment and no-one knows what the likely outcome will be, least of all the Government' (Hunter 1993: 40).[9]

2   The (in)significance of nursing

Government pronouncements about policy change in the NHS in the 1980s and academic commentaries on these have one thing very clearly in common. Neither gives nurses or nursing more than cursory and passing mention. From his vantage point at the head of the RCN, Trevor Clay observed that in the Griffiths Report, save for a whimsical reference to Florence Nightingale, nursing was deemed 'monumentally unimportant' (Clay 1987: 57). A close look at *Working for Patients* for the number and nature of mentions of nursing suggests something very similar.[10] And while some of the health policy analysts hint from time to time at distinct effects on and reactions from nurses to some of the key changes, in the main they either assume that nursing is affected in similar ways to medicine, but to a lesser degree, or they leave nursing altogether out of account.

In respect of the Griffiths reforms, however, there was a major difference between medicine and nursing. The introduction of general managers was in large measure a device to change the doctors. Whether by enticing, cajoling, persuading or ultimately forcing them, the aim was to bring them into the managerial process and to instil managerial values. Nurses, however, were already in managerial positions in their own area. From the 1974 reorganization, they had been directly responsible for the massive budgets that covered the provision of nursing staff. The structures of nursing management that this entailed were swept clean away by the Griffiths reorganization. Instead of bringing nurses in, the reforms apparently shut them out – hence the campaign of resistance mounted by the RCN which was noted earlier. How could this be? For one thing, the pattern of professional control that was represented by nursing management was now suspect; budgets were not to be in the hands of a professional group as such, but to shift more directly towards each care group. For another thing, as we have already seen in Chapter 4, the competence of nurses as managers was in question. Third, and this perhaps requires the greatest emphasis, nursing was unimportant – it was, as we have repeatedly seen in Part Two of this book, a matter of staffing the service, providing support to the costly business of medical care, and it was this latter which was deemed the real focus.

The creation of a Nursing Policy Studies Centre gave some recognition to the profound imbalance in attention given to medicine and to nursing, and a series of studies of the impact of the Griffiths reforms was set in train.[11] Having completed two rounds of interviews with a wide variety of staff in seven health authorities, and having carried out a national survey of those in the newly created Chief Nursing Advisor posts, the Centre's researchers concluded that while nursing had been 'caught in the crossfire' of changes targeted at medicine, these changes nevertheless had major consequences for nursing. The framework of reform may have denied any consideration to nurse management but it did acknowledge that professional nursing advice would be needed in the new regime and hence protected this function. The result was a 'hotchpotch of jobs', with the role of Chief Nursing Advisor often made into a hybrid post and linked with other functions (Strong and Robinson 1988). There had been a huge change in a very short time. But as far as the researchers could see, there was neither rhyme nor reason in the 29 job titles they found for the nurse advisor at District level. 'No common principles or unifying factors for the management of nursing or for the provision of nursing advice could be identified at District level' (Robinson *et al.* 1989: 97).

The same team was later to expand this work into a broader account of the effects of the Griffiths reforms, concentrating in equal measure on the two 'clinical trades' of nursing and medicine. They emphasized the different styles of the doctors and the nurses, the one group confident and assertive, regularly given to bursting in on the manager and making demands; the other, unconfident, hesitant and deferential, apparently hiding behind the hierarchy, unable to turn its numbers and budgetary importance into the clout to make things happen. Strong and Robinson (1990: ch. 3) suggested that these two styles reflected enormous differences of power between the two groups, where nurses, though many deeply resented it, continued to act as handmaidens to the doctors, and where the two groups were locked together in a mirror image of each other. While nurses were often strong critics of their own profession, the researchers pointed to weaknesses in basic nurse education and to the lack of opportunity nurse managers had had to develop their education and training for the massive task of nurse management as factors contributing to their sense of inadequacy and to the disparagement of others. Vivid examples of that disparagement come in some of the quotations the researchers produce. One general manager observed to his senior nurse colleague that he was going to be very busy, and asked pointedly 'What are you going to do?' Another, responding to the RCN's advertising campaign that claimed that general managers did not know their coccyx from their humerus, retorted that his outpatient manager was not a nurse – the reason being that he could not find one 'who knew her debit from her credit'! (ibid.: 56).

Strong and Robinson at one point sum up the dilemma of 1980s reorganization in the comment that '[d]octors would not be led. Nurses did not know how to lead' (ibid.: 65). But their work, taken together with the material in Part Two of this book, suggests that the position was more complex. Underlying the lack of developed expertise and the defensiveness and uncertainty of nurse managers themselves is surely *a failure to acknowledge that there is a management job to be done*. This is entirely consistent with the devaluation of the work of nursing which has been the theme of the book. NHS leaders have resolutely refused to look at nursing; they have misunderstood the recruitment and supply problem, ignored the Polo mint problem at the heart of practice and failed to see the wider picture of educational improvement. Without this acknowledgement, nurse management becomes transformed into reactive coping – a matter of ensuring that 'pairs of hands' are in the right place at the right time. The Audit Commission (1991) recognized this when they wrote of contrasting styles of management, a 'traditional one' where the aim was 'solve staffing problems' and a 'progressive' one where the issue was 'develop the service'. They were convinced of the need for progressive nurse management, and were able to find a certain number of examples of it at work. I myself have tried to trace the dynamics which sustain the traditional model, where nursing managers, unable to gain acceptance of the value of the work of nursing or understanding of the dilemmas of its development, become defensive and inward-looking. They then develop a coping style of management which exacerbates their isolation, worsens their resource levels and prompts them to demand ever more from staff (Davies 1992). Making a transition to the progressive model is not something that will come about by exhorting nurses alone to change – it is part and parcel of the dilemma of devaluation of their work as 'women's work' – something we are not used to seeing as in need of management. The work that women do, after all, is noticed when it is not there, and taken for granted when it is.

In principle, it would have been possible for general managers to blow this apart. Fresh eyes concentrated on the specification of objectives, fresh ears attuned to questions of customer satisfaction, a perspective sceptical about the claims of medicine, all these could have resulted in a new acknowledgement of the place of nursing in health care and of the urgent need for organizational reform. They did not do so. In practice, therefore, the 'ideological foreign body' that was general management was not quite so foreign after all. Questioning administrative bureaucracy and medical professionalism were sharp jolts to central features of the NHS, market principles may have seemed inconceivable as a basis for day-to-day health care delivery; but alongside all this change, the assumption that nursing would 'just happen' remained more or less intact. Instead of new structures to address the fundamental issues of supply and demand and of the organization of practice and its management, old structures were dismantled with nothing coherent put in their place. Nurses with a vision of what progressive nurse management might be were left to promote this vision locally, with little in the way of support. And indeed, good nurse managers were creamed off and recruited into general management.[12]

The health reforms of the 1980s were thus predicated on a continuing assumption that it was the relations amongst men that needed reform, and that women would continue in their silent support. How else can we explain the widespread neglect of nursing? The new system, with its stress on the entrepreneur rather than the bureaucrat or the professional, might be seen as representing a 'clash of masculinities'. More accurately, however, it would seem that it involves a rearrangement of the elements in the model of masculinity that we discussed in Part One of this book. The next section explores this further.

3   Of managers, markets and masculinity

What is 'new managerialism'? At one level the answer can be stated quite briefly and simply. New managerialism means the injection of business principles into areas of activity in the public sector. New and unfamiliar job titles, activity costing, devolved budgeting, staff appraisal and merit pay are part of the cluster of practices which can be involved (see for example Pollitt 1990; Hood 1991). Perhaps the single most influential and accessible text of the 1980s purporting to set out those principles was that by Peters and Waterman (1982). Their bestseller, *In Search of Excellence*, documented the practice of a wide range of successful corporations under eight main headings. The really successful firms had a 'bias to action'. Managers spent little time on standing committees and lengthy reports, instead they blitzed problems as they arose. They remained at all times 'close to the customer', they valued 'autonomy and entrepreneurship' and developed a culture that expressed a belief in 'productivity through people'. The style was 'hands-on and value-driven'. They concentrated on doing well that which was basic to their success, delegating and subcontracting other work. This was expressed in the formula 'stick to

Table 8.1   Changing management styles in the public sector

	Administrative management	The 'new' managerialism
Goals	System maintenance and stability	System performance and change
Resource strategy	Reliance on state resources	Pro-active search for non-state resources
Resource allocation	Rationed by bureaucratic rules of eligibility and professional needs judgements	Rationed by target and charges
Financial management objectives	To ensure accountability and probity	To inform management decision making
Cost reduction pressures	Internal search for control of production/ allocation	External search for 'opportunities'
Supervision style	Role-procedure-based	Review-based
Incentives	Rewards for conformity	Rewards for innovation achievement
Orientation to consumers	Defensive, paternalistic	Receptive, responsive
Accountability	To electorate or representative board	To a management board of executives
Employment relationship	Long career hierarchy	Short-term contracts

Source: Kelly (1991: 134)

the knitting'. And above all, and by way of summary, such firms had a 'simple form, lean staff'. Once it was well understood what had to be controlled tightly, the rest, in an overall competitive environment, could be let loose – on this principle, the number of staff at the centre in the successful companies had often been quite dramatically reduced. Less often mentioned is a more recent text that applies similar themes, albeit critically, directly to government itself. *Reinventing Government* (Osborne and Gaebler 1992), though again an American text, has been acknowledged as a major influence in government circles in the UK (Allsop and May 1993: 13).

A useful tabulation, contrasting old and new styles of management as they have appeared in social service delivery and in health has been drawn up by Kelly (1991) (see Table 8.1). Setting the new 'performance culture' alongside the older bureaucratic model as Kelly does, shows that there is much in it, in principle, to which nursing can respond positively. A stance that explores goals and asks just what it is that the Service is trying to achieve instead of continuing without question as before, has a potential benefit to those who want to put caring more firmly on to the agenda. The premium placed in the new model on innovation and particularly on responsiveness to patient need, could work in a similar direction. But, as we have seen in the last section, nursing is largely squeezed out of any discussion and influence in this area. What has given these changes their strength and appeal has, of course, in large measure been the potential they hold for greater efficiency and resource cuts. But a cost-driven agenda of organizational transformation needs to have some content. This, I will argue, is where gender imagery comes in. The new organizational forms that are envisaged take the form that they do as a function of lauding the relations of the marketplace against the assumed 'degeneracy' of both bureaucracy and profession. However, while ostensibly rejecting the two older models, they remain focused on the masculine values that both have expressed.

NHS reform is a direct attack on bureaucrats and bureaucracy. The criticism of bureaucrats underlying the contrasts that Kelly draws out is that in their tenured and salaried positions, they have grown lazy, indifferent in their management of public funds and unresponsive to the needs of the public. Emphasizing the shortcomings of bureaucracy, as Pollitt has pointed out, is a good strategy in the face of public support for health care and the NHS, since it is the bureaucrats not the professionals who have little public sympathy. But the analysis can be extended without much difficulty to encompass professionals in the employ of the state. Thus it is an excess of 'provider power' that we are said to experience in 'the indifference, unresponsiveness or downright arrogance of the clerks, teachers, doctors (etc.) who actually dealt with the public' (Pollitt 1990: 40). And it is a short step then to present a public service bureaucracy such as the NHS as a double evil – 'a budget-maximising monopolist that was likely to be both unnecessarily costly and deeply inadequate' (ibid.: 43), undermining enterprise and self-reliance and threatening individual freedom. Put in these terms, a solution is not hard to see. Provider power must be curbed, and if their central planning and controls have proved costly and ineffective, exposure to the discipline of the market, to the winds of competition and real consumer choice, provide the key elements of the answer. A new kind of leader, the manager with a market-orientated ethos, is needed.

The new manager, however, turns out to have many of the same characteristics as the old. Like the other two, he remains distant and controlled. He takes a critical stance towards the arguments and established practices of others, asking constantly for outcome data, cost information and performance measures. He follows his own convictions, is tough-minded in that he must take hard decisions about 'what market to be in', without being swayed by appeals to sympathy or particular cases. Above all, he is a strong and active decision-maker who will not dodge controversy and confrontation, be it with staff or the public. At his fingertips he has not the rulebook of the bureaucrat or the expert clinical knowledge of the doctor, but the performance information about the costs of the overall service, and about the performance of competitors. David Cox (1992) has emphasized the 'no nonsense', 'down to earth' stance of the manager, his focus on 'getting things done' if necessary through force and his emphasis on speed and decisiveness. The manager is a definite leader; he stands out from the crowd – he is another hero.[13]

The result of this new style is that everyone has to give an account of their performance, for no one can be relied upon not to be profligate with resources. New managerialism involves a challenging and questioning, if not aggressive style of interaction. It replaces the 1970s model of consent and consensus and at times welcomes overt conflict. In providing incentives to staff, it assumes that money is the main motivational currency. The performance culture demands this; everyone is aware that individual appraisal and performance review are never far round the corner for the general manager, and pay and indeed the continuation of an employment contract depend on the achievement of acceptable out-comes. In terms that hark back to the assumptions discussed in Chapter 2 of a world of 'hostile strangers', some writers have begun to refer to a culture of 'distrust' (Harrison *et al.* 1992: 68), and have questioned the appropriateness of it for health care (Cousins 1987, Strong and Robinson 1990). Certainly it would seem that the very factors which often bring nurses into nursing – commitment, altruism, service ideals, the same factors which encourage them to come in early, go home late, and work their breaks – are without a place in this model.

There are a number of further points to be made about this new man-agement of the NHS. In the first place, as Cox has suggested, there are two contradictory models intertwined here, the one linked with the ideo-logical influence of large-scale corporate capital, the other with *laissez-faire* and the New Right. Thus there is the managerialism of big business:

> Here the emphasis is on speed of decision-making, co-ordination, accountability, setting and reviewing objectives, good financial controls and information, cost improvement, consumer loyalty and public image and responsiveness.
>
> (Cox 1992: 28)

And there is the vision of the entrepreneur in the competitive market-place:

> Here the model is small business . . . [f]rom these roots comes the emphasis on market criteria, prices (not costs), competition, tendering, privatization and casualization of manual and managerial labour.
>
> (ibid.: 28)

Many commentators have stressed the apparently irresistible pressures from the centre to control and to manage the competition that has been created, though they do not often locate it in two models in this way. What is of interest to us, however, is to draw out not so much the differences, but the underlying similarities between tycoon and entrepreneur, and between both of these and bureaucrat and professional. All four call for a cool head and independent judgement, all four stress heroic leadership and demand close forms of control over others. All work on a model of the world as populated by 'hostile strangers'. The difference is that the marketplace models lay bare the notion of hostility and warring, encourage it, celebrate it and aim to work with it, rather than seeking to contain, hide or transcend it in some way.

It may well be that it is this very overt celebration of masculinity in new managerialism which provides the conditions for a backlash. For this model, in a way much less true for the bureaucratic or the professional one, is beginning to be questioned in direct gender terms. We hear health service staffs referring to new managerialism as a style that is aggressive, harsh and confrontational. There is a form of critical 'gender talk' in the NHS, unknown a decade ago, which makes disparaging references to the new army of 'men in suits', and questions the relevance of a 'grey suit' mentality to the NHS which generates and brings to bear an economic calculus that is devoid of human warmth and sympathy and that distances itself from the personal dilemmas and the suffering that those in the frontline of health care must face on a daily basis. It seems that Christine Hancock, General Secretary of the RCN, is not alone when she says, '[Y]ou cannot use the sterile philosophies of the accountant and the economist, or even the entrepreneurial acumen of an industrialist, as the blueprint for a social service dealing with people' (Hancock 1992). Others are thinking in a similar way.[14]

Furthermore, the new managerialism, in its big or small business variant, is not always an entirely welcome gender identity for those who take on senior and public positions. It suited Kenneth Clarke as a Minister, it would seem, much more than it did William Waldegrave. The present Prime Minister, John Major, seems to have inaugurated something of a different trend in the form of his personal backing for the Citizen's Charter initiative.[15] Managerialism does not square altogether easily either with the values of an array of clinicians, of some trade unionists, or of a number of long-serving NHS staff who started their careers as NHS administrators (see for example Cousins 1987). There are question marks also around the ways in which the growing numbers of women in middle ranks of management in health, social welfare and local government will respond to aspects of managerialism – its aggressive, 'macho' style and the culture of 'putting in long hours' were quickly questioned by attendees at a conference designed for women in public management.[16] Some women undoubtedly will take new managerialism as their own and will feel that they have to do so in order to survive in a men's world; others, however, especially as their numbers increase in the context of a continuing equal opportunities campaign, may well feel able to bring in new lines of approach and deeper questioning of the rationales for existing practices.

Another feature which has been the subject of much critical comment though as yet it has not been overtly linked with masculinity, is the belief in the availability of rational decision criteria and hence in the neutrality of managerial action. Gray and Jenkins refer specifically to the 'comforting' idea of neutrality present in bureaucracy and professionalism and ask whether the new form of management has not simply 'assumed a different mantle of neutrality', trading old values for new values and operational-izing these under a cloak of objectivity, cost minimization, accountability and the achievement of results' (Gray and Jenkins 1993: 23). Harrison and his colleagues refer in a similar way to a 'retreat into technique', and argue that this is 'an example of the kind of instrumental rationality in which profoundly political questions of priority are transposed into apparently scientific or technical issues' (Harrison *et al.* 1992: 69). While all appears to be rational and neutral, the first and controversial step, of defining the specific nature of the service need has not been addressed. The language of managerialism, with its targets and indicators, its performance culture, its apparently calm, measured and scientific approach, in other words, turns out to have areas of blindness. These blind spots, of course, relate centrally to the business of caring and to the questions of interdependence, uncertainty and vulnerability that masculinist visions reject. In principle it would seem that a contract culture could enable care to be specified and written into contracts if competencies in care could be defined (see Ellis 1988, Ellis and Whittington 1993; and Chapter 7). In practice, in a gender-blinkered context, it will need a particular effort for this to occur.

Additionally, we may well need to bring a wider perspective to bear, and to see contemporary change as influenced by a concept of welfare that is itself driven by metaphors of gender. To sketch this in briefly: the programmatic vision of William Beveridge that brought the NHS and the contemporary welfare state into being in the post-war era, rested, as feminist analysts have emphasized, on a strong notion of male independence and female dependency (see Wilson 1977; Lewis 1983). Talk of universal rights and benefits notwithstanding, the vision was that the working man could retain his independence, his sense of dignity and worth and protect and provide for his wife and his family through social insurance. His contributions while working would give him entitlements that kept him in a breadwinner role through unemployment, sickness and old age. Married women, on this model, were to play their part through the care of children and through unpaid labour in the home. Their relation to insurance reflected this. Education for all and health care free at the point of use underpinned this vision of a society where citizenship turned out to mean something different for women and men. By the 1980s, however, all this was under strain. Costs had escalated; unemployment was high. Families had broken up through divorce, rising numbers of children were being cared for by single parents, mostly single mothers. The New Right analysis, in a nutshell, was that the very growth of welfare provision was to blame. Men had grown irresponsible and lazy in face of state handouts. Symbolically and through the ever useful gender lens, the problem was encapsulated in the scornful and dismissive reference to the 'nanny state' – men were not grown, they had not left home, they were still looking for the protection of 'nanny'. In short, they had been feminized! In these ways, a celebration of the masculinity/femininity split was still inscribed into the very heart of social policy. The analysis of welfare that was on offer, an analysis that included health policy, sought not to transcend this split but to find ways of ensuring its reinstatement.

The world of health policy, as was argued in Part One, is a gendered world in more than one sense. It is not simply a matter, important as this is, of the predominance of men in positions of power, it is also a matter of metaphors of masculinity and how these have come at all levels of activity to shape visions of what is to be achieved. We have just seen these masculinist visions, however, starting to come under challenge – sometimes fairly direct challenge. Today's potential for resistance and change is different from what it was in an era of strong professional dominance. Just what are the critics saying and how closely does it align with an interest in nursing care?

4   Health care allies and alliances

One important strand of criticism that is emerging amongst writers on the NHS is insisting that the focus on the costs and benefits of market arrangements, important as it is, is not the whole of the story. Alongside the emphasis on markets and managers is a 'more profound and less explicit shift from the ethos and values of the NHS' (Allsop and May

1993: 6). Sociologist David Cox (1992) has represented this line of thought extensively in the article already quoted in the previous section. He notes the 'moralistic' tone of discussions about health and health care and defends this; we do need to be explicit, to state and affirm the values that are being supported in the public provision of health care. While the underlying values were clear at the outset of the NHS, we have witnessed a set of changes that amount to a retreat into technique and into purely economic objectives. This, in effect, has rendered the whole project of public services suspect. The source of the problem lies in part in the way the NHS developed; its positive vision of a service to the community became caught up in a 'paternalistic bureaucracy', where being a patient or client came to have connotations of 'passivity, gratitude and relative powerlessness' (Cox 1992: 36). In such a context, the alternative model of the health service consumer, actively choosing between providers, has seemed both viable and attractive. What we need instead, he argues, is a revalorization of the idea of public services and of the citizen rights and obligations which accompany this. If we pay serious attention to the quality of services and to consumer satisfaction, values, after all, that were alluded to in the Griffiths Report itself, management can then take its rightful place as being necessary but also being grounded in and driven by a set of fundamental values. Such values, Cox claims, 'cannot be set in the emotivism of market preferences. They have to be set in the intrinsic worth of all citizens in a pluralistic society and in a commitment to equity and service' (ibid.: 40). It is notable that while the key policy documents repeatedly reaffirm the necessity of health care as promoting independence and as responding to individual needs and to a local community, the mechanisms for delivering this regularly disappear in the determined emphasis on market competition.

Outside the NHS, some strikingly similar arguments are being developed. Local government is a case in point. Stewart and Ranson (1988), for example, make a number of points which parallel the above and develop the overall theme of the distinctiveness of public management. Selecting just a few of these will give a flavour of their line of thinking. Organizational arrangements, they argue, should be designed to learn from citizens rather than to contain public debate; 'strategy' should be understood not as taking a competitive stance but as putting into effect a set of aspirations which have been articulated through public debate; reconciling political control and staff potential and the need to be responsive to customers or citizens is a balancing that is part of the job of public management; the public manager needs not only to be held to account, but to find ways of actively giving account so that the issues and dilemmas of a public service can be more properly and fully the subject of debate.

Other political scientists have joined the debate about what is beginning to be called public management or a new public service ethos. Hood (1991), for example, in a particularly influential article, suggests that there are perhaps three clusters of values that can be promoted in areas of public management. First, there is the 'lean and purposeful' value set that underlines the importance of sparingly matching resources to the task, of eliminating waste and concentrating on success indicators in terms of time and money. Second, there is a cluster of values around 'honesty, fairness and mutuality' that stresses reporting relationships, appeal mechanisms and independent scrutinies of activities. Success here is in terms of rectitude in how the job is done and in terms of the maintenance of public confidence and trust. Third, there are values that cluster around 'reliability, robustness and adaptability', where resilience is a crucial criterion. Hood suggests that any two of these might be pursued at the same time, but not all three. A debate like this about what public services should now achieve and hence about what public management is, finds an echo in many places. It is there in the rather slow and cautious efforts of opposition parties to reconstruct their overall approaches to questions of justice and social welfare as well as to develop a more pragmatic response to the implementation of markets in health care. It is there also in the success of an organization like the Office of Public Management, which emphasizes in its consultancy the importance of 'managing for social result' and of recognizing that there is no single bottom line in the public sector.[17]

All this points to a revival of collectivist values after a period of insistent emphasis on individualism, and the very strength and aggressive pursuit of market ideas itself may be playing some part in this. A public service ethos is certainly still discernible among many managers in the NHS, as was clear in the extensive quotations Strong and Robinson provide showing managers at different levels and in different contexts grappling with the new emphasis on costs and competition and trying to reconcile this with the values that had brought them into NHS administration in an earlier era. It is there, too, in the continuing support in opinion polls for the NHS, and in insistent media attention to the ways things go wrong in the new managerial NHS. The many critical comments that have been offered on the consumer model and its inappropriateness to the circumstances which generate a need for health care point in the same direction.[18]

What does this mean for nursing? Providing a service that is equitable, accessible, free at the point of use and permeable to influence by the user are key elements of the evolving public management/public service ethos perspective;[19] putting in place a service that is devoted to 'caring' figures less often, though it is not entirely absent from or inconsistent with these debates. In the light of the themes of this book, and given its association with 'femininity' it should come as no surprise that caring is at present the theme sketched in most lightly in the debates about revitalizing public services and restructuring the welfare state. Interestingly, however, and in a way that was not present when bureaucracy and professionalism had reign, we have seen that managerialism has provoked more overt gender talk, which starts to question and to some extent unmask the values associated with masculinity. Such an unmasking holds out a hope that the new debate about the nature of work and organization in public service institutions will become one that can recognize vulnerability and interdependence and respond positively to such human qualities rather than demonizing and denying dependency by feminizing it. I have found one text, where, in a parallel debate in the USA concerned with 'refounding public administration', an effort is made to uncover and explore the masculine gender images at the heart of the notion of a public servant, and where an alternative, more feminine image is proposed to describe the work, that of the midwife (Stivers 1993).[20]

The nursing agenda, in the light of policy changes in the NHS which have been discussed in this chapter, has several aspects. Nurses must continue to discuss the nature of caring and to articulate the requirements of a service which will enable caring to take place. Nurses must deepen their knowledge of the history of health care and current organization of the NHS. Nurses must take part in the new public management/public service ethos debates. These are some of the essentials if nurses are to play a part in the important process of retrieval and revitalization of the values of a health service which is already beginning to occur. Nursing cannot afford to remain on the sidelines of these crucial changes in the delivery of health care. If it does, these debates will remain couched in terms of a masculinist vision that represses and denies the very vulnerabilities that health care in practice has to address.

Notes

1 Discussions of the transformation of welfare and the welfare state are legion. For some recent examples see Loney *et al.* (1991), Sullivan (1992), Taylor-Gooby and Lawson (1993). These relate to and overlap with discussions of Thatcherism, the New Right and welfare; see, for example, Brown and Sparks (1989), McCarthy (1989).

2 Butler (1993) makes reference to the reviews of potential changes to the funding base of the NHS in the first term of the Conservative government. For a flavour of some of the debate generated, see McLachlan and Maynard (1982).

3 This is discussed in standard health policy texts (see, for example, Harrison *et*

al. 1990, Ham 1992, Levitt and Wall 1992). Brief accounts can also be found in Harrison *et al*. (1992: ch. 2) or Strong and Robinson (1990: ch. 2).

4 These 'Rayner scrutinies' were so called after Sir Derek Rayner, Managing Director of Marks & Spencer, who had been appointed efficiency adviser and had carried out a number of studies initially in the civil service.

5 For an account which emphasizes the lack of an overall strategic determination for change at the point of contacting Griffiths, and an interpretation of the likely factors at work in the short-term political thinking of the period, see Harrison (1988: ch. 6) who draws up a fictional address by the Secretary of State to his junior ministerial colleagues.

6 The members of the Management Inquiry Team were: Roy Griffiths, Deputy Chairman and Managing Director, J. Sainsbury; Michael Bett, Personnel Director, British Telecom; Jim Blythe, Group Finance Director, United Biscuits; Sir Brian Bailey, Chairman of Television South West and a former NALGO official.

7 I came to this view with particular reference to a government handbook produced as early as 1981 for those who were to chair the new DHAs, where the idea of a mix of providers was quite clearly articulated (Davies 1987: 305–6). The question of how far there was a 'grand plan' remains contentious however. Harrison (1988), for example, contrasts his own more sceptical view with that of Petchey (1986); Jobling (1989) is still questioning the extent of intentional change remarkably much later. Le Grand and Bartlett (1993: 2) point out that the basic structure of the welfare state was still much the same in 1987 as it had been in 1979, and that the overall proportion of national resources going into public welfare had remained the same.

8 I have concentrated in this section and in what follows less on community health services and more on the hospital sector. For a particularly accessible account of the changes in community care since 1979, and a critical evaluation, see Walker (1993).

9 The literature on markets in health and social care is already voluminous and is now growing very fast indeed. For some recent routes into this material with special reference to health care, see, for example, Paton (1992), Le Grand and Bartlett (1993), Hoyes and Means (1993), Hughes (1993), Tilley (1993).

10 Nurses receive a number of passing references in *Working for Patients*, but do not have a section of the report devoted to them in the way that doctors do. After acknowledging that nurses are the largest single staff group, the report goes on to refer to better training for non-professional support staff and to hint at reappraisals of skill mix in a way that can only have given nurses cause for alarm (para. 2.12). Later, there is an explicit recognition of the need to protect and develop 'medical, nursing and other training' in the new arrangements. The next paragraph expands on this – but it does so solely with reference to medicine (para. 4.29).

11 The Nursing Policy Studies Centre was set up in January 1985 at the University of Warwick with funding from the King Edward's Hospital Fund for London. The money was intended however only to be pump-priming, and the resources of the Centre were very limited. Notwithstanding a very creditable output of challenging analyses, the Centre only survived for a

period of four and a half years (for details, see Robinson J. 1992). The fate of the Centre serves to underline the message of the devaluation of nursing that it so eloquently demonstrated through its academic work.

12 Readers might like to compare the analysis of this section with that offered by Owens and Glennerster (1990). Their study was carried out over much the same period as Strong and Robinson; it contains a number of similar elements but seems to look more resolutely to nursing itself and its internal divisions and failures of leadership. While the authors refer to 'the gender issue', it is not quite clear what place this has in the analysis as a whole (see especially ch. 2). Overall, the study uncovers a myriad of issues of strain and difficulty in adjustment, yet concludes on a surprisingly optimistic note about the likely capacity of nursing to develop and adjust.

13 Pollitt recognizes this; in seeing managerialism as an ideology that privileges certain groups and marginalizes others, he refers explicitly to managers as heroes – white middle-class men – and notes, in brackets, that there is a gender issue here (Pollitt 1990: 8). Later he includes a brief discussion of a range of gender issues under the heading of unequal opportunities, suggesting that economic liberalism and social conservatism are particularly inimical to equal rights and acknowledging a form of 'passive discrimination' at work here (ibid.: 140–2).

14 This is not to say, however, that all who are questioning business values are contrasting these with caring values. Cox, for example, seems to imply this when he refers to the early distaste for the intrusion of managerialism into 'the sacrosanct ethical world of professional and caring values' (Cox 1992: 32). The arguments about professionalism developed in earlier chapters of this book suggest that professionalism and caring cannot be automatically equated in this way, and the point of this section and the remarks that follow is to encourage thinking about how such a unity might be forged and facilitated.

15 Debates about consumerism, citizenship and the idea of citizens' charters are very much a contemporary issue. In the second edition of his work on managerialism, however, Pollitt has added a chapter pointing to a 'new mood' signalled by John Major's *Citizen's Charter* initiative and by an escalation of interest in issues of quality in public services (see Prime Minister 1991, Treasury 1991). He quotes Major's introductory comments and now suggests that '[g]eneralised public-servant bashing has all but ceased' and that the service user has become the 'rhetorical pivot upon which many new devices and initiatives are said to balance' (Pollitt 1993: 186). How much is rhetoric and how much real change, seems impossible yet to say.

16 Women in Public Management – a networking conference, 21–23 October 1992, London, Office for Public Management. See note 17 below.

17 The Office for Public Management was established in London in 1989 to carry out consultancy with public sector organizations and to develop theory and practice in this area. The Public Management Foundation was created shortly thereafter as its 'theory wing'. Publications and conferences have developed the theme of linking efficiency and requisite investment with 'righting the balance of intended values', where such values include

social outcomes, locally developed objectives and, particularly interestingly, identifying allowable trade-offs by working with politicians and professionals. See Parston (1992).

18 The many discussions of the characteristics of health care markets routinely cover the question of the amount of consumer choice that is realistically available in relation to a complex commodity like health. Critics often refer to the inappropriateness of a model of a 'supermarket-style shopper' in this regard. Flynn (1990) provides a more extended discussion than most under the heading of a user-orientated service. The question is a fundamental one that can take us back to the nature of care and of service and to the issues of empowerment and activity. It is a debate that Margaret Stacey encouraged medical sociology to tackle some time ago, arguing that the entire managerial model was seriously misleading (see Stacey 1976, 1988: 6–7).

19 The terminology of this debate is somewhat confused, in particular whether 'new public management' refers to managerialism or whether it refers to a new ethos supplanting this is unclear. Pollitt in his 1993 edition, for example, seems to equate new public management with managerialism, whereas the Office for Public Management clearly uses public management in the sense of an alternative to managerialism.

20 The relevant excerpt reads as follows:

> The image of the midwife is of a skilled and caring person who facilitates the emergence of new possibilities by means of embodied and embodying action. The good midwife has deep knowledge and vast experience, which she brings to bear on each unique situation, using them to help her sense the nuances of a process that she can only facilitate rather than steer. The process is an embodied, life or death affair (no distanced contemplation here!), one on which she brings to bear both her own body and her mind, one that requires both connection and a certain level of detachment in order to be of greatest service.
>
> (Stivers 1993: 132)

nine

CONCLUSION

Nursing has always been a much conflicted metaphor in our culture, reflecting all the ambivalences we give to the meaning of woman-hood.

(Reverby 1987: 207)

At the 1994 RCN annual congress in Brighton, six years on from the jubilation at government acceptance of Project 2000, the tone was more sombre. Broadcasting at the beginning of conference week, Radio Four picked up the mood; speaker after speaker insisted that the NHS had to save money – that highly skilled nurses were not needed for jobs such as shifting paper in the outpatients' department, giving baths to patients, or holding the hand of a dying person whose family was around and was coping. Christine Hancock, General Secretary of the College, came across as a lone voice, arguing that nurses were angry with denials and misunderstandings of the essence of their work and that those who had recently received nursing care knew very well and valued the contri-bution that a highly trained and skilled nurse can make. Once again, it seemed that nurses were on the defensive. Once again, the language that they use of skilled nursing care was finding no obvious echo in terms of the language of debate in the public arena.

The difficulty encountered by nurses in trying to place their work on the agenda of public policy and to do so in a fashion that both reflects the lived experience of nurses and offers a constructive way of developing work to which they are committed has been the central theme of this book. The argument throughout has been that this problem cannot be addressed simply by giving attention to the supposed deficiencies of nurses themselves – their internal divisions, their lack of hard-headedness or whatever – but instead has to be seen in terms of the gendered world in which nursing is embedded. An understanding of the development of nursing must be sought in the gendering of social institutions, in the dynamics of devaluation of nursing work that this produces and in the discourses of diminishment which accompany this. Together these factors trivialize the work of nursing, belittle the people who carry it out, putting them in a position of impossible choices which in turn conduces to doubt about the calibre of their leaders and of themselves.

Three steps were needed to prepare the way for such an analysis. First, it was necessary to direct attention to the cultural baggage of gender, to the content of masculinity and femininity, each as a partial expression of human qualities and experience, the two as locked together in ways that can demean and sometimes altogether erase the qualities associated with femininity. Second, it was crucial to understand the multiple levels at which cultural codes of gender come into play. They help to create gendered identities, they encourage gendered interaction, but most importantly, they play a part in shaping the very logic of organizations and organizing. Third, it was important to emphasize that all this was a starting point only and that interaction of gendered identities and gendered institutions would take different specific forms, forms that would vary with time and place and would need detailed analysis in their own right.

The presentation of these themes in Part One began as a work of exegesis, selecting some of the key writers to demonstrate how an argument about the gendering of institutions could be put together for those unfamiliar with work in this area. It then developed significantly further. If gendering was built into the notion of bureaucracy, if it was in essence a masculine logic that valued and called forth the impersonality, impartiality and hierarchical character of bureaucratic organizations, then might it not be that a similar gendering underpinned the notion of profession? This line of questioning led to a re-examination of key features of profession, its emphasis on expertise, on detachment and autonomy as linked to the project of masculinity. Chapter 3 suggested that nursing functioned as an adjunct to profession understood in this way, enabling medicine to retain a masculine gendered character. The analysis went no further at this point. It was already beginning to be clear, however, that some of the struggles of nursing were both to become a profession in the masculine gendered sense and to work against it. Perhaps, then, the dilemmas of nursing in its bids to shape its own history could be newly understood in this context.

Part Two turned attention directly to the policy dilemmas that nursing as a profession has faced in recent years. It considered three areas in which nursing has been enmeshed in apparently convoluted and unproductive debate – first, in relation to the question of recruiting and retaining staff and enabling them to achieve career progression, second, in relation to the organization of nursing work, and third in relation to educational improvement. Seeing all this through the lens of gender, situating the debates in a world already gendered, showed how the parameters of the debate were fixed in ways that never worked to the advantage of nurses and nursing.

Chapter 4 demonstrated that underpinning the 'manpower' planning techniques of nursing in the NHS was a model of supply and demand that derived from and continued to orientate to the lifelong, uninterrupted participation of the male career. On this model, nurses became a nuisance. Career breaks and part-time working had to be a feature of the management of a nursing labour force, and they were so, but they were seen as expedients, as a 'hassle'. Instead of womanpower planning being seen as the challenge that it is, instead of allocating the best minds and significant resources to it, it was left to nurses themselves to try to tackle the matter as best they could. When they ran into difficulty, as well they might, protest rang out both from within nursing and outside it. All this was hardly the recipe that would facilitate the new conceptual develop-ments and associated routines of data-gathering and monitoring that would be necessary actively to manage nursing numbers and positively to facilitate women's participation in a nursing career. The management of staff seemed to be a matter of crisis management, of harassed nurse managers filling gaps as they arose and constantly finding a new expedient to achieve 'cover'.

In planning terms, nursing was being treated as an adjunct to the 'real' business of providing medical care, a support function that was a mere matter of pairs of hands and sufficient 'cover'. This had a knock-on effect in terms of the delivery of care and the organization of work on the hospital ward. In practice, care is delivered by a mix of staff, qualified, unqualified and in training, with the qualified staff often not delivering nursing care themselves, but carrying out the more technical procedures and arranging that the rest of nursing care should be delivered through others. This trivializes nursing and works against individualized patient care. But the real and painful irony in this context, as Chapter 5 argued, is that there is no clear professional practice role at all. Once again, nurses feel they are constantly dealing in expedients, not getting to the real business of nursing at all, not ever able to demonstrate what it is they have been trained to do. The paradox of nursing, it seems, is that nurses rarely feel that they are in a position to do nursing!

Educational reform of the late 1980s is seen variously from within nursing as a great success or as a questionable step in the direction of elitism. Chapter 6 pursued a different theme. It emphasized reluctance of government, the minimal nature of the resources given, and the well-nigh impossible timetable of change. More important than these was the resounding silence about the nature and conditions of practice. Nurses were dubbed unrealistic when they made a bid for a practice-based division of labour to accompany educational change. One of the most important outcomes of the whole process of policy development, however, was the confirmation with clear numerical data of the constant recruitment, high intake/high wastage model of nursing. It confirmed that nurses were treated as a disposable labour force, that if it was no longer acceptable to use young women in training as cheap labour in the same way as in the past, nothing dramatic was going to be done to ensure their fullest participation in the nursing labour force and their opportunities to pursue careers in their chosen work area. The government was exceedingly circumspect in what it said about this; the doctors, some of them at least, angered as they were by nurses' pretensions to a better education, were much less so. The devaluation of nursing work was still alive and well in that quarter.

Some of the themes in all this will be only too familiar to students of women's studies. There is the sheer invisibility of nurses in debates about the future of the NHS and the absence of information about them that is collected and examined in a systematic way. There is the matter of the male yardstick, of men's lives as the template, the constant point of comparison against which women can rarely measure up – not least because it is the pre-existing sexual division of labour and specifically the servicing work of women that allows men to present themselves as 'unencumbered' in the labour market. Negative stereotyping of women relates to this. This was particularly clear in Chapter 5 in relation to women's career-building strategies, where their different strategies in face of a system that had not allowed for clinical career development and did not acknowledge the complexities of their lives, were deemed lack of commitment, and the pejorative tone of concepts such as 'lateral movement syndrome', or 'migrant certificate gatherers' was not acknowledged or confronted. Behaviour which displayed by men might be lauded and applauded, or at the least taken as cause for investigating a possible organizational restructuring, displayed by women can be seen in a much less positive light. Victim-blaming arguments, ones which focus attention on individuals, finding them at fault rather than giving attention to the structures in which they are enmeshed, are a well-known problem in much academic work on women. It is difficult to read the chapters of Part Two, however, and still to conclude, as many, including nurses do, that the whole of the problem is that 'nurses are their own worst enemies'.

A reader might be forgiven for being cast at this point in gloom and despondency. First, the argument has been put forward that social institutions, including organizational forms for the delivery of health care, are profoundly affected by cultural codes of gender, and that it is images of masculinity that are tied up with activity, achievement and social relations in the public sphere. Next, many of the contradictions that a world so deeply gendered in this way produces for nurses have been set out. It is apparent that within a masculinist gaze, the supply of nurses becomes a problem without resolution, the delivery of care becomes a daily balancing act that produces frustration for all concerned, and bids for educational improvement become a logistic and financial nightmare. Nurses find that the nature of their work cannot be easily described, the dilemmas that it produces just cannot be seen, and the results are arrangements that satisfy no one and that undermine nurses and contribute to self-doubt.

A close reading of the initial analysis of masculinity and femininity and the relations between them only deepens this sense of despondency. For the argument was that these two are closely interlocked, and that we need to understand how femininity represents not just a pleasurable complementarity and difference, but a relation that is more complex, ambiguous and sinister. Within a Western cultural heritage, femininity – with its stress on dealing with dependency, acknowledging emotions and intimacy and nurturing others – comes to represent qualities that are feared and denied in masculinity, qualities that at best are seen as to be contained and allocated to a different sphere, and at worst are repressed or treated with contempt. It is not simply that nursing is allocated and comes to stand for work that is 'natural' to the sphere of women – it is also that nursing stands for a set of qualities that are feared and denied. Nursing, in other words, reminds us of the very vulnerabilities and dependencies that are edited out of masculinity. From this perspective, to be nursed is to admit to being less than 'a man'. Can nursing ever take its rightful place in policy debates about health care if this is what is at stake? Is it doomed forever to be devalued?

The previous two chapters were designed to counter extreme pessimism of this sort and they do so by extending and developing the theoretical perspective presented earlier, paying attention to the cautions, the caveats and the hints of controversies that emerged as the argument unfolded. Making the initial case for a gendered world necessarily meant overemphasizing the solidity and the unitary character of gendering, and giving attention to (static) form, rather than to (dynamic) transformation and change. A gendered world must constantly be re-created, and in this process the levers for change are several.

   In the first place, it is real people who as nurses undertake this process of re-creating their worlds, reflective people who are not perfectly socialized into the gendered identities that we have described, who have other identities in terms of class, ethnicity, sexuality and so on and who use all of these actively to analyse, interpret and adapt to the changing circumstances they face. Chapter 7 opened with nurses' doubts about professionalization, and showed how these might be linked both to debates about 'new professionalism' and to feminist understandings of the work of care. Nurses in the academy are already playing a part in weaving the threads of these arguments together. What is at stake here is nothing to do with ivory towers. It is a very practical business of reconceptualization – a vital enterprise of *putting nursing into words* – the kind of words that will enable nurses to give voice to the work that they do, give them dignity and allow them to take their proper place at the policy-making table.

   If new spaces for change are opening up in the academy, they are also there in the apparently unpromising contract culture of the NHS. Managerialism has meant that a questioning of the masculinity of organization is creeping onto the agenda in a way that was never previously so overt. And with this the potential is there for new alliances to be forged and new questions raised. Contact with others – radical doctors, new-style managers, groups running feminist health care facilities, international movement groups devoted to guardianship of public health and so on provides opportunities for collective reflection and redefinition of the division of labour, including the sexual division of labour in health care. The difficulties of making the links should not be underestimated, but the clash of masculinities in the new system is an important and unprecedented opportunity. Figure 9.1 will perhaps serve now as a convenient summary, albeit in somewhat abstract terms, of the key elements of the overall argument, emphasizing the possibilities it contains for change.

   It was something of a surprise to me to find myself returning so centrally in this book to the concept of profession. I had struggled too long with it, finding it altogether too arid and too demeaning when set in the context of nursing. Thinking about gender, however, has allowed a 'different take' on the debate about professions. The key has been to consider the professional ideal as forged with the tools of a gendered culture, as an expression of that same masculinist vision that gave us bureaucracy, and the elevation of mastery, control and technical rationality as the only principles of organizing. I have come to see that this is a model that has been historically and socially constructed, that its flaws can be understood in relation to masculinity and these aspects can be addressed and can be changed. The new model, I suggested, involves a

1 Binary thinking associated with gender forms a fundamental basis for social relations.
2 This confirms men as active subjects in the public sphere, elaborates a language for reflecting on their experience and separates and underplays sexuality, reproduction and emotions.
3 It also devalues women – as objects – as the unbounded and unspecified 'other' – as carriers of uncontrolled emotions.
   But:
4 The jobs women hold often 'stand for' gendered characteristics. In this case, women are not excluded from social institutions but are included via a truncated and unacknowledged understanding of gender.
5 Women's contribution both in the public and private sectors, however, remains unacknowledged and misunderstood.
   Thus:
6 Women are rendered marginal and will find it difficult to account for themselves.
7 Women will meet with failures of understanding and resistance to change.
   However:
8 Gendering is a social fiction, a defective vision which is not sustainable as a basis for daily practice.
9 Women as located on the 'fault line' are well placed to uncover the tacit gendering of institutions.
10 Men may also resist the existing forms of the masculine vision; in doing so they may create a clash of masculinities, or ally with women in a bid for change.

Figure 9.1   The gendering of social institutions

reflective practitioner who is engaged, embodied and creating an active problem-solving environment (see pages 149–50). Some of the conditions for this to be developed are now beginning to be met. Nurses could be amongst those who now take these ideas forward.

There is a further point. The principal aim of the book and its main contribution has been to provide an analysis of nursing, for nurses. Chapter 8 began with this in mind. I was convinced that nurses needed to pay more attention to the contract culture of the NHS, not as a given of 'high politics' that they could criticize but in the main keep their heads down and ignore, but as an arena in which they had to take a more active part. And for this, the prerequisite was information about what changes had occurred, how and why. As I began to address this, it became clear that my account of these changes was going to depart from much of the existing wisdom. The gender lens not only brings nurses back on to the stage but shows things in a different light, opening up themes such as the 'clash of masculinities' and pressing for a consideration of the potential alliances for change in the present situation, rather than focusing, as so many health policy analysts now seem to be doing, almost solely on a power struggle between the medical profession and the state. A gender analysis of the kind produced here can provide much more than the 'gender count' that much equal opportunities work has facilitated and can offer a fresh perspective, of relevance not only for nursing but for the direction of the health care system as a whole.

What then of the limitations of this approach? First, there is the matter of the strong prioritization of gender. This is clearly the strength of the book, but it is also its weakness. Correcting for the marginalization of gender issues runs the risk of overstatement, creating an impression that gender is the principal or even the only dimension of analysis. I do not mean to deny the relevance of class and of race as key structuring principles that have shaped nursing and the health care system, and important work is in hand in social policy in trying to work with these in the integrated fashion that must ultimately be correct. Next, there is the particular form of gender analysis that is used here. Nothing that has been said should be read as suggesting that mine is the only approach to studying gender in nursing. Much work is under way at the different levels of analysis set out in Chapter 3, and I have included an Appendix as a guide for the reader on the broader developments of which this book is a part, and as an indicator of the many directions which feminist work in this area is beginning to pursue.

Of the different directions in which to go, I would single out in the context of nursing the importance of pursuing the theme of masculinity and in particular the ideas of fear and repression which have been outlined here. A critical look at the explosion, in the last year or two, of men's writing on masculinity, which I have not covered in this book is an obvious starting point. On this score, a comment from a nurse who was closely involved with the RCN work on 'The Value of Nursing' (described in Chapter 7) has remained with me. Her comment was as follows:

Do you remember that story in 'The Value of Nursing', the one about the man who was to have a colostomy, the one who told the surgeon that he'd rather die than have his wife and family see anything so disgusting? Do you remember how he could hardly bear the nightmare of having nurses wash and wipe him, how the nurse got him to talk about what it was that was really bothering him, and it turned out to be how you could possibly make love with a bag of faeces dangling from your stomach? And she liaised with the stoma nurse, and got another man who had had a stoma to come and talk to him, and how he then consented to have the operation?

Well, it is a great story, isn't it – but I want to tell you what happened next – the bit that isn't in the book. There he is, you see, six months on, in the pub, having a drink, and in come his mates. The colostomy has been reversed. He is feeling fine. 'You've lost weight', they say, 'but you are looking fine. What has been happening to you?' 'Ah well', he replies, 'I've had a pretty rough time. In hospital, you know. But the surgeons, they put me right. They were great.'

The message of this book is neatly encapsulated in this tale. That message is not just that nurses need to be appreciated for what they do. It is not just that they need to be better rewarded for their work. The story directs attention back to the nature and the limitations of the cultural code of masculinity. Masculinity fears and feminizes dependency. It handles vulnerability and indeed any emotional expression by handing it over to women, and repressing and denying the need for any discussion of such matters in the 'rational' forum of a public place or space. And because, as Reverby puts it in the quotation that opens this chapter, nursing is a metaphor for much of this, nurses will often feel bruised and confused when they enter the arena of public policy debate. We must understand all this better. We need nurses to take their place in debates about public policy in health care, not only for their own good, but for the good of us all. Their more confident entry to this arena will signal a revitalization of public life and a rethinking of the key institutions of social welfare which moves on from the limited visions of reform that characterized the 1980s.

APPENDIX: GENDER AND NURSING: A BRIEF GUIDE TO THE LITERATURE

As far as I am aware, there is as yet no systematic and extended review article available covering the diversity of approaches that have begun to emerge with respect to the study of gender and nursing. Since it has been the intention of this book to develop one particular approach rather than to explore the range of material, the impression given may have been that the literature base is narrower than is actually the case. This appendix provides a brief corrective and gives an indication to those who wish to pursue this topic further of the several forms of analysis of gender and nursing which are now available. The account is developed with special reference to literature produced in the UK, though reference is also made to studies carried out elsewhere, particularly in the USA.

The question of the attitudes, motivation and behaviour of the minority of men in nursing has long been a focus of comment and of detailed empirical research in Britain. R. Brown and R. Stones (*Men in Nursing*, London, G. Bell and Sons, 1973) provided a substantial and detailed empirical study noting the rapid rise of men of fairly humble social origins to positions in nurse management. It has been criticized, however, for tending to reproduce stereotyped thinking about men and women rather than providing a critical analysis. Robert Dingwall published an article in the nursing press a year earlier which had noted a potential trend towards male domination in a classically female profession ('Nursing: towards a male-dominated occupation?', *Nursing Times*, **68**: 1585–6, 1972), but it was Mick Carpenter who had a particularly strong influence with his examination of the Salmon restructuring of nurse management and his observation that the official report amounted to 'an implicit critique of female authority, [which] . . . as such is sexist' ('The new managerialism and professionalism in nursing', in M. Stacey and M. Reid (eds) *Health and the Division of Labour*, London, Croom Helm, 1977). Carpenter has continued to emphasize gender divisions; he does so throughout his history of the trade union, COHSE, exploring, for example, the militancy of female asylum nurses (*Working for Health: The History of the Confederation of Health Service Employees*, London, Lawrence and Wishart, 1988). Recently he has synthesized and developed his thinking about the interrelation of gender with class and race, in what he calls a 'social divisions' approach ('The subordination of nurses in health care: towards a social divisions approach', in E. Riska and K. Wegar (eds) *Gender, Work and Medicine*, London, Sage, 1993).

A year after Carpenter's pioneering commentary on Salmon, came the publication, in a collection of feminist essays, of an early product from Eva Gamarnikow's doctoral studies on the history of nursing ('Sexual division of labour: the case of nursing', in A. Kuhn and A-M. Wolpe (eds) *Feminism and Materialism*, London, Routledge and Kegan Paul, 1978). This article, much cited subsequently, captured imaginations with its documentation of the turn of the century family metaphors which served effectively to subordinate nurses to doctors and to give an ideological affirmation of their position as assistants in relation to the more powerful medical profession. Carpenter, Gamarnikow, and a lively and critical piece on the history of women healers – bringing the controversial historical interpretations of Barbara Ehrenreich and Deirdre English (*Witches, Midwives and Nurses: A history of women healers*, Old Westbury, New York, The Feminist Press, 1973) to the attention of scholars (Margaret Versluysen, 'Old wives' tales? Women healers in English history', in C. Davies (ed.) *Rewriting Nursing History*, London, Croom Helm, 1980) – were among the writers at this point who signalled that a new and critical focus on gender and nursing was under way.

A strand of historical scholarship on gender and nursing began to flourish in the 1980s. While Gamarnikow completed her doctorate on the history of British nursing (*Women's Employment and the Sexual Division of Labour: the case of nursing 1860–1923*, London School of Economics, PhD thesis, 1985), she did not publish in full at the time, but has more recently made available further parts of her material ('Nurse or Woman: gender and professionalism in reformed nursing, 1860–1923', in P. Holden and J. Littlewood (eds) *Anthropology and Nursing*, London, Routledge, 1991). Other historical studies with a strong emphasis on gender include work by Ann Summers ('Pride and prejudice: ladies and nurses in the Crimean War', *History Workshop*, **16**: 33–56, 1983), by A. Simnett ('The Pursuit of Respectability: Women and the Nursing Profession 1860–1900', in R. White (ed.) *Political Issues in Nursing*, Vol.2, Chichester, Wiley, 1986) and a piece on the history of health visiting by C. Davies ('The health visitor as mother's friend: a woman's place in public health 1900–1914', *Social History of Medicine*, **1**: 38–57, 1988). The landmark in this field, however, was Susan Reverby's study of American nursing (*Ordered to Care: The dilemma of American Nursing 1850–1945*, Cambridge, Cambridge University Press, 1987). An historian, based at one of the foremost centres of women's studies in the USA, her work was a pioneering blend of the two disciplines; her notion that nursing was 'ordered to care in a society that did not value caring' struck an instant chord on these shores, and her wide-ranging scholarship and ability to synthesize set a daunting precedent. Reverby acknowledges a much earlier feminist study in the USA by Jo Ann Ashley (*Hospitals, Paternalism and the Role of the Nurse*, New York, Teachers College Press, 1976); see also E. Lewin ('Feminist ideology and the meaning of work: the case of nursing', *Catalyst*, 10–11, 1977). Interestingly, comparative historical studies of gender and nursing may now be beginning to emerge, and this is clearly an area where there is much that could be learned (see K. Melby, 'Women's ideology: difference, equality or a new femininity: women teachers and nurses in Norway 1912–1940', in T. Andreasen *et al.* (eds), *Moving on. New Perspectives on the Women's Movement*, Aarhus, Aarhus University Press).

Reverby had remarkably little in the way of a sociological, anthropological or women's studies tradition on which to build. The pre-war Chicago School of interactionist sociology of work under the leadership of Everett Hughes had given at least passing attention to nurses (E. C. Hughes, *The Sociological Eye: Selected papers*, New York, Atherton, 1971); an insightful analysis in the era of functionalist sociology had been produced at mid-century, but was thereafter largely ignored (G. Devereux and F. Weiner, 'The Occupational Status of Nurses', *American Sociological Review*, **15**: 1028–634, 1950). A half tongue-in-cheek observation by a doctor, published in a medical journal in the mid-1960s, captured attention on both sides of the Atlantic for its accurate observation of the 'game' between doctors and nurses which preserved the sense of superiority and knowledge on the part of the former (L. Stein, 'The doctor–nurse game', *Archives of General Psychiatry*, **16**: 699–703, 1967; reprinted in R. Dingwall and J. McIntosh (eds) *Readings in the Sociology of Nursing*, Edinburgh, Churchill Livingstone, 1978; see also for a direct update, L. Stein *et al.*, 'The doctor–nurse game revisited', *New England Journal of Medicine*, **322**(8): 546–9, 1990).

In 1982, however, Janet Muff had brought together a very wide-ranging collection of contributors to examine women's development, career choices and political and psychological issues for nurses (J. Muff (ed.) *Socialisation, Sexism and Stereotyping*, St Louis, Missouri, C. V. Mosby, 1982). Surprisingly little attention, however, seems to have been paid to it, and it is still more than worthwhile as a key text for coursework. Feminist sociologists Ann Game and Rosemary Pringle in Australia produced a series of case studies on gender at work which included a chapter on nursing and the health industry focusing on the sexual division of labour, setting all this in a wider perspective on gender divisions in the labour market (A. Game and R. Pringle, *Gender at Work*, London, Pluto Press, 1984). Such direct attention focusing on nurses from feminist sociologists is rare. Ann Oakley, writing for the *Nursing Times* ('The importance of being a nurse', 12 December 1984: 24–7) admitted that in all her work on medicine, health and gender, she had taken the presence of nurses for granted. Having made this admission, however, she has not taken any steps to rectify it. Two works, however, that would repay further study in terms of some of the themes of the book surrounding cultural embarrassment that nursing represents are J. Lawler, *Behind the Screens: Nursing, sociology and the problem of the body*, London, Churchill Livingstone, 1991, and M. F. Colliere, 'Invisible care and invisible women as health-care providers', *International Journal of Nursing Studies*, **23**(2): 95–109, 1985. See also anthropological work in this area, for example R. Littlewood, 'Gender, role and sickness: the ritual psychopathologies of the nurse', in P. Holden and J. Littlewood (eds) *Anthropology and Nursing*, London, Routledge, 1991.

One area where there has been an important strand of development has been in regard to professions. A. Etzioni's immensely influential collection of essays on 'semi-professions' (*The Semi-Professions and their Organisation; teachers, nurses and social workers*, New York, New York Free Press, 1969) contained a chapter on nursing which, like the concept itself, teetered on the brink of being an apology for rather than an analysis of the status quo (R. C. Simpson and I. H. Simpson, 'Women and bureaucracy in the semi-professions'). Jeff Hearn later provided a pioneering new theoretical development of professionalization and gender ('Notes on patriarchy, professionalization and the semi-professions', *Sociology*, **16**(2): 184–201, 1982) in a decade in which most authors continued to see class as the only axis of professional power. Anne Witz (*Professions and Patriarchy*, London, Routledge, 1992) has developed and extended a set of ideas around case studies of women's professionalizing projects as influenced particularly by male closure of the professions. This work contains chapters on both nursing and midwifery. An author who provides a recent and extended review of the literature on professions, discussing the above matters and emphasizing their relevance to gender and caring, is R. Hugman (*Power in the Caring Professions*, London, Macmillan, 1991).

Meanwhile, with the effects of sex discrimination legislation and equal opportunity thinking beginning to permeate, the circumstances were right for more empirical research to be commissioned within the NHS on the position of women in various occupational groups. C. Davies and J. Rosser (*Processes of Discrimination: A study of women working in the NHS*, London, DHSS, 1986) applied equal opportunity thinking to nurses on the one hand and administrative and clerical staff on the other, finding that this thinking had rather less purchase, however, when it came to nursing, already heavily numerically dominated by women. Rosemary Hutt (*Chief Officer Career Profiles: A study of the backgrounds, training and career experiences of Regional and District Nursing Officers*, IMS Report No. 111, Brighton, Institute of Manpower Studies, 1985) was commissioned to study the careers of senior men and women in nursing and produced important findings, as did Lesley Hardy ('Career politics: the case histories of selected leading female nurses in England and Scotland', in R. White (ed.) *Political Issues in Nursing: Past, Present and Future*, Vol. 2, London, Wiley, 1986) whose 'lateral movement syndrome' is discussed at length in Chapter 5 of this book. Concern about men's apparent promotion advantage has continued into the 1990s with much discussion in the nursing press (see C. Davies and L. Conn, *Creating Compatible Careers: a report and a selected bibliography on career paths in nursing*, London, Department of Health, Women's Unit, 1994), and new thinking about the distinctive nature of women's careers, if not about the gendering of the concept of career, has begun to be applied – for example to the case of midwives (R. Mander, 'Carers' careers: contingencies and crises', *Midwives' Chronicle and Nursing Notes*, 1989), and to permeate into discussions, as we saw in Chapter 4, about the active management of career breaks and the promotion of personnel practices to facilitate women (see for example, R. Waite *et al.*, *Career Paths of Scotland's Qualified Nurses*, Brighton, Institute of Manpower Studies, 1990). Midwifery is also a focus of a growing body of work exploring men entering areas of work formerly a women's preserve; for a guide see H. McKenna, 'The developments and trends in relation to men practising midwifery: a review of the literature', *Journal of Advanced Nursing*, **16**(4): 480–9, 1991). It is particularly notable that nurses are beginning to demand more recognition of their needs as women and nurses. Lesley Mackay's study (*Nursing a Problem*, Milton Keynes, Open University Press, 1989) relies heavily on the words of nurses themselves, and in doing so strongly prioritizes gender issues. This is followed up again in a later text discussing both doctors and nurses (L. Mackay, *Conflict in Care: Medicine and nursing*, London, Chapman and Hall, 1993).

Perhaps it is not surprising, then, that for the most part it has been nurses themselves who have begun to take forward the analysis of gender and nursing in the last decade. Jane Salvage (*The Politics of Nursing*, London, Heinemann, 1985), as we saw in Chapter 7, opened up a debate about the value of professionalization as a route for nursing; she covered much more besides, questioning the value accorded by others to nurses and discussing the misleading images of nurses as angels, battleaxes and sex symbols (see also J. Holloway, 'The media representation of the nurse: the implications for nursing', in K. Soothill, C. Henry and K Kendrick (eds) *Themes and Perspectives in Nursing*, London, Chapman and Hall, 1992); Pam Smith documented in detail students' experiences of the emotional side of caring work and made important recommendations for more recognition of this in training programmes (*The Emotional Labour of Nursing*, London, Macmillan, 1992); first Christine Webb (*Sexuality, Nursing and Health*, London, Wiley, 1985), and then Jan Savage (*Nurses, Gender and Sexuality*, London, Heinemann, 1987) opened up the question of how nurses might attend to sexuality in their work. Several of these writers had been active in the Radical Nurses Group in the early 1980s, and this had provided an important discussion and consciousness-raising forum among nurses sympathetic to feminist ideas.

Additional work has now developed in relation to the nature of the caring relationship, to empowerment and information sharing – some of this directly influenced by the women's alternative health movement and by women's demands for greater control over reproductive activity and over their health more generally (see for example, J. Orr, *Women's Health in the Community*, Chichester, Wiley, 1985; J. Orr, 'Women's health: a nursing perspective', in R. White (ed.) *Political Issues in Nursing: past, present and future*, Vol. 3, Chichester, Wiley, 1988; C. Webb (ed.), *Feminist Practice in Women's Health Care*, Chichester, Wiley, 1986; C. Webb, 'Mothers and daughters: a powerful spell', *Journal of Advanced Nursing*, **17**(11), 1992; D. Hennessey, 'The restrictive and wanting policies affecting health visitors' work in the field of emotional health', in R. White (ed.) *Political Issues in Nursing: Past, present and future*, Vol. 2, Chichester, Wiley, 1986; E. Rolls, 'Do health visitor's professional training and bureaucratic responsibilities separate her from the women she is serving?', *Women's Studies International Forum*, **15**(3): 397–404, 1992).

By the early 1990s, at least three trends had become clear: first, nurses with strong links to academic departments of sociology had developed a detailed knowledge of the work of relevant social scientists and students of Women's Studies and had begun themselves to develop a gender theme in a more sustained way, publishing theoretically informed work about gender and nursing in mainstream sociology journals. Nicky James' doctoral studies of the nature of carework in hospice settings is one important example (Care and Work in Nursing the Dying, University of Aberdeen, PhD thesis, 1986; 'Care = organisation + physical labour + emotional labour', *Sociology of Health and Illness*, **14**(4): 488–509, 1992; 'Emotional Labour: skill and work in the social regulation of feelings', *Sociological Review*, **37**: 15–42, 1989); Sam Porter's close observation of the interaction between male and female doctors and nurses and the gendered experience of nurses is another ('A participant observation study of power relations between doctors and nurses in a general hospital', *Journal of Advanced Nursing*, **16**(6): 728–35, 1991; 'Women in a women's job: the gendered experience of nurses', *Sociology of Health and Illness*, **14**(4): 510–27, 1992). Second, sociology was becoming more hospitable to work on gender and nursing in other ways, witness the inclusion of commissioned articles in two recent collections of readings, one on the caring professions, and another on gender and organization more broadly (M. Lorentzon, 'Professional status and managerial tasks: feminist service ideology in British nursing and social work', in P. Abbott and C. Wallace, *The Sociology of the Caring Professions*, Brighton, Falmer Press, 1990; C. Davies, 'Gender, history and management style in nursing: towards a theoretical synthesis', in M. Savage and A. Witz (eds) *Gender and Bureaucracy*, Oxford, Blackwell, 1992). See also in this context, A. Witz, 'The challenge of nursing', in J. Gabe, D. Kelleher and G. Williams (eds) *The Challenge to Medicine*, London, Routledge, in press. Third, the importance of a gender dimension to the understanding of a wide array of professional issues was being noted with a growing insistence. It would be a small project in its own right to trace this, but the work of Jane Robinson is the most prominent (see, for example, 'Nursing in the future: a cause for concern', in M. Jolley and P. Allan (eds) *Current Issues in Nursing*, London, Chapman and Hall, 1989; and 'Power, politics and policy analysis in nursing', in A. Penny and M. Jolley (eds) *Nursing: A Knowledge Base for Practice*, London, Edward Arnold, 1991).

Sociological discussions, and more explicit use of feminist theorizing, of gender and nursing are evident in the American literature too. An edited volume in 1988 on the worth of women's work contained two contributions based on nursing (S. K. Collins, 'Women at the top of women's fields: social work, nursing and education', in A. Statham *et al.* (eds) *The Worth of Women's Work*, Albany, NY, SUNY Press, 1988; M. Corley and H. Mauksch, 'Registered nurses, gender and commitment', in the same volume); a later volume seeking to theorize carework contains much of relevance to nursing in its section on care in formal organizations including a further historical essay by S. Reverby, and articles by T. Diamond and by K. B. Saks (E. Abel and M. Nelson, *Circles of Care: Work and identity in women's lives*, Albany, NY, SUNY Press, 1990). A growing theme, reflecting developments in feminist theorizing recognizing the diversity of women is represented in studies of nursing on both sides of the Atlantic; Carpenter's recent study of social divisions in nursing was mentioned at the outset; the importance of class and ethnic divisions within the nursing labour force and the contribution of nursing leadership in enhancing those divisions is also discussed in recent publications both in Britain (K. Robinson, 'The nursing workforce: aspects of inequality', in J. Robinson *et al.* (eds) *Policy Issues in Nursing*, Buckingham, Open University Press, 1992) and in the USA (N. Y. Glazer, 'Between a rock and a hard place: women's professional organizations in nursing and class, racial and ethnic inequalities', *Gender and Society*, **5**(3): 351–72, 1991). A glimpse of how feminism and the political economy of health care can be fused to give an understanding of recent developments in the management and delivery of care is afforded in an article from a Canadian (M. Campbell, 'Accounting for care: a framework for analysing change in Canadian nursing', in R. White (ed.) *Political Issues in Nursing: Past, present and future*, Vol. 3, Chichester, Wiley, 1988).

There is no doubt that nursing is being examined more critically by nurses themselves and is becoming more visible and more acceptable as a subject of study in social science disciplines and to some extent too in women's studies. Attention to the theme of gender therefore is both increasing and diversifying. While the approach of Hagell, for example, opening up the question of a gendered knowledge base in nursing (E. Hagell, 'Nursing knowledge: women's knowledge. A sociological perspective', *Journal of Advanced Nursing*, **14**(3): 226–34, 1989), remains a somewhat isolated example in a British context, I suspect that a systematic search of some of the American journals would produce a clearer trend towards contesting the masculinist knowledge base on topics of women's health and producing woman-centred alternatives. *Advances in Nursing*, for example, is one candidate among the journals for such a search. Interestingly, too, direct pleas for a rapprochement between nursing and Women's Studies, and efforts to identify points of contact, are starting to emerge in the US context (see S. Speedy, 'The contribution of feminist research', in G. Gray and R. Pratt (eds) *Towards a Discipline of Nursing*, London, Churchill Livingstone, 1991; and J. Mulligan, 'Together we go, separate we stay: women's studies and nurses' studies', in B. Flynn and M. Miller (eds) *Current Perspectives in Nursing*, St Louis, Miss., C. V. Mosby, 1980). A more recent piece by Joan Mulligan ('Nursing and Feminism: caring and curing', in C. Kramarae and D. Spender (eds) *The Knowledge Explosion: Generations of feminist scholarship*, London, Harvester Wheatsheaf, 1993) is an encouraging sign of changing times as well as a useful indicator of new areas of work.

As this book was being prepared, an immensely successful conference was organized by the Nursing Department at the University of Nottingham, under the title 'Nursing, women's history and the politics of welfare' (July 1993); as it went to press, the programme of the annual conference of the British Sociological Association, in March 1994, listed five papers on nursing, three of which were explicitly concerned with gender and nursing (R. Startup and A. Wilson, 'Nursing and gender'; C. Williams, 'Nurses' voices – Men in nursing'; C. Wright, 'Nursing(s) work and social identity').

In all this, however, the relation between nurses and feminist ideas remains an uneasy one, where movement between the two is still a minority interest. A more systematic examination of the literature than has been possible here, however, may provide a firmer basis for classifying and evaluating what is starting to be a range of different approaches under the broad heading of gender and nursing, each with its own potential for an enhanced critical understanding of the project that is nursing and the dilemmas of its contemporary practice.

BIBLIOGRAPHY

Abel, E. and Nelson, M. (eds) (1990). *Circles of Care: Work and identity in women's lives*. Albany, NY, SUNY Press.

Acker, J. (1989). 'Making gender visible', in R. Wallace (ed.) *Feminism and Sociological Theory*. London, Sage.

Acker, J. (1990). 'Hierarchies, jobs, bodies: a theory of gendered organisations', *Gender and Society*, **4**(2), 139–58. (Reprinted in J. Lorber and S.A. Farrell (eds) (1991). *The Social Construction of Gender*. London, Sage.)

Acker, J. (1992a). 'Gendering organisational theory', in A.J. Mills and P. Tancred (eds), *Gendering Organisational Analysis*. London, Sage.

Acker, J. (1992b). 'From sex roles to gendered institutions', *Contemporary Sociology*, **21**(5), 565–9

Adkins, L. (1992). 'Sexual work and the employment of women in the service industries', in M. Savage and A. Witz (eds) *Gender and Bureaucracy*. Oxford, Blackwell.

Alleway, L. (1987). 'Make or break?', *Nursing Times*, **83**(18), 207–28.

Allsop, J. and May, A. (1993). 'Between the devil and the deep blue sea: managing the NHS in the wake of the 1990 Act', *Critical Social Policy*, **38**, 5–22.

Alvesson, M. and Billig, Y.D. (1992). 'Gender and organisation: towards a differentiated understanding', *Organisation Studies*, **13**(1), 73–103.

Argyris, C. and Schön, D.A. (1989). *Theory into Practice: Increasing professional effectiveness*. San Francisco, Jossey-Bass.

Audit Commission for Local Authorities and the NHS in England and Wales (1991). *The Virtue of Patients: Making best use of ward nursing resources*. London, HMSO.

Bacchi, C. (1990). *Same Difference: Feminism and sexual differences*. London, Unwin Hyman.

Bakan, D. (1966). *The Duality of Human Existence*. Boston, Beacon.

Bardwick, J. (1980). 'The seasons of a woman's life', in D. McGuigan (ed.) *Women's Lives: New theory, research and policy*. Ann Arbor, Centre for Continuing Education of Women, University of Michigan.

Baruch, G., Barnett, R. and Rivers, C. (1983). *Lifeprints: New patterns of love and work for today's woman*. New York, New American Library.

Baxter, C. (1988) *The Black Nurse: An endangered Species*. Cambridge, National Extension College for Training in Health and Race.

Beardshaw, V. and Robinson, K. (1990). *New For Old? Prospects for Nursing in the 1990s*, Research Report No. 8. London, King's Fund Institute.

Belenky, M.F., Clinchy, B.F., Goldberger, N.R. and Tarule, J.M. (1984). *Women's Ways of Knowing: Development of self, voice and mind*. New York, Basic Books.

Benhabib, S. (1987). 'The Kohlberg–Gilligan controversy and feminist theory', in S. Benhabib and D. Cornell (eds) *Feminism as Critique*. Oxford/Cambridge, Blackwell/Polity.

Benjamin, J. (1988). *The Bounds of Love*. New York, Pantheon.

Benner, R. and Wrubel, J. (1989). *The Primacy of Caring: Stress and coping in health and illness*. New York, Addison-Wesley.

Berliner, H.S. (1975). 'A larger perspective on the Flexner Report', *International Journal of Health Services*, **5**(4), 573–92.

Bledstein, B. (1976). *The Culture of Professionalism: The middle class and the development of higher education in America*. New York, Norton.

Bolger, T. (1990). 'Project 2000: From Worried, of London', *Nursing Times*, **86**(24), 19.

Bologh, R.W. (1990). *Love or Greatness: Max Weber and masculine thinking – a feminist inquiry*. London, Unwin Hyman.

Brown, E.R. (1979). *Rockefeller Medicine Men*. Berkeley, University of California Press.

Brown, J. (1993) *Contract Culture and Professional Practice*. Sheffield and North Trent College of Nursing and Midwifery Student Conference, *Which Way Now? The Future of Nursing Work*, Rotherham, March.

Brown, J.M., Kitson, A. and McKnight, T. (1987). *Challenges in Caring: explorations in nursing and ethics*. London, Chapman and Hall.

Brown, P. and Sparks, R. (eds) (1989). *Beyond Thatcherism: Social policy, politics and society*. Milton Keynes, Open University Press.

Brubaker, R. (1984). *The Limits of Rationality: An essay on the social and moral thought of Max Weber*. London, Allen and Unwin.

Buchan, J. (1992). 'Nurse manpower planning: role, rationale and relevance', in J. Robinson, A. Gray and R. Elkan (eds) *Policy Issues in Nursing*. Buckingham, Open University Press.

Buchan, J. and Seccombe, I. (1991a). *Nurse Turnover Costs*, IMS Report No. 212. Brighton, Institute of Manpower Studies.

Buchan, J. and Seccombe, I. (1991b). *Nurses' Work and Worth*, IMS Report No. 213. Brighton, Institute for Manpower Studies.

Buchan, J., Bevan, S. and Atkinson, J. (1988). *Costing Labour Wastage in the NHS*, Report No. 157. Brighton, Institute for Manpower Studies.

Buchan, J., Waite, R. and Thomas, J. (1989). *Grade Expectations: Clinical grading and nurse mobility*, IMS Report No. 176. Brighton, Institute for Manpower Studies.

Burrell, G. (1984). 'Sex and organisational analysis', *Organisation Studies*, **5**(2), 97–118.

Burton, L. (1975). *The Family Life of Sick Children*. London, Routledge and Kegan Paul.

Butler, J. (1993). 'A case study in the NHS: working for patients', in P. Taylor-Gooby and R. Lawson (eds) *Markets and Managers: New issues in the delivery of welfare*. Buckingham: Open University Press.

Campbell, A.V. (1984). *Moderated Love: A theology of professional care*. London, SPCK.

Campbell, M. (1988). 'Accounting for care: a framework for analysing change in Canadian nursing', in R. White (ed.) *Political Issues in Nursing: Past, present and future. Vol. 3*. Chichester, Wiley.

Carpenter, M. (1977). 'The new managerialism and professionalism in nursing', in M. Stacey and M. Reid (eds) *Health and the Division of Labour*. London, Croom Helm.

Carr-Saunders, A.M. and Wilson, P.A. (1933). *The Professions*. London, Oxford University Press.

Castledine, G. (1986). 'Clinical nurse specialists', *Nursing Practice*, **31**(4), 213–14.

Chapman, C. (1985). 'Advanced nurse education', *Journal of Advanced Nursing*, **10** (Janforum), 88–90.

Chapman, P. (1989). 'Another view of Project 2000', *COHSE Journal*, **1**(3), September/October.

Chodorow, N. (1978) *The Reproduction of Mothering: Psychoanalysis and the sociology of gender*. London, University of California Press.

Chodorow, N. (1989). *Feminism and Psychoanalytic Theory*. London, Yale University Press.

Clarke, M. (1986). 'Action and reflection: theory and practice in nursing', *Journal of Advanced Nursing*, **11**(1), 3–12.

Clay, T. (1987). *Nursing: Power and politics*. London, Heinemann.

Cockburn, C. (1983). *Brothers: Male dominance and technological change*. London, Pluto Press.

Cockburn, C. (1985). *Machinery of Dominance: Women, men and technical knowhow*. London, Pluto Press.

Cockburn, C. (1991). *In the Way of Women: Men's resistance to sex equality in organisations*. London, Macmillan.

Committee on Nursing (1972). *Report of the Committee on Nursing (Chairman: Asa Briggs)*, Cmnd 5115. London, HMSO.

Corley, M.C. and Mauksch, H.O. (1988). 'Registered nurses: gender and commitment', in A. Statham, E. Miller and H. Mauksch (eds) *The Worth of Women's Work*. Albany, NY, SUNY Press.

Cousins, C. (1987). *Controlling Social Welfare*. Brighton, Wheatsheaf Books.

Cox, D. (1992). 'Crisis and opportunity in health service management', in R. Loveridge and K. Starkey (eds) *Continuity and Crisis in the NHS*. Buckingham, Open University Press.

Crail, M. (1990). 'Project 2000 off to a shaky start', *COHSE Journal*, **2**(4), 10–11, July/August.

Dalley, G. (1988). *Ideologies of Caring*. London, Macmillan.

Daniels, A.K. (1987). Invisible Work, *Social Problems*, **34**(5), 403–13.

Davies, C. (1980). 'A constant casualty', in C. Davies (ed.) *Rewriting Nursing History*. London, Croom Helm.

Davies, C. (1983). 'Professions and bureaucracy', in R. Dingwall and P. Lewis (eds) *The Sociology of the Professions: Lawyers, Doctors and Others*. London, Macmillan.

Davies, C. (1985). 'Policy in nursing education: plus ça change . . .?', *The Politics of Progress: Proceedings of the 19th Annual Study Day of the Nursing Studies Association*. Edinburgh, University of Edinburgh.

Davies, C. (1987). 'Viewpoint: things to come: the NHS in the next decade', *Sociology of Health and Illness*, **9**(3), 302–17.

Davies, C. (1988). 'The health visitor as mother's friend: a woman's place in public health 1900–1914', *Social History of Medicine*, **1**, 39–59.

Davies, C. (1989). 'Workplace action programmes for equality for women: an orthodoxy examined', in C. Hussey (ed), *Equal Opportunities for Men and Women in Higher Education. Proceedings of a Conference*. Dublin, University College Dublin.

Davies, C. (1992). 'Gender, history and management style in nursing: towards a theoretical synthesis', in M. Savage and A. Witz (eds) *Gender and Bureaucracy*. Oxford, Blackwell.

Davies, C. (1993). 'The equality mystique, the difference dilemma and the case of women academics', *Women's Studies Centre Review*, *2*, 53–72. University College Galway.

Davies, C. (in preparation). Conventional careers and conventional theorising: the challenges of gender analysis.

Davies, C. and Conn, L. (1994). *Creating Compatible Careers: A report and a selected bibliography on career paths in nursing*. London, Department of Health, Women's Unit.

Davies, C. and Parkyn, A. (1992). *Realising Potential – a practical guide to equality of opportunity in management development*. Bristol, NHSTD.

Davies, C. and Rosser, J. (1984). Career Paths of Men and Women in Nursing (II) – A View from Below. Coventry: University of Warwick (unpublished).

Davies, C. and Rosser, J. (1986). *Processes of Discrimination: A study of women working in the NHS*. London, DHSS.

Dean, M. (1992). 'Nursing's identity crisis', *Lancet*, 339, 1160–1, 9 May.

Delamothe, T. (1988). 'Nursing grievances: (v) women's work', *British Medical Journal*, **296**, 271–4, 30 January.

Department of Health (1989). *Working for Patients*, Cm 555. London, HMSO.

Department of Health (1990). *NHS Workforce in England* (1990 edn). London, Department of Health.

Department of Health and Social Security (DHSS) (1979). *Patients First: Consultative paper on the structure and management of the NHS in England and Wales*. London, HMSO.

Department of Health and Social Security (DHSS) (1987a). *The Role and*

Preparation of Support Workers to Nurses, Midwives and Health Visitors and the Implications for Manpower and Service Planning. London, DHSS.

Department of Health and Social Security (DHSS) (1987b). *Promoting Better Health: The government's programme for improving primary health care*, Cm 249. London, HMSO.

Devlin, B. (1987). 'An unreal brave new world', *Nursing Times*, **83**(18), 29–30, 6 May.

Diamond, T. (1990). 'Nursing homes as trouble', in E. Abel and M. Nelson (eds) *Circles of Care: Work and identity in women's lives*. Albany, NY, SUNY Press.

Dickson, N. (1987). 'A Top Priority', *Nursing Times*, **83**(18), 23, 6 May.

Dingwall, R., Rafferty, A.M. and Webster, C. (1988). *An Introduction to the Social History of Nursing*. London, Routledge.

Dolan, B. (ed.) (1993). *Project 2000: Reflection and celebration*. London, Scutari Press.

Dominelli, L. (1988). *Anti-Racist Social Work*. London, Macmillan.

Dominelli, L. and McLeod, E. (1989). *Feminist Social Work*. London, Macmillan.

Doyal, L. (1979). 'A matter of life and health: medicine, health and statistics', in J. Irvine, I. Miles and J. Evans (eds) *Demystifying Social Statistics*. London, Pluto Press.

Dyson, R. (1988). 'Project 2000: the numbers game', *Nursing Times*, **84**(22), 15, 1 June.

Eichenbaum, L. and Orbach, S. (1985). *Understanding Women*. London, Penguin.

Eichler, M. (1988). *Nonsexist Research Methods: A practical guide*. London, Allen and Unwin.

Eisenstein, H. (1984). *Contemporary Feminist Thought*. London, Unwin Paperbacks.

Elkan, R. and Robinson, J. (1991). *The Implementation of Project 2000 in a District Health Authority: The effect on the nursing service. An interim report*. Nursing Policy Studies 7. Nottingham, University of Nottingham, Department of Nursing and Midwifery Studies.

Elkan, R., Hillman, R. and Robinson, J. (1993). *The Implementation of Project 2000 in a District Health Authority: The effect on the nursing service*, Nursing Policy Studies 10. Nottingham, University of Nottingham, Department of Nursing and Midwifery Studies.

Ellis, R. (ed.) (1988). *Professional Competence and Quality Assurance in the Caring Professions*. London, Croom Helm.

Ellis, R. and Whittington, D. (1993). *Quality Assurance in Health Care: A handbook*. London, Edward Arnold.

Equal Opportunities Commission (EOC) (1991). *Equality Management: Women's employment in the NHS*. Manchester, EOC.

Evers, H. (1981). 'Care or custody? The experiences of women patients in longstay geriatric wards', in B. Hutter and G. Williams (eds) *Controlling Women: The normal and the deviant*. London, Croom Helm.

Ferguson, K. (1984). *The Feminist Case against Bureaucracy*. Philadelphia, Temple University Press.

Flynn, N. (1990). *Public Sector Management*. Hemel Hempstead, Harvester Wheatsheaf.

Francis, B., Peelo, M. and Soothill, K. (1992). 'NHS nursing: vocation, career, or just a "job"', in K. Soothill, C. Henry and K. Kendrick (eds) *Themes and Perspectives in Nursing*. London, Chapman & Hall.

Freidson, E. (1970a). *Profession of Medicine*. New York, Dodd Mead.

Freidson, E. (1970b). *Professional Dominance*. New York, Atherton.

Fuss, D. (1989). *Essentially Speaking: Feminism, nature and difference*. New York, Routledge.

Gallos, J.V. (1989). 'Exploring women's development: implications for career theory, practice and research', in M. Arthur, D. Hall and B. Lawrence (eds) *Handbook of Career Theory*. Cambridge, Mass., Cambridge University Press.

Gamarnikow, E. (1978). 'Sexual division of labour: the case of nursing', in A.Kuhn and A.-M. Wolpe (eds) *Feminism and Materialism*. London, Routledge and Kegan Paul.

Gaze, H. (1987). 'Men in nursing', *Nursing Times*, **83**(20), 24–7, 20 May.

Gaze, H. (1988). 'For better or worse', *Nursing Times*, **85**(38), 48–9, 21 September.

Gherardi, S. (1994). 'The gender we think, the gender we do in our everyday organisational lives', in J. Rothschild and C. Davies (eds) *Gender and Organisational Life, Human Relations* (special issue), **47**(6).

Gibberd, B. (1988). 'Project 2000 – the only option', *Health Service Journal*, **98**, 182–3, 11 February.

Gibbs, I., McCaughan, D. and Griffiths, M. (1991). 'Skill mix in nursing: a selected review of the literature', *Journal of Advanced Nursing*, **16**(2), 242–9.

Gilligan, C. (1982). *In a Different Voice: Psychological theory and women's development*. London, Harvard University Press.

Glazer, N.Y. (1991). 'Between a rock and a hard place: women's professional organizations in nursing and class, racial, and ethnic inequalities', *Gender and Society*, **5**(3), 351–72.

Glazer, P. and Slater, M. (1987). *Unequal Colleagues: The entrance of women into the professions, 1890–1940*. New Brunswick, Rutgers University Press.

Glendinning, C. (1983). *Unshared Care: Parents and their disabled children*. London, Routledge and Kegan Paul.

Gomm, R. (1993). 'Issues of power in health and welfare', in J. Walmsley, J. Reynolds, R. Shakespeare and R. Woolfe (eds) *Health, Welfare and Practice: Reflecting on roles and relationships*. London, Sage.

Goss, S. and Brown, H. (1991). *Equal Opportunities for Women in the NHS*. London, Office for Public Management/NHSME.

Graham, H. (1983). 'Caring: a labour of love', in J. Finch and D. Groves (eds) *A Labour of Love: Women, work and caring*. London, Routledge and Kegan Paul.

Graham, H. (1993). 'Feminist perspectives on caring', in J. Bornat, C. Pereira, D. Pilgrim and F. Williams (eds) *Community Care: A reader*. London, Macmillan/ Open University.

le Grand, J. and Bartlett, W. (eds) (1993). *Quasi-Markets and Social Policy*. London, Macmillan.

Grant, J. and Tancred, P. (1992). 'A feminist perspective on state bureaucracy', in A. J. Mills and P. Tancred (eds) *Gendering Organisational Analysis*. London, Sage.

Gray, A. and Jenkins, B. (1993). 'Markets, management and the public service: the changing of a culture', in P. Taylor-Gooby and R. Lawson (eds) *Markets and Managers: New issues in the delivery of welfare.* Buckingham, Open University Press.

Greenwood, J. (1993). 'Reflective practice: a critique of the work of Argyris and Schön', *Journal of Advanced Nursing*, **18**(8), 1183–8.

Gregory, J. (1988). *Sex, Race and the Law.* London, Sage.

Griffiths, E. Roy (1983). NHS Management Inquiry (letter to the Secretary of State). London, The Team.

Ham, C. (1992). *Health Policy in Britain: The politics and organisation of the NHS.* Basingstoke, Macmillan (3rd edn).

Hancock, C. (1992). 'Expectations of Management', *Senior Nurse*, **12**(3), 4–7, May/June.

Hansard Society (1990). *The Report of the Hansard Society Commission on Women at the Top.* London, The Hansard Society for Parliamentary Government.

Hanson, M. and Patchett, T. (1986). 'When the tap runs dry', *Nursing Times*, **82**(52), 26–8, 31 December.

Harding, S. (1986). *The Science Question in Feminism.* Milton Keynes, Open University Press.

Hardy, L. (1986). 'Career politics: the case of career histories of selected leading female nurses in England and Scotland', in R. White (ed.) *Political Issues in Nursing: Past, Present and Future. Vol. 2.* London, Wiley.

Hare-Mustin, R. and Marecek, J. (eds) (1990). *Making a Difference: Psychology and the construction of gender.* London, Yale University Press.

Harrison, A. and Wistow, G. (1993). 'Managing Health Care: balancing interests and influence', in B. Davey and J. Popay (eds) *Dilemmas in Health Care.* Buckingham, Open University Press.

Harrison, S. (1988). *Managing the NHS: Shifting the frontier?* London, Chapman and Hall.

Harrison, S., Hunter, D. and Pollitt, C. (1990). *The Dynamics of British Health Policy.* London, Allen and Unwin.

Harrison, S., Hunter, D., Marnock, G. and Pollitt, C. (1992). *Just Managing: Power and Culture in the NHS.* London, Macmillan.

Hart, L. (1991). 'A ward of my own: social organisation and identity among hospital domestics', in P. Holden and J. Littlewood (eds) *Anthropology and Nursing.* London, Routledge.

Hartsock, N. (1985). *Money, Sex and Power.* Boston, Northeastern University Press (first published 1983).

Hawkins, C. (1986). 'Pursuing the Medical Model', *Senior Nurse*, 5(4) October.

Hearn, J. (1982). 'Notes on patriarchy, professionalization and the semi-professions', *Sociology*, **16**(2), 184–201.

Hearn, J. (1987). *'Sex' and 'Work': The power and paradox of organisational sexuality.* Brighton, Wheatsheaf.

Hearn, J. (1992). *Men in the Public Eye.* London, Routledge.

Hearn, J., Sheppard, D., Tancred-Sheriff, P. and Burrell, G. (eds) (1989). *The Sexuality of Organization.* London, Sage.

Hochschild, A.R. (1983). *The Managed Heart: Commercialization of human feeling*. London, University of California Press.

Hoffman, L. (1989). *The Politics of Knowledge: Activist movements in medicine and planning*. Albany, NY, SUNY Press.

Holloway, J. (1992). 'The media representation of the nurse: the implications for nursing', in K. Soothill, C. Henry and K. Kendrick (eds) *Themes and Perspectives in Nursing*. London, Chapman and Hall.

Homans, H. (1989). *Women in the NHS: Report of a case study into equal opportunities in clinical chemistry laboratories*, EOC Research Series. London, HMSO.

Hood, C. (1991). 'A public management for all seasons?', *Public Administration*, **69**(1), 3–40.

House of Commons (1981). *Seventeenth Report from the Committee of Public Accounts. Session 1980–1*. London, HMSO.

House of Commons (1984). *Sixteenth Report from the Committee of Public Accounts. Session 1983–4*. London, HMSO.

House of Commons (1985). *Thirty-second Report from the Committee of Public Accounts. Session 1984–5. NHS: Hospital Based Medical Manpower*. London, HMSO.

House of Commons (1986). *Fourteenth Report from the Committee of Public Accounts. Session 1985–6. Control of Nursing Manpower*. London, HMSO.

Hoyes, L. and Means, R. (1993). 'Markets, contracts and social care services: prospects and problems', in J. Bornat, C. Pereira, D. Pilgrim and F. Williams (eds) *Community Care: A reader*. London, Macmillan/Open University.

Hughes, D. (1993). 'Health policy: letting the market work?', *Social Policy Review*, **5**, 105–24.

Hugman, R. (1991). *Power in the Caring Professions*. London, Macmillan.

Hunter, D. (ed.) (1991). *Paradoxes of Competition for Health*. Leeds, Nuffield Institute for Health Service Studies/European Healthcare Management Association.

Hunter, D. (1993). 'The internal market: the shifting agenda', in I. Tilley (ed.) *Managing the Internal Market*. London, Paul Chapman.

Hutt, R. (1985). *Chief Officer Career Profiles: A study of the backgrounds, training and career experiences of regional and district nursing officers,* Report 111. Brighton, Institute of Management Studies.

Irigaray, L. (1993). *Je, Tu, Nous: toward a culture of difference*. London, Routledge.

Jackson, J.A. (ed.) (1970). *Professions and Professionalization*. London: Cambridge University Press.

James, N. (1989). 'Emotional labour skill and work in the social regulation of feelings', *Sociological Review*, **37**, 15–42.

James, N. (1991). 'Care, work and carework: a synthesis', in J. Robinson, A. Gray and R. Elkan (eds) *Policy Issues in Nursing*. Buckingham: Open University Press.

James, N. (1992). 'Care = organisation + physical labour + emotional labour', *Sociology of Health and Illness*, **14**(4), 488–509.

Jenkins, M. (1994). Occupational Therapy: perspectives on the effectiveness of practice, D.Phil. dissertation. University of Ulster.

Jewson, N. and Mason, D. (1986). 'The theory and practice of equal opportunities policies: liberal and radical approaches', *Sociological Review*, **34**(2), 307–34.

Jobling, R. (1989). 'Health care', in P. Brown and R. Sparks (eds) *Beyond Thatcherism: Social Policy, Politics and Society*. Milton Keynes: Open University Press.

Johnson, T.J. (1972). *Professions and Power*. London, Macmillan.

Jolley, M. (1989). 'The professionalisation of nursing: the uncertain path', in M. Jolley and P. Allan (eds) *Current Issues in Nursing*. London, Chapman and Hall.

Jones, K.B. (1993). *Compassionate Authority: Democracy and the representation of women*. London, Routledge.

Jourard, S. (1971). *The Transparent Self*. 2nd edn. New York, Van Nostrand.

Jowett, S. (1992). 'Project 2000 – research on its implementation', *Nursing Times*, **88**(26), 24 June.

Jowett, S., Walton, I. and Payne, S. (1992). *Implementing Project 2000: An interim report*. Slough, NFER/DOH.

Jowett, S., Walton, I. and Payne, S. (1994). *Challenges and Change in Nurse Education: A study of the implementation of Project 2000. Executive Summary*. Slough, NFER.

Kelly, A. (1991). 'The enterprise culture and the welfare state: restructuring the management of health and personal social services', in R. Burrows (ed.) *Deciphering Enterprise Culture*. London, Routledge.

Kerber, L., Green, C., Maccoby, E., Luria, Z., Stack, C. and Gilligan, C. (1986). 'On "In a Different Voice": an interdisciplinary forum', *Signs*, **11**(2), 304–33.

Kimball, B.A. (1992). *The 'True Professional Ideal' in America: A history*. Oxford, Blackwell.

King Edward's Hospital Fund for London (1990) *Racial Equality: The nursing profession*. Equal Opportunities Task Force, occasional paper No. 6. London, King Edward's Hospital Fund for London.

Klein, R. (1984). 'The politics of ideology vs the reality of politics: the case of Britain's NHS in the 1980s', *Millbank Memorial Fund Quarterly*, **62**(i).

Kohlberg, L. (1969). 'Stage and sequence: the cognitive-development approach to socialization', in D.A. Goslin (ed.) *Handbook of Socialization Theory and Research*. Chicago, Rand McNally.

Kohlberg, L. (1973). 'Continuities and discontinuities in childhood and adult moral development revisited', in *Collected Papers on Moral Development and Moral Education*. Cambridge, Mass., Moral Education Research Foundation, Harvard University.

Kurzweil, E. (1989). 'Psychoanalytic feminism: implications for sociological theory', in R. Wallace (ed.) *Feminism and Sociological Theory*. London, Sage.

Levitt, R. and Wall, A. (1992). *The Reorganised NHS*. London, Chapman and Hall.

Lewis, J. (1983). 'Dealing with dependency: state practices and social realities', in J. Lewis (ed.) *Women's Welfare, Women's Rights*. London, Croom Helm.

Lewis, J. and Davies, C. (1992). Protective Legislation in Britain: equality, difference and their implications for women, *Policy and Politics*, **19**(1), 13–25.

Lewis, J. and Meredith, B. (1988). *Daughters who Care: Daughters caring for their mothers at home*. London, Routledge.

Lewis, P. (1989). 'Male midwives: reasons for training and subsequent career paths', in J. Wilson–Barnett and S. Robinson (eds) *Directions in Nursing Research. Ten Years of Progress at London University*. London, Scutari.

Loney, M., Bocock, R., Clarke, J., Cochrane, A., Graham, P. and Wilson, M. (eds) (1991). *The State or the Market: Politics and welfare in contemporary Britain*. 2nd edn. London, Sage.

Long, A. and Mercer, G. (1987). *Health Manpower, Planning, Production and Management*. London, Croom Helm.

Lorber, J., Cosner, R., Rossi, A. and Chodorow, N. (1981). 'On "The Reproduction of Mothering": a methodological debate', *Signs*, **6**(3), 482–514.

Lorde, A. (1984). *Sister Outside: Essays and Speeches*. New York, The Crossing Press, Feminist Series.

Lovenduski, J. (1989). 'Implementing equal opportunities in the 1980s: an overview', *Public Administration*, **67**, 7–18.

McAuley, J. (1987). 'Women academics: a case study in inequality', in A. Spencer and D. Podmore (eds) *In a Man's World: Essays on women in male-dominated professions*. London, Tavistock.

McCarthy, M. (ed.) (1989). *The New Politics of Welfare: An agenda for the 1990s?* London, Macmillan.

Mackay, L. (1989). *Nursing a Problem*. Milton Keynes, Open University Press.

McLachlan, G. and Maynard, A. (eds) (1982). *The Public/Private Mix for Health*. London, Nuffield Provincial Hospitals Trust.

Markham, G. (1988). 'Special cases', *Nursing Times*, **84**(36), 29–30, 29 June.

Marshall, J. (1984). *Women Managers: travellers in a male world*. Chichester, Wiley.

Mayeroff, M. (1972). *On Caring*. New York, Harper and Row.

Meehan, E. (1985). *Women's Rights at Work: Campaigns and policy in Britain and the United States*. London, Macmillan.

Meehan, E. and Sevenhuijsen, S. (1991). *Equality, Politics and Gender*. London, Sage.

Melia, K. (1987). *Learning and Working: the occupational socialization of nurses*. London, Tavistock.

Menzies, I. (1960). 'A case study in the functioning of social systems as a defence against anxiety: a report on a study of the nursing service of a general hospital', *Human Relations*, **13**(2), 95–121.

Miller, A. (1984). *Thou Shalt Not Be Aware: Society's betrayal of the child*. New York, New American Library.

Mills, A. (1992). 'Organization, gender and culture', in A. Mills and P. Tancred (eds) *Gendering Organizational Analysis*. London, Sage.

Mills, A. and Murgatroyd, S. (1991). *Organizational Rules*. Buckingham, Open University Press.

Mills, A. and Tancred, P. (eds) (1992). *Gendering Organizational Analysis*. London, Sage.

Ministry of Health (1966). *Report of the Committee on Senior Nursing Staff Structure (Chairman: B. Salmon)*. London, HMSO.

Mitchell, J. (1975). *Psychoanalysis and Feminism*. Harmondsworth, Penguin (first published 1974).

National Audit Office (NAO) (1985a). *Report by the Comptroller and Auditor General. NHS: Control of Nursing Manpower*. London, HMSO.

National Audit Office (NAO) (1985b). *Report by the Comptroller and Auditor General. NHS: Hospital Based Medical Manpower*. London, HMSO.

National Audit Office (NAO) (1992). *Nursing Education. Implementation of Project 2000 in England*, Report by the Comptroller and Auditor General. London, HMSO.

National Steering Group on Equal Opportunities for Women in the NHS (1987–9). *Resource Information Pack*. London, North West Thames Regional Health Authority.

Newell, R. (1992). Anxiety, accuracy and reflection: the limits of professional development, *Journal of Advanced Nursing*, **17**(11), 1326–33.

NHS Management Executive (NHSME) (1992). *Women in the NHS: An action guide to Opportunity 2000*. London, HMSO.

Nursing and Midwifery Staffs Negotiating Council: Staff Side (no date). Action Towards Equality. London, NMSNC.

Nuttall, P. (1983). 'Male takeover or female giveaway?', *Nursing Times*, **72**(2), 10–12, 12 January.

O'Neill, E., Morrison, H. and McEwan, A. (1993). *Professional Socialisation and Nurse Education: An evaluation. Report prepared for the National Board for Nursing, Midwifery and Health Visiting for Northern Ireland*. Belfast, School of Education, Queen's University.

Osborne, D. and Gaebler, T. (1992). *Reinventing Government: How the entre-preneurial spirit is transforming the public sector*. New York, Addison-Wesley.

Owens, P. and Glennerster, H. (1990). *Nursing in Conflict*. London, Macmillan.

Pape, R. (1978). 'Touristry: a type of occupational mobility', in R. Dingwall and J. McIntosh (eds) *Readings in the Sociology of Health and Illness*. Edinburgh, Churchill Livingstone.

Parston, G. (1992). *Managing for Social Result: A new framework for public management*. London, Office for Public Management.

Pateman, C. (1988). *The Sexual Contract*. Oxford, Blackwell/Polity Press.

Paton, C. (1992). *Competition and Planning in the NHS: The danger of unplanned markets*. London, Chapman and Hall.

Pearson, A. (1983). *The Clinical Nursing Unit*. London, Heinemann.

Pearson, A. (1988). 'Trends in clinical nursing', in A. Pearson (ed.) *Primary Nursing: Nursing in the Burford and Oxford Nursing Development Units*. London, Chapman and Hall.

Pembrey, S. (1985). 'A framework for care', *Nursing Times*, 47–9, 11 December.

Petchey, R. (1986). 'The Griffiths reorganisation of the NHS: Fowlerism by stealth?', *Critical Social Policy*, **17**, 87–101.

Peters, T. and Waterman, R. (1982). *In Search of Excellence*. London, Harper and Row.

Phillips, A. and Taylor, B. (1980). 'Sex and skill: notes towards a feminist economics', *Feminist Review*, **6**, 79–88.

Pollitt, C. (1990). *Managerialism and the Public Services: the Anglo-American Experience*. Oxford, Blackwell.

Pollitt, C. (1993). Managerialism and the Public Services: the Anglo–American Experience, 2nd edn. Oxford, Blackwell.

Porter, S. (1992). 'Women in a women's job: the gendered experience of nurses', *Sociology of Health and Illness*, **14**(4), 510–27.

Price Waterhouse (1987). *The UKCC: Report on the Costs, Benefits and Manpower Implications of Project 2000*. London, Price Waterhouse.

Price Waterhouse (1988). *Nurse Retention and Recruitment: Report on the Factors Affecting the Retention and Recruitment of Nurses, Midwives and Health Visitors in the NHS*. London, Price Waterhouse.

Prime Minister (1991). *The Citizen's Charter: Raising the standard*, Cm 1599. London, HMSO.

Pringle, R. (1989). *Secretaries Talk: Sexuality, Power and Work*. London, Verso (first published 1988, Sydney, Allen and Unwin).

Proctor, S. (1989). 'The functioning of nursing routines in the management of a transient workforce', *Journal of Advanced Nursing*, **14**(3), 180–90.

Purtilo, R. (1993). 'Meaningful Distances', in J. Walmsley, J. Reynolds, P. Shakespeare and R. Woolfe (eds) *Health, Welfare and Practice: Reflecting on roles and relationships*. London, Sage.

Rafferty, A.M. (1992). 'Nursing policy and the nationalization of nursing: the representation of "crisis" and the "crisis" of representation', in J. Robinson, A. Gray and R. Elkan (eds) *Policy Issues in Nursing*. Buckingham: Open University Press.

Ramsay, K. and Parker, M. (1992). 'Gender, bureaucracy and organisational culture', in M. Savage and A. Witz (eds) *Gender and Bureaucracy*. Oxford, Blackwell.

Rees, T. (1992). *Women and the Labour Market*. London, Routledge.

Reid, N.G. (1985). *Wards in Chancery?* London, Royal College of Nursing.

Reverby, S. (1987). *Ordered to Care: The dilemma of American nursing 1850–1945*. Cambridge, Cambridge University Press.

Robinson, J. (1991). 'Project 2000: the role of resistance in the process of professional growth', *Journal of Advanced Nursing*, **16**(7), 820–4.

Robinson, J. (1992). 'Introduction: beginning the study of nursing policy', in J. Robinson, A. Gray and R. Elkan (eds) *Policy Issues in Nursing*. Buckingham, Open University Press.

Robinson, J., Strong, P. and Elkan, R. (1989). *Griffiths and the Nurses: A national survey of CNAs, Nursing Policy Studies 4*. Coventry, University of Warwick, Nursing Policy Studies Centre.

Robinson, Jill (1992). 'Mixed feelings', *Nursing Times*, **88**(40), 28–30, 30 September.

Robinson, K. (1992). 'The nursing workforce: aspects of inequality', in J. Robinson, A. Gray and R. Elkan (eds) *Policy Issues in Nursing*. Buckingham, Open University Press.

Rodgers, J. (1983). *The Career Patterns of Nurses who have Completed a JBCNS Certificate. Report of the Follow-Up Study*, Vols. I and II. London, DHSS.

Rosener, J. (1990). 'Ways women lead', *Harvard Business Review*, **68**(6), 119–25.

Rosser, J. and Davies, C. (1987). '"What would we do without her?": invisible women in NHS administration', in A. Spencer and D. Podmore (eds) *In a Man's World: Essays on women in male-dominated professions.* London, Tavistock.

Rossi, A. (1980). 'Life span theories and women's lives', *Signs,* **6**(1).

Roth, J. (1974). 'Professionalism: the sociologist's decoy', *Sociology of Work and Occupations,* **1**(1), 6–23.

Rothschild, J. and Davies, C. (eds) (1994). *Gender and Organisational Life, Human Relations* (special issue), **47**(6).

Royal College of Nursing (RCN) (1985). *Commission on Nursing Education (Chairman: H. Judge). The Education of Nurses: A New Dispensation.* London, The College.

Royal College of Nursing (RCN) (1992). *The Value of Nursing.* London, The College.

Royal Commission on the NHS (1979). *Royal Commission on the NHS, Report,* Cmnd 7615. London, HMSO.

Ruddick, S. (1990). *Maternal Thinking: Towards a politics of peace.* London, The Women's Press.

Saks, K.B. (1990). 'Does it pay to care?', in E.K. Abel and M.K. Nelson (eds) *Circles of Care: Work and Identity in Women's Lives.* New York, SUNY Press.

Saks, M. (1983). 'Removing the blinkers? A critique of recent contributions to the sociology of professions', *Sociological Review,* **31**(1), 1–21.

Salvage, J. (1985). *The Politics of Nursing.* London, Heinemann.

Salvage, J. (1992). 'The new nursing: empowering patients or empowering nurses?', in J. Robinson, A, Gray and R. Elkan (eds) *Policy Issues in Nursing.* Buckingham, Open University Press.

Savage, M. and Witz, A. (eds) (1992). *Gender and Bureaucracy.* Oxford, Blackwell.

Saylor, C.R. (1990). 'Reflection and professional education: art, science and competency', *Nurse Educator,* **15**(2), 8–11.

Schofield, M. (1987). 'A welcome attempt at reform', *Nursing Times,* **83**(18), 27–8, 6 May.

Schön, D. (1983). *The Reflective Practitioner: How professionals think in action.* London, Temple Smith.

Scott, J. (1988). 'Deconstructing equality versus difference', *Feminist Studies,* **1**, 33–50.

Seccombe, I. and Ball, J. (1992). *Motivation, Morale and Mobility: A Profile of Qualified Nurses in the 1990s,* IMS Report No. 233. Brighton, Institute for Manpower Studies.

Secretaries of State for Health (1989a). *Working for Patients,* Cm 555. London, HMSO.

Secretaries of State for Health (1989b). *Caring for People: Community care in the next decade and beyond,* Cm 849. London, HMSO.

Secretary of State for Health (1989). Letter to Dame Audrey Emerton, UKCC Chairman, 18 May, *RCN Newsline.*

Segal, L. (1987). *Is the Future Female? Troubled Thoughts on Contemporary Feminism.* London, Virago.

Shipp, P.J. (1979). *Nurse Manpower Systems for South West Thames RHA.* Brighton, Institute for Manpower Studies.

Slevin, O. and Buckenham, M. (eds) (1992). *Project 2000: The teachers speak.* Edinburgh, Campion.

Smith, D.E. (1987). *The Everyday World as Problematic: A feminist sociology.* Milton Keynes, Open University Press.

Smith, P. (1992). *The Emotional Labour of Nursing.* London, Macmillan.

Stacey, M. (1976). 'The health service consumer: a sociological misconception', in *Sociology of the NHS, Sociological Review Monograph 22.* Keele, University of Keele.

Stacey, M. (1981). 'The division of labour revisited or overcoming the two Adams', in P. Abrams, R. Deem, J. Finch and P. Rock (eds) *Practice and Progress: British Sociology, 1950–1980.* London, Allen and Unwin.

Stacey, M. (1988). *The Sociology of Health and Healing: A textbook.* London, Unwin Hyman.

Stacey, M. (1992). *Regulating British Medicine: The General Medical Council.* Chichester: Wiley.

Stack, C. (1986). 'The culture of gender: men and women of color', *Signs*, **11**(2), 321–4.

Stein, L. (1967). 'The doctor–nurse game', *Archives of General Psychology*, **16**, 699–703.

Stein, L., Watts, D. and Howell, T. (1990). 'The doctor–nurse game revisited', *New England Journal of Medicine*, **322**(8), 546–9.

Stewart, J. and Ranson S. (1988). 'Management in the public domain', *Public Money and Management*, **8**(2), 13–18.

Stivers, C. (1993). *Gender Images in Public Administration.* London, Sage.

Strong, P. and Robinson, J. (1988). *New Model Management: Griffiths and the NHS*, Nursing Policy Studies 3. Coventry, University of Warwick, Nursing Policy Studies Centre.

Strong, P. and Robinson, J. (1990). *The NHS: Under New Management.* Milton Keynes, Open University Press.

Sullivan, M. (1992). *The Politics of Social Policy.* London, Harvester Wheatsheaf.

Tancred-Sheriff, P. (1989) 'Gender, sexuality and the labour process', in J. Hearn, D. Sheppard, P. Tancred-Sheriff and G. Burrell (eds) *The Sexuality of Organization.* London, Sage.

Tannen, D. (1991). *You Just Don't Understand: Women and men in conversation.* London, Virago.

Taylor-Gooby, P. and Lawson, R. (eds) (1993). *Markets and Managers: New issues in the delivery of welfare.* Buckingham, Open University Press.

Thomas, C. (1993). 'De-constructing concepts of care', *Sociology*, **27**(4), 649–70.

Thompson, P. and McHugh, D. (1990). *Work Organisation.* London, Macmillan.

Tilley, I. (ed.) (1993). *Managing the Internal Market.* London, Paul Chapman.

Tong, R. (1989). *Feminist Thought: A Comprehensive Introduction.* London, Unwin Hyman.

Treasury (1991). *Competing for Quality: buying public services*, Cm 1730. London: HMSO.

Uden, G., Norberg, A. and Lindseth, A. (1992). 'Ethical Reasoning in Nurses' and Physicians' Stories about Care Episodes', *Journal of Advanced Nursing*, **17**(9), 1028–35.

Ungerson, C. (1983). 'Why do women care?', in J. Finch and D. Groves (eds) *A Labour of Love: Women, work and caring*. London, Routledge and Kegan Paul.

Ungerson, C. (1987). *Policy is Personal: Sex, gender and informal care*. London, Tavistock.

Ungerson, C. (ed.) (1990). *Gender and Caring: Work and welfare in Britain and Scandinavia*. London, Harvester Wheatsheaf.

United Kingdom Central Council on Nursing, Midwifery and Health (UKCC) (1986a). *Project 2000: A New Preparation for Practice*. London, The Council.

United Kingdom Central Council on Nursing, Midwifery and Health (UKCC) (1986b). *Project 2000: The Project and the Professions: Report of the UKCC Consultation on Project 2000*, Project Paper 7. London, The Council.

United Kingdom Central Council for Nursing, Midwifery and Health Visiting (UKCC) (1987a). *Project 2000: Counting the Cost: Is Project 2000 a practical proposition?*, Project Paper 8. London, The Council.

United Kingdom Central Council for Nursing, Midwifery and Health Visiting (UKCC) (1987b). *Project 2000: The Final Proposals*, Project Paper 9. London, The Council.

Van Herik, J. (1982) *Freud on Femininity and Faith*. Berkeley, University of California Press.

Waerness, K. (1992). 'On the Rationality of Caring', in A. Showstack Sassoon (ed.) *Women and the State*. London, Routledge (first published in 1984).

Waite, R. and Hutt, R. (1987). *Attitudes, Jobs and Mobility of Qualified Nurses: A Report for the RCN*, IMS Report No. 130. Brighton, Institute for Manpower Studies.

Waite, R., Buchan, J. and Thomas, J. (1989). *Nurses In and Out of Work. A Tracing Study, 1986–88, for the RCN of the Attitudes, Employment and Mobility Rates of RCN Members*, IMS Report No. 170. Brighton, Institute for Manpower Studies.

Waite, R., Buchan, J. and Thomas, J. (1990). *Career Paths of Scotland's Qualified Nurses*. Brighton, Institute for Manpower Studies.

Walker, A. (1993). 'Community care policy: from consensus to conflict', in J. Bornat, C. Pereira, D. Pilgrim and F. Williams (eds) *Community Care: A reader*. London, Macmillan/Open University.

Walmsley, J., Reynolds, J., Shakespeare, P, and Woolfe, R. (eds) (1993). *Health, Welfare and Practice: Reflecting on roles and relationships*. London, Sage.

Watkins, S. (1987). *Medicine and Labour: The politics of a profession*. London, Lawrence and Wishart.

Webb, J. and Liff, S. (1988). 'Play the white man: the social construction of fairness and competition in equal opportunities policies', *Sociological Review*, **36**(3), 532–51.

West, C. and Zimmerman, D. H. (1991). 'Doing gender', in J. Lorber and S. A. Farrell (eds) *The Social Construction of Gender*. London, Sage.

White, R. (1985). *The Effects of the NHS on the Nursing Profession 1948–1961*. London, King's Fund.

Wiebe, R. (1968). *The Search for Order*. New York, Hill and Wang.

Williams, C., Barry, J. and Soothill, K. (1992). 'Nursing wastage from the nurses' point of view', in K. Soothill, C. Henry and K. Kendrick (eds) *Themes and Perspectives in Nursing*. London: Chapman & Hall.

Williams, J. (1993). 'What is a profession? Experience versus expertise', in J. Walmsley, J. Reynolds, P. Shakespeare and R. Woolfe (eds) *Health, Welfare and Practice: Reflecting on roles and relationships*. London, Sage.

Wilson, E. (1977). *Women and the Welfare State*. London, Tavistock.

Witz, A. (1992). *Professions and Patriarchy*. London, Routledge.

Wright Warren, P. (1986). *Mix and Match: A Review of Nursing Skill Mix* (a report presented to Mrs A.A.B. Poole, Chief Nursing Officer (Chair: P. Wright Warren)). London, DHSS.

Young, I.M. (1987). 'Impartiality and the civic public: some implications of feminist critiques of moral and political theory', in S. Benhabib and D. Cornell (eds) *Feminism as Critique*. Oxford/Cambridge, Blackwell/Polity.

INDEX

RESEARCH INTO PRACTICE
A READER FOR NURSES AND THE CARING PROFESSIONS
Pamela Abbott and Roger Sapsford (eds)

This book is a collection of examples of research, all concerned in some way with nursing or the study of health and community care. It illustrates the kind of research that can be done by a small team or a single researcher, without large-scale research grants. The editors have selected papers which show a great diversity of approaches: differing emphasis on description or explanation, different degrees of structure in design and different appeals to the authority of science or the authenticity of empathic exploration. They show the limitations typical of small-scale projects carried out with limited resources and the experience of applied research as it occurs in practice, as opposed to how it tends to look when discussed in textbooks. The papers have been organized into three sections representing three distinct types of social science research – 'observing and participating', 'talking to people and asking questions' and 'controlled trials and comparisons'. Each section is provided with an editorial introduction.

Contents
Section A: Observing and participating – Introduction – Labouring in the dark – A postscript to nursing – Working with women's health groups – Section B: Talking to people and asking questions – Introduction – Leaving it to mum – Planning research: a case of heart disease – Hospital visiting on two wards – How do women and men in nursing perceive each other? – Section C: Controlled trials and comparisons – Introduction – Treatment of depressed women by nurses – Health visitors' and social workers' perceptions of child-care problems – Health and material deprivation in Plymouth – Postscript – Author index – Subject index.

Contributors
Pamela Abbott, Joyce Bernie, George Choon, Robert Dingwall, Susan Fox, Verona Gordon, Nicky James, Mavis Kirkham, Jean Orr, Geoff Payne, Roger Sapsford, Suzanne Skevington.

176pp   0 335 09742 1 (Paperback)   0 335 09743 X (Hardback)

RESEARCH METHODS FOR NURSES AND THE CARING PROFESSIONS

Roger Sapsford and Pamela Abbott

This book is about the appreciation, evaluation and conduct of social research. Aimed at nurses, social workers, community workers and others in the caring professions, the book concentrates on relatively small-scale studies which can be carried out by one or two people, rather than large and well-resourced teams. The authors have provided many short, practical exercises within the text and particular emphasis is given to evaluative research including the assessment of the reader's own professional practice. Their clear, accessible style will make this the ideal introductory text for those undertaking research or the evaluation of research for the first time.

This book may be read in conjunction with *Research into Practice: A Reader for Nurses and the Caring Professions* (Open University Press) by the same authors.

Contents
Section 1: Introduction – Finding out and making sense – Section 2: Assessing research – Reading research reports – Reading open interviewing research – Reading observation research – Reading about controlled trials – Reading survey research – Reading secondary-source research – Section 3: Doing research – Using secondary sources – Survey research: design and sampling – Experimental practice – Open interviewing – Analysing text – Participant observation and self-evaluation – Evaluation of single cases – Section 4: In conclusion – Writing up – In conclusion – References – Index.

192pp   0 335 09620 4 (Paperback)   0 335 09621 2 (Hardback)

CARERS PERCEIVED
POLICY AND PRACTICE IN INFORMAL CARE
Julia Twigg and Karl Atkin

Carers are the bedrock of community care, and yet our understanding of how they do and do not fit into the care system is limited. Concern is often expressed about the need to support carers, but the best way to do this is not always clear.

This book breaks new ground in exploring the reality of how service providers like doctors, social workers, and community nurses respond to carers. It looks at which carers get help and why, analysing how age, relationship, class and gender structure the responses of service providers and carers. It examines the moral and policy issues posed by trying to incorporate carers' interests into service provision. What would services look like if they took the needs of carers seriously? How far can they afford to do so? Is this only achieved at the expense of disabled people? What is the proper relationship between carers and services? Carers pose in acute form many of the central dilemmas of social welfare, and the account presented here has the widest significance for the analysis of community care.

Focusing on the views of carers as well as service providers, the book looks at caring across a variety of relationships and conditions, including people with mental health problems and learning disabilities.

Contents
Informal care – Carers in the service system – The carers' experience – Social services – The health sector – Services in a mixed setting – Carers of people with learning disabilities – Carers of adults with mental health problems – Mediating – Structuring – Carers in the policy arena – Appendix – References – Index.

192pp   0 335 19111 8 (Paperback)   0 335 19112 6 (Hardback)